Achiel Peelman

Christ Is
a Native American

Cover design: Christiane Lemire

Cover photo: Marc Audette

Author photo: K. Heiberg

Layout: Gilles Lépine

The illustrations of Leland Bell are taken from sixteen paintings by the native artist which are featured in full colour in the book by Greg J. Humbert and George Leach sj, *Beedahbun: First Light of Dawn*, available from Tomiko Publications, P.O. Box 502, North Bay, Ontario P1B 8J1 Canada. Used with permission.

Copyright © 1995, Novalis-Saint Paul University, Ottawa.

First published in Canada in 1995 by Novalis, 49 Front Street East, 2nd floor
    Toronto, Ontario, Canada M5E 1B3

Published in the United States of America by Orbis Books, Maryknoll, New York 10545-0308.

The Catholic Foreign Mission Society of America (Maryknoll) recruits and trains people for overseas missionary service. Through Orbis Books, Maryknoll aims to foster the international dialogue that is essential to mission. The books published, however, reflect the opinions of their authors and are not meant to represent the official position of the society.

Manufactured in Canada.

Library of Congress Cataloging-in-Publication Data

Peelman, A.
Christ Is a Native American / Achiel Peelman.
    253 p. 15.5 x 22.8 cm.
    Includes bibliographical references.
    ISBN 1-57075-047-5

    1. Jesus Christ--Person and offices. 2. Christianity and culture.
3. Indians of North America--Religion. I. Title
BT205.P37   1995
277′ .0089′97--dc20   95-22933
                                              CIP

Cataloguing in Publication Data

Peelman, Achiel, 1942-

Christ Is a native American

Translation of: Le Christ est amérindien.

Includes bibliographical references.

ISBN 2-89088-743-X (Novalis)

ISBN 1-57075-047-5 (Orbis)

    1. Christianity and culture. 2. Jesus Christ – Person and offices. 3. Indians of North America – Canada – Religion. I. Title.
BT205.P4313 1995   261   C95-900452-1

Contents

Part 1

List of Illustrations

Encounters with the Great Mystery.
Little Red River, Alberta, 1984
Photo: Achiel Peelman

Introduction

During his 1984 visit to the Shrine of the Canadian Martyrs in Midland, Ontario, Pope John Paul II declared: "Thus the one faith is expressed in different ways. There can be no question of adulterating the word of God or of emptying the Cross of its power, but rather of Christ animating the very centre of all cultures. Thus, not only is Christianity relevant to the Indian peoples, but *Christ, in the members of his Body, is himself Indian.*"[1] In the immediate context of the papal visit, this declaration was first given an ecclesiological interpretation. It was perceived by many Native Americans as an encouragement and an invitation to build a truly Amerindian church. I have had the privilege of observing this development over the years at the Canadian Summer Institutes for the promotion of Amerindian leadership in the church, in the publications and the assemblies of the *Tekakwitha Conference* in the United States, and during many encounters with native persons across Canada.

During these encounters I soon came to the conclusion that an ecclesiological renewal of this kind cannot occur without an in-depth reflection on the relationship between Christianity and the Amerindian cultures, and without a corresponding christological vision. There can be no Amerindian church without an Amerindian Christ. But who is this Indian Christ Pope John Paul II referred to in Midland? What is his place in the spiritual universe of the Amerindian peoples? How do they visualize him? What impact does his gospel have on their life?

The basic purpose of this research

These are the questions to be considered in this research. To answer them I will adopt the deductive method to present and analyze the testimonies from native witnesses which I have been gathering in field studies since 1982. I have sought out the witness of native Americans who are deeply involved in the renewal of their church. I have been interested in the unique contribution of those who are achieving a personal integration of their ancestral spirituality and the Christian faith, inside or outside the current structures of the church. In line with the religious pluralism that characterizes the native scene, I will also adopt an

ecumenical approach. This essay is not limited to Catholic Native Americans. I
will also consider the fact that, within the contemporary ecumenical movement,
the christological challenge (the vertical relationship between the churches and
Christ) is slowly replacing merely ecclesiological preoccupations. This christological challenge also inspires the larger ecumenical dialogue between Christianity and other religions.[2]

To grasp the precise meaning of this research the reader should also note that
the postconciliar evolution of Catholic theology is profoundly influenced by the
massive migration of the People of God to the western and southern regions of our
planet. Demographic inquiries indicate that the majority of Christians already live
in the Third World. The "Third Church" has arrived, wrote Walbert Bühlmann in
1974.[3] This evolution, hardly foreseen by Vatican II (1962-1965), represents an
enormous challenge for theology. We are witnessing the passage from a theology
which was almost exclusively associated with western cultures to a more international and planetary theology.[4] We observe the emergence of local theologies
based on the life experience of those who welcome the gospel and let Christ
challenge them in the Spirit.[5]

This is the situation in which the majority of the North American native
peoples find themselves. Even though the historical encounter of the Christian
missionaries with the Amerindians has not yet produced a truly Amerindian
church, Christ is profoundly incarnated in the Indian consciousness. His gospel
has become an endogenous factor in the Amerindian cultures on which Christianity has exercised a tremendous impact. The purpose of this research is to
demonstrate that this incarnation of Christ among the aboriginal peoples of North
America is producing a unique kind of christology. Our concern is not to show
how the Amerindians have integrated our western images of Christ, but to under-
line the specific contributions they are making to a deeper and larger vision of the
Christ mystery.

Anthropological and theological presuppositions

This research presupposes the encounter or confrontation between different
cultures which anthropologists call "acculturation." This is a widespread phenomenon in native North America. Acculturation is not limited here to the historical
encounter of Amerindian cultures with western civilization and Christianity.
Before and after this encounter occurred there was much cultural interaction
between the different aboriginal peoples of North America. In the twentieth
century, this cultural interaction gave rise to the pan-Indian movement which is
rapidly spreading across the continent.

This research also presupposes a particular theological approach to the
Christian mission among the Amerindian peoples. We will try to assess the results
of this missionary adventure by concentrating on those elements which are often
overlooked or ignored by the main missionary actors in native North America. We

intend to interpret these elements as particular signs of the mysterious presence and action of Christ among the Amerindian peoples.

It is currently thought that the native peoples first arrived in North America from Asia during the Pleistocene age via a land bridge across what is now the Bering Strait. Archaeological research has been pushing the date for their arrival in North America further and further back. There is no consensus among scholars, but estimates vary from about 10,000 to 50,000 B.C.E. It is now held as conclusive that, by 8,000 B.C.E. (end of the Ice Age), native peoples could be found in all parts of the Americas. This constitutes a remarkable fact from the point of view of the history of civilizations. We no longer undertake a theological interpretation of Amerindian cultures and Amerindian history as though nothing significant happened before 1492! At that time our own ancestors entered into contact with a wide variety of aboriginal cultures whose internal organization, cross-cultural interaction and adaptation to new situations were most impressive. They met with very spiritual peoples who knew God well before the arrival of the first Christian missionaries. These native cultures and their God-experience have not disappeared from the face of the earth. The fact that they have survived the colossal shock of western civilization and that they are now enjoying a remarkable rebirth constitutes a "moral victory" of unique dimensions. We consider this "moral victory" to be one of the key aspects of this christological research.[6] We will examine where Christ situates himself with respect to the contemporary Amerindian search for identity (cultural continuity) and with respect to the political and socio-economic transformations of the Amerindian communities (cultural discontinuity).

Permit me to point out that, from the theological viewpoint, this research presupposes a particular way of looking at the Christian mission adventure among the Amerindian peoples (evangelization). We should not be misled by the fact that the majority of the North American native peoples have become Christian. This fact does not say anything about the historical and present confrontation between aboriginal religious experience and Christianity. One fact stands out very sharply: Christianity has not been able to displace the traditional Amerindian religions. Ancestral spirituality continues to play a significant role in the lives of many native Americans and in their communities. It is a vital factor even in the lives of many Amerindians who consider themselves faithful members of the Christian church.

We are dealing here with a complex religious situation. Must we interpret it as a missionary failure?[7] Should we speak of it as merely "pre-evangelization"?[8] Or can this situation be interpreted as a profound but unexpected result of the churche's own missionary effort? If so, are we not then confronted with one of the mysterious fruits of the ongoing interaction between the gospel and the Amerindian cultures?

We will attempt to answer these questions by using a new theological term, inculturation. In a previous study, we explained that this technical term must not be understood as a new missionary method, but as a new vision of the church's evangelizing mission.[9] We remain convinced that the term inculturation is the key concept for a truly theological interpretation of the encounter between Christ and the Amerindian cultures. The church's missionary activity (evangelization) does not end with the proclamation of the gospel and the integration (assimilation) of new members in a dogmatic and religious system whose boundaries have been fixed once and for all. The church's evangelizing mission also includes the capacity to welcome and to harvest the new (and sometimes unexpected) fruits that each "cultural soil" produces when it has received the seeds of the gospel. Surely it is not necessary to insist here on the fact that these "new fruits" are not limited merely to the external aspects of Christianity (structures, ministries and rituals), but that they also concern its very centre and foundation: the mystery of the crucified and risen Christ as perceived and visualized by different peoples and cultures?

The structure of the book

In this research on the Amerindian vision of Christ we will adopt the dynamics of local or contextual theologies. Within the larger perspective of theology as *fides quaerens intellectum* (faith searching for understanding), the term "local theology" represents an important change of perspective. The term does not refer to the creation of new theological systems, but to new ways of doing theology from the grassroots. Local theology starts with the concrete life situation of the ethnic communities, cultures, peoples, and social groups who have welcomed the gospel and for whom the message of Christ has become an important source of community building and social consciousness. Local theology can therefore be understood as a dynamic process involving three realities: cultures (the global situation of a people or group of persons), the missionary church (the evangelizing Christian communities), and the Christic mystery (the presence and action of Christ's Spirit in the world). Local theology represents a contextual way of thinking by the Christian community itself to the extent that it becomes aware of its concrete situation in the world and makes a conscious effort to interpret that situation in the light of the gospel, while being attentive to the presence of Spirit.[10]

To account for these contextual christologies among North American native peoples, in Part I of this book we will present an overview of the contemporary Amerindian cultures and of their historical interaction with Christianity. We will not present a summary of the churches' missionary enterprise in North America, but concentrate rather on those elements which lead to the contemporary Amerindian vision of Christ. Because the native peoples understand themselves basically as spiritual peoples, we will pay particular attention to the religious dimension of the Amerindian cultures. We know, however, that it is almost impossible to isolate this religious dimension from the other political, social and economic aspects of the Amerindian reality. Amerindian cultures have remained holistic or homogeneous cultures notwithstanding the pressures of modern and postmodern, fragmented western society. We must remain attentive to all the aspects of the Amerindian cultures.

In Part II of the book we will first listen to the voices of Amerindian women and men who shared their vision of Christ with us on various trips we made across Canada in 1982 and the following years. A short note about the way in which this vision is presented: Even though the amount of written literature by native American authors is increasing, oral tradition remains a cultural trademark of their communities. Native American theology, therefore, remains experiential in orientation. It is not a matter of doctrine but of life experienced in the immediate context of extended family, clan, tribe, people and nation. This theological life experience is seldom committed to paper. Amerindian theology, furthermore, is not the product of individual thinkers or writers. Like the contextual theologies of the Third World, it remains a communitarian enterprise. Our presentation of the Amerindian vision of Christ will respect, as much as possible, these particular aspects of the native American theological process. This presentation of oral reports will be followed by an analysis of the theological themes to which the Amerindian Christian communities offer particular contributions. But, once again, we will remain more attentive to the process than to content as such. We will be able to show that because this Amerindian theological process is experiential, it can help non-native Christians better understand the cultural and contextual aspects of their own christologies.

A contemporary issue

A concluding remark on the contemporary significance of this research. It will be evident that the nascent Amerindian christologies experience the same strain as all other "contextualized" christologies: the tension between the historical figure of Jesus, whom we accept in faith as the unique and decisive revelation of God but from whom we are culturally more and more separated, and the Christic mystery which transcends the boundaries of the Christian churches. The Amerindian vision of Christ respects this fundamental tension. We will see, for example, that interreligious dialogue is perceived by many native Americans, not as the encounter between parallel religious systems, but as a personal experience of integration. These men and women who are fascinated by the historical person of Jesus wonder if there is truly a place in their spiritual universe for the one who said: "I have not come to abolish but to fulfill" (Mt 5:17b).

It is also important to note that this christological questioning is an intrinsic dimension of the contemporary Amerindian renaissance with all its political, social and economic implications. This fact cannot be ignored by any attentive observer of the Amerindian reality in Canada. The aboriginal peoples of North America cannot escape the impact of western culture and the dominant society, but they claim the right to be different and to control their own future. This is not just a political, social and economic challenge, but a spiritual adventure. The Amerindian peoples have understood that to find the necessary energies for the revitalization of their cultures and their communities they have to look first of all to their own traditions. Once again, they want to drink from their own wells without necessarily turning their back on Christianity.

Canada is now facing a decisive historical moment. Just and equitable relationships must be woven between the first nations and the other Canadian peoples for the total well-being of all. We dare to believe that this essay on the Amerindian visions of Christ will assist the Christian churches in redefining their mission among the Amerindian peoples with whom they want to establish a new covenant.[11]

Acknowledgements

In the past several years I have met with many native persons across Canada who have shared their vision of Christ with me. This study would not have been possible without their hospitality and their willingness to introduce me into their spiritual universe. This book belongs to them. A special word of gratitude to the elders who encouraged me to become a bridge builder between the native spiritual experience and Christianity. A special word of thanks to Eva Solomon, CSJ, and Daryold Winkler, CSB, of the Ojibway or Anishnabe people, for their friendship and support; to Thomas Novak, OMI, and Jean-Guy Goulet (Anthropology, University of Calgary), who shared with me his love for the Dene Tha people. Dr. Kenneth Russell (researcher at the Faculty of Theology, Saint Paul University) reviewed the English translation and adaptation of this book.

To all my relations.

PART I

THE NATIVE AMERICAN PEOPLES AND CHRISTIANITY

In the first part of this research on the Amerindian vision of Christ we will focus on the encounter between the spiritual universe of the Amerindians and Christianity. This encounter began in 1492 with the "discovery" of the Americas by Christopher Columbus. All the controversies which developed on both sides of the Atlantic on the occasion of the 500th anniversary of this discovery seem to indicate that we are still unsure about the implications of an historical event which seemed inevitable. Sooner or later, the "New World" of the Amerindians, which was in fact much older than the already "Old Continent" of the discoverers, was destined to meet with western civilization and Christianity. In what is now called Canada, the first contact took place on July 20, 1543 with the planting of a cross by Jacques Cartier in Gaspé. This symbolic gesture was followed in 1610 by the arrival of Father Jessé Fléché, a priest from the diocese of Langes in France, who can claim the honour of being the first true missionary in Indian territory. The first Récollets (a congregation of reformed Franciscans) settled in Quebec in 1615. The Jesuits followed in 1625. The beginning of the Canadian missionary adventure is often said to coincide with the establishment of a trading post in 1608 in what is now the city of Quebec and with the arrival of the Jesuits among the Hurons in

1634. This missionary adventure ended symbolically in 1967 when, by a decree of the Holy See, the Apostolic Vicariates (depending on the Sacred Congregation *De Propaganda Fidei*) were transformed into archdioceses and dioceses. From that date Canada ceased to have any "missionary territory." Three and a half centuries sufficed to implant the Catholic church in Canada from the Atlantic to the Pacific Oceans and from the American frontier to the North Pole!

In the pages which follow we will not attempt to offer an assessment of this remarkable missionary adventure. We will concentrate instead on what seems to be a key issue of the encounter between the Amerindians and Christianity: the extraordinary vitality of the Amerindian religious experience. Many historical and anthropological studies of the Indian missions in Canada demonstrate that the Amerindian spiritual universe did resist the formidable confrontation with western civilization and Christianity, even though the churches fulfilled their mission in a culturally aggressive way. In the first part of this study we offer a theological interpretation of the Amerindian religious experience. We will show that, throughout the unfolding of the church's missionary enterprise in Canada, this Amerindian religious experience has remained a true *preparatio evangelica* (gospel preparation) in view of the manifestations and the incarnation of Christ in native North America. Even after the definite implanting of the Christian churches in Canada, the Indians' ancestral spirituality must be considered as the principal axis of their nascent christology. Whether we consider the Indian missions of Canada a success or failure, we must recognize that this ancestral spirituality remains the true place where we will eventually discover the hidden face of the Amerindian Christ.

CHAPTER I

The Amerindian Reality

I. The Return of a Vanishing People

1. The turning point of the 1980s

Although their disappearance was almost a *fait accompli* at the beginning of this century, the aboriginal peoples of North America are currently experiencing a veritable cultural renaissance. Fifty years ago, many anthropologists, missionaries, medical doctors and politicans rightly described the Indians as "vanishing peoples." They did not hesitate to conclude that the only survival open to them was through total assimilation or individual integration into the Canadian or North American society. In 1923, Father Pierre Duchaussois, author of the famous book *Mid Snow and Ice: The Apostles of the North-West*, could write that because of sickness and government policies "the Indians of the reserves have become fewer in number, and their inevitable intermarriages seem to foretell that they will not be stretched out on this world's rack much longer."[1] Famous anthropologists Franz Boas and George Hunt raided the native villages of the Pacific coast in a desperate attempt to supply Chicago's Field Museum and the Smithsonian Institute in Washington, D.C., with Indian artifacts. Nor did they have any compunction about raiding and digging up native burial grounds. European and American museums were competing hard to obtain as much Indian material as possible.[2] Everybody seemed convinced that these Indian art treasures would soon disappear forever in the North American forests. If they couldn't save the Amerindian people, they could at least try to save their cultural treasures, their spiritual heritage, legends and myths, their songs and music, their ceremonial and ritual art. After contact with western civilization, the cultural and social disintegration of the native communities seemed inevitable. Indeed this is what the Canadian government of those days had in mind. In 1920, Duncan Campbell Scott, superintendent-general of the Indian Affairs Branch (and a well-known poet), could state in public testimony concerning a proposed bill on Indian policy: "Our object is to continue until there is not a single Indian in Canada that has not been absorbed into the body politic and there is no Indian question and no Indian problem."[3]

But the Indians are still here! They are more visible than ever throughout Canada.[4] We are no longer dealing with vague, weak or vanishing groups of individuals who are on the verge of total assimilation into our political, economic, social and religious structures, but with members of distinct societies who strongly desire to maintain their cultural identity. William Means of the *International Treaty Council* rightly stated: "As the 1960s saw the emergence of the black man on the world scene; the 1970s saw the emergence of the Arab peoples; the 1980s will see the red man take his rightful place on the world stage."[5]

This prophecy is confirmed by the movement of cultural revitalization which has been underway since the sixties. This movement has many political, social, economic and religious ramifications. Indeed it nourishes the hope that the Amerindians will be able to remain distinct peoples within the multicultural universe of North America. In fact, one of the immediate effects of this revitalization consists in the growing awareness that the Amerindian culture is more than a few scattered native artifacts that have survived the wear and tear of time. Cultures are history in the making. Throughout the western hemisphere, the Indians are intensifying their consciousness of cultural identity. They want to become once again the makers of their own history and to contribute to the well-being of the other peoples who now share their land.

It is important to note that, notwithstanding its socio-political implications, this Amerindian revitalization is above all a spiritual movement. In the Amerindian mind there is a close connection between the land, culture and religion. Emma Laroque, a native historian, wrote as early as 1975: "If there is any Indian renaissance today, it is in the world of religion. Young people are coming to the elders for spiritual guidance and the elders are once again sharing their secrets."[6] In the course of our research we met a considerable number of native women and men who did not hesitate to travel across North America in search of spiritual guides who could help them reconstruct their personal life and revivify their communities. Religion or spirituality remains the quintessence of the Amerindian reality. Even though the native languages do not possess technical terms to designate what we call theology, philosophy, religion or church, the Amerindians define themselves, basically, as *spiritual peoples*. The Navajo, for example, call themselves *the Children of the Holy People (Diyin dine'é)*. In 1983, while visiting a remote Dene community in northwestern Alberta, a middle-aged Dene mother told us: "The most important thing about our native way is that it is a spiritual way. We are a spiritual people. No one can take this spirituality away from us."

Although most western observers of the native scene see only the political and economic dimensions of the "Indian problem," statements like this can be heard all over North America. More attention ought to be paid to the astonishing vitality of the Amerindian spiritual traditions. All over Canada these ancestral religions are developing new forms of visibility, and traditional Indian medicine is becoming popular.[7] This revaluation of ancestral spirituality appears to be an essential dimension of the development of peoples whose history is marked by a long period of political, cultural and religious oppression. Insofar as the suppression of traditional religions was one of the factors that contributed to the social collapse of the exploited and colonized peoples, the revitalization of their traditional religion, in the wake of the growing pressures of secularization and technology, has become an indispensable element in their integral development.[8]

This "return to ancestral spirituality" is the most fascinating and disconcerting aspect of the Amerindian revitalization. Many Euro-Canadian observers, especially Christian missionaries, find it difficult to understand why the Amerindians borrow technology, communication advances and all kinds of material things from western society, while, in the religious domain, they seem to return to the past. They want the Amerindians to be successful in the field of education, politics and commerce, but, at the same time, they spontaneously wish that these "civilized" Indians would proclaim at the end of the assimilation process: "Now, we have become just like you. Thank you for your civilizing efforts!" But, usually, these "civilized" Indians don't fall on their knees to thank their western educators. They forcefully express the desire to maintain and to enhance their cultural identity. They claim the right to be Indian *today* as members of the modern world and see the return to their traditional values as the best guarantee for their cultural survival.[9] To grasp the implications of this particular cultural process, we will briefly consider the international context of the Amerindian renaissance.

2. An international movement

It is difficult to gauge the current number of indigenous peoples in the western hemisphere (the Americas and the Pacific Islands). Because of several demographic and historical factors it is sometimes not easy to determine who is an Indian and who is not. In 1983, a Working Group on Indigenous Populations, established by the United Nations Sub-Commission on the Prevention of Discrimination and the Protection of Minorities, adopted the following definition of "indigenous peoples": "indigenous populations, communities, peoples and nations are those which, having a historical continuity with pre-invasion and pre-colonial societies that developed on their territories, consider themselves distinct from the other sections of the societies now prevailing on those territories or parts of them. They form at present non-dominant sectors of society and are determined to preserve, further develop and transmit to future generations their ancestral territories, and their ethnic identity as the basis of their continued existence as peoples, in accordance with their own cultural patterns, social institutions and legal systems."[10] Reliable sources place the indigenous population in the western hemisphere at approximately 40 million people: 20.5 million in Latin America and 15 million in the Pacific Islands. In some countries, like the United States of America (1%) and Canada (2%), the indigenous populations constitute very small minority groups. In many Pacific island nations, they comprise the majority of the population. They make up more than half the population of Bolivia, almost half the population in Peru and about a third of the people in Mexico. Yet in none of these nations do the aboriginal peoples hold any significant political power. Rightfully, they consider themselves to be oppressed minorities.

Since its "discovery" by the Europeans in the fifteenth century, the indigenous population has decreased dramatically. Historians and anthropologists estimate that there may have been 10 million Indians in what is now the United States of America at the moment of contact with the Europeans. Now they are about 1.5 million. The same decline is evident in many other countries. In Colombia, for example, there were 5 million Indians in the sixteenth century. Today, there are less than 500,000. Amnesty International reports periodically that thousands of Indians continue to be massacred in several Latin American countries.[11] In 1983, the Center for Defense Information in Washington reported that, during the thirty-eight years following the end of the Second World War, more than 16 million people had been killed in civil wars and wars between states. The so-called period of "peace," following the Second World War, has been as costly as any world war in terms of human lives and human misery. The weight of human misery has fallen especially hard on the indigenous nations since the beginning of the 1960s. From 1960 to 1983 more than 4 million indigenous people were killed.[12]

Yet, many of these indigenous peoples or nations are now making a remarkable return to the central stage of world history. In Canada, for example, the rebirth of the native peoples really began during the 1960s, when their communities seemed to have reached a point of no return in terms of social disintegration. This was a crucial moment for them to recognize the almost complete failure of all "foreign interventions" in the native world. The many social programs created by the government, the churches and the native organizations themselves were unable to redress the situation. The Amerindians then understood that the only way out was to gain full control of their own destiny and to return to their own spiritual traditions.[13]

This native revitalization movement rapidly caught the attention of the international political community because of two major events: the eighteen-month occupation of Alcatraz Island in San Francisco Bay in 1969-1970 and the 1973 ten-week siege at Wounded Knee in South Dakota by the *American Indian Movement*.[14] The movement began to have a deeper and wider impact with the creation of two international organizations: the *International Indian Treaty Council* (1974), an organization which promotes solidarity among the indigenous peoples of the Americas, and the *World Council of Indigenous Peoples* whose inaugural meeting took place in Port Alberni, British Columbia, in 1975. George Manuel, a Shuswap Indian and president of the *National Indian Brotherhood of Canada*, had a critical role in the emergence of this international indigenous movement. The 1960s saw the creation of other important international organizations such as the *Interamerican Indian Congress* (Peru), the *Central American Indian Council* (Costa Rica), the *Inuit Circumpolar Conference* (Canada), and the

International Workgroup for Indigenous Affairs (Denmark), an international organization promoting action and contacts, now recognized by the Economic and Social Council of the United Nations.

The United Nations reacted. Until the beginning of 1970 no organization in the United Nations other than the International Labour Office had paid any serious attention to the indigenous or tribal populations. But in 1971, the United Nations Sub-Commission on Prevention of Discrimination and Protection of Minorities appointed José R. Martinez Cobo as Special *Rapporteur* to prepare a study on the problem of discrimination against indigenous populations. Following the completion of that study, a decade later, the United Nations decided to entrust the dossier of the indigenous peoples to the international Non-Governmental Organizations (NGO). The next step was the international NGO Conference on Discrimination against indigenous Populations in the Americas, held in Geneva in 1977. This conference prepared a Draft Declaration of Principles for the Defence of the Indigenous Nations and Peoples in the Western Hemisphere, dealing with issues such as the indigenous peoples and international law, treaty rights, the jurisdiction of states over their indigenous populations, the settlement of disputes, national and cultural integrity, and the protection of the environment.[15] A second conference in 1981, which also met in Geneva, was entitled Indigenous Peoples and the Land. Meanwhile, the Russell Tribunal in Rotterdam had received the complaints of the North American Indians in 1980.[16] From that moment on several Canadian native groups multiplied their efforts to heighten the public awareness of the European populations concerning their land claims, their fishing and hunting rights, and especially their opposition to the U.S. missile tests in northwestern Canada, and the NATO Tactical Fighter Weapons Training Centre in Labrador or Nitassinan, the land of the Innu.[17]

All these efforts led the United Nations Sub-Commission on the Prevention of Discrimination and the Protection of Minorities to establish a special Working Group on Indigenous Populations, which has met annually since 1982 to collect information on the treatment and the rights of the indigenous peoples. Since 1985, as a consequence of the study prepared by Martinez Cobo, this Working Group has been elaborating a Universal Declaration on the Rights of the Indigenous Peoples which will eventually be proposed to the General Assembly. In its present state, this Declaration contains thirty paragraphs dealing with issues such as the indigenous peoples' fundamental rights, their collective rights (culture, language, education), their rights of private and collective ownership (land claims, compensations, participation in collective decision-making concerning the exploitation of natural resources), environmental rights (subsistence economies, habitat), and political rights (self-government, juridical systems).[18]

We remain convinced that it was awareness of the vitality of aboriginal cultures, interest in Amerindian spirituality and concern about the fundamental values which are at stake in the present evolution of North America that got this international movement underway. The contemporary drama of the Amerindian peoples is evolving within the context of the larger North American society which is questioning its own political, social and economic creeds. It comes, therefore, as no surprise that when aboriginal peoples participate at national or international meetings, they insist on the need to elaborate new visions of society, before they focus on their political or economic rights.[19] Almost always, culture and spirituality come first. This should not be interpreted as a return to a "primitive past" or as an unqualified rejection of modernity, but as a rediscovery of the essential values which all North American peoples need to survive in a highly technological environment. We do, of course, detect traces of the aboriginal peoples' progressive disenchantment with many aspects of the Euro-American culture. For example, the nuclear arms race of modern states has generated distrust and cynicism about western society. No wonder that the messages of some contemporary native spiritual leaders have frequently sounded "apocalyptic." Thomas Banyacya, a great Hopi spiritual leader, does not hesitate to predict the end of the world, unless all peoples commit themselves to a profound spiritual renewal.[20] Behind the message of many native leaders and prophets one detects a deep concern for the ecological crisis and the materialistic orientation of western society. This explains to some extent the real explosion of interest in Amerindian spirituality among native and non-native peoples to which Joseph Epes Brown refers in his well-known book, *The Spiritual Legacy of the American Indian*. He suggests that this phenomenon is associated with the refusal by many individuals to consider henceforth western society as the normative model of civilization for all peoples. The Amerindian and other peoples are now involved in a common search for their spiritual roots. Have we lost the spiritual heritage of our ancestors? Are we truly concerned about our cultural impoverishment? What are the values guiding our personal life and our societies?[21] Philosophers, such as Thomas Berry of the *Riverdale Center for Religious Research*, do not hesitate to declare that North America needs the unique contribution of the aboriginal peoples to guarantee its own future. The fates of the American continent, native Americans, and the white population are finally identical. None of these can be saved except in and through the others. Berry recognizes that the rhythm of Indian civilizational development has been broken since the fifteenth century. But it has not been destroyed. The "psychic structure" of the Indian mind has remained intact. He is already forecasting a further development of the Amerindian renaissance: the gradual unification of all the Indians of the western hemisphere from which a new power may well emerge. The power of this movement, Berry writes, may affect the development of civilization in the western hemisphere more extensively than anyone can now foresee.[22]

It must be noted, in conclusion, that the "return" of the Amerindians to their own traditions can be accompanied by a severe critique of the western society which continues to dominate their lives. In fact, one of the greatest challenges faced by the Amerindian nations in the United States and Canada is their ongoing confrontation with governments which seem to have no "vision" of their own future, but are pretentious enough to impose a new world order on the rest of humanity! Would it be an exaggeration to speak of a crisis of civilization in this case? If this is true, we can rely on Brown and Berry to insist on the unique advantage of the Amerindian peoples: their relationship with the land. This central aspect of Amerindian spirituality has remained intact, notwithstanding the erosion and the disintegration of many native communities. The relationship with the land remains the axis for the essential values at stake in the present Amerindian renaissance which has so many implications for North America.

3. Ramifications

We will now briefly consider some of the most important ramifications of the Amerindian renaissance. We shall limit ourselves to the Canadian context which will be considered in detail in the second part of this chapter. The examples presented reflect the life experience of most of the Amerindians we met in connection with this christological research. In fact, even though this research is theological in orientation, the people we met were unable to share with us their vision of Christ without first referring to their own life experience. They instinctively knew what "contextual" theology is all about.

Native education and aboriginal languages

In June 1987 we attended the first international conference on aboriginal education, organized by the *World Council of Indigenous Peoples* in Vancouver. During the evening of June 8, about 1,500 people, most of them native people from seventeen countries, gathered behind the Museum of Anthropology of the University of British Columbia where a *Grand Entry* marked the official opening of the conference. Next day, they were received by the Squamish Nation of Xwmelch'sten, north of the city of Vancouver. In the early morning, they gathered at the Longhouse, where the sacred fires were burning, for the official welcome by the Squamish elders and chiefs. The opening prayers, the exchange of gifts, and the speeches by the elders set the tone for the entire conference. Even though most of the meetings and workshops took place on the campus of the university, the day at Xwmelch'sten had a special meaning. It clearly demonstrated that the aboriginal peoples no longer wanted to consider native education without its link to the land and to their traditional values. In fact, the overall goal of the conference was to examine how indigenous beliefs and values (the past) could be applied to the changing practices of contemporary education (the present), for the survival and further development of the native communities (the future). The theme of the conference, "Tradition, Change and Survival," symbolized a major turning point in the orientation of aboriginal education. It is not enough to introduce native cultural elements into the educational system created by the dominant society. From now on, native education (process and content) must be constructed on the basis of the aboriginal cultures as they present themselves today in the global context of North America.

This congress was a potent "sign of the times" and marked the return of the Indian peoples to centre stage. The promotion of aboriginal education is one of the main ramifications of the Amerindian renaissance. It was in the field of education that the first nations of Canada were first able to take control of their destiny. Following centuries of domination and the imposition of alien values and life-styles, most native groups now control the educational process of their own children. Canada's aboriginal peoples have always given high priority to educa-tion. They want to give their children the best of both worlds, the Indian world and the western world where they now live, in order to thwart the negative aspects of the almost inevitable process of acculturation.[23] The contemporary Amerindian renaissance has helped to define a "bicultural" philosophy of Indian education which blends the old and the new into a unique synthesis. This "bicultural" philosophy sharply contrasts with the assimilationist approach of the days when the entire native education process was controlled by the government and the Christian churches. A painful controversy has recently developed in Canada over the so-called residential and industrial schools where many generations of native children, separated from their families and their tribes, were forced to learn the culture of a dominant society. Almost inevitably they were in danger of losing their native language and culture. In June 1991, we attended a national conference in Vancouver, organized by the *Cariboo Tribal Council*, one of the most impor-tant native groups in British Columbia, on the tragic history of these schools. An official request was made to the Canadian government and to the Christian churches to recognize their share of responsibility for past cultural hurts, and to participate in the process of healing the victims of this cultural aggression.[24] During the last stage of this christological research we met several native persons who shared their residential school experience with us. Their confidence in the churches seems to have been permanently shaken by the experience.

There is a close connection between native control in the field of education and the promotion of the aboriginal languages. Native language teaching has, only recently, become part of the curricula in the aboriginal school systems, in an effort to stop present trends towards language loss. It is within this context that native peoples from all over Canada attended the Aboriginal Language Policy Confer-ence held in Ottawa in January 1988. While it was recognized by the participants that educational institutions play an important role in native language retention, they also felt an urgent need for the native communities to be committed totally to giving new life to their languages. They were aware of the vital link between language and culture and of the rapid deterioration of several native languages across Canada.[25] Special emphasis was put on the role of the elders who, as "keepers of the knowledge," pass on the traditions and wisdom that come from years of experience. Given the fact that the oral traditions and the experiential mode of learning remain basic characteristics of the contemporary native cultures, communication between the elders and the new generations is crucial for the further development of the native cultures.[26]

Social welfare and health care

Social welfare, especially child welfare, and health care are two other important fields where Indian self-determination is becoming a reality. The aboriginal peoples are now assuming responsibility for programs which make an effort to combine modern, technological medicine with traditional, native healing methods.

Notwithstanding the fact that the Indian population in Canada has constantly increased since the 1960s, Canada's native population is still dying from so-called "Third World" diseases such as tuberculosis, gastroenteritis, and pneumonia—diseases that rarely cause death among non-native Canadians. The millions of dollars invested by the Canadian government in native health care seem unable to redress this situation. The shocking degree of ill-health among Indian people has been widely documented. Most studies reveal the interrelationship between health care and other factors such as poor housing, unemployment and the breakdown of community structures. Many of the diseases in native North America are the result of the tremendous impact western technological civilization has had on the traditional lifestyle of the Amerindians. This calls for a holistic approach that considers all the dimensions of this cultural situation: environment, psychological development, physical condition, emotional states, ethics and spirituality. The fundamental purpose of this holistic approach is the restoration of the social and cultural integrity of the native person.

The rediscovery of traditional native healing practices is an important dimension of the present Amerindian renaissance. During the consultations on Indian self-government in Canada (1980-1983), representatives of the Department of National Health and Welfare acknowledged: "We have come to appreciate very much the relevance and the utility of traditional approaches, particularly to mental health problems—approaches which address the suicide rate, approaches which address addiction problems. We believe that in areas such as those the application of traditional medicine and native culture perhaps can be more successful than anything we could offer in terms of contemporary psychiatric approaches to those kinds of problems."[27] In 1984, a spokesperson of the department confirmed that the representatives of the Assembly of First Nations, one of Canada's most important aboriginal organizations, had been asked to establish formal relations between the department and traditional native healers. One year later, Correctional Service Canada, in charge of the federal prison system, approved a Directive on Traditional Native Spirituality Practice. The approval of this policy was based largely on the conviction that native inmates should have access to their own spiritual leaders, elders and medicine persons. Native spirituality is accorded status and protection equal to that of other recognized religions.[28]

Medicine persons have once again assumed a more active role in their communities. New programs are developing all over Canada to allow increasing interaction between traditional native medicine and western medical techniques. A leading role in this field has been assumed by the Edmonton-based *Nechi*

Institute.[29] In 1981, the *Winnipeg Free Press* (August 20) reported how a Cree Medicine Man, John Daniel Blacksmith, was inundated by letters from people seeking cures for all kinds of diseases. In 1987, the *Globe and Mail* (March 2) reported on the collaboration between 87-year-old Indian medicine man, Nazar Linklater, and Manitoba doctors and nurses. According to a study by a University of Manitoba nursing professor, 38.5% of northern Manitoba nurses were referring patients to medicine men, and 52% to native elders. The survey found that 59% of patients sent to elders received relief from their medical problem. In 1988, the *Globe and Mail* (July 28) reported on the creation of a new clinic in Wikwemikong, the largest reserve on Manitoulan Island (Ontario), which uses both traditional and modern medicine. In 1993, *The Ottawa Citizen* (March 14) carried an important article by Robert Mason Lee *(The Vancouver Sun)* on Ovide Mercredi's decision to focus the attention of the *Assembly of First Nations* on community healing instead of constitutional reform. In the article Mercredi, president of the AFN, describes his own spiritual relationship with the famous Cree medicine man Peter O'Cheese.

One of the major contributions to the recognition of the value of traditional native medicine has been made by psychiatrist Wolfgang Jilek and his wife Louise Jilek-Aall, a psychiatrist and anthropologist, in relation to the Spirit Dance of the Salish Indians and other West coast tribes.[30] An important study, sponsored by the University of Alberta, demonstrated the extraordinary healing capacities of the Woods Cree shaman Russell Willier (Mehkwasskwan or Red Cloud) regarding psoriasis, an incurable disease.[31]

Political self-determination

Even though the first nations of Canada now have their own political organizations, the negotiations on political self-government are progressing very slowly. In fact, since the beginning of the Canadian confederation in 1867, the Indians have been systematically ignored by the federal and the provincial governments in negotiations about the future political and economic development of Canada. In the field of politics, the Amerindians continue to face a kind of "Berlin Wall," even though the question of aboriginal rights is in the news more than ever. The Amerindians continue to resist any form of assimilation. They are more and more determined to defend their rights to the land, especially when faced with the industrial megaprojects which have been developing in the northern part of Canada since the 1960s. We will come back to this question in more detail in the second part of this book when we deal with the basic aspects of the Amerindian theology of liberation.

It is important to note that, over the last two decades, a new mentality has developed among the Amerindians in Canada, especially among their political leaders. Before that, most of them seemed convinced that the economic development of the North would eventually benefit their communities. The mood has changed today, as the Amerindians claim sovereignty over immense territories which contain enormous natural resources. It is not easy to determine when this change of mind occurred. But the focus is now on political self-determination and on the economic self-sufficiency of the aboriginal communities, rather than on their participation in megaprojects which are planned by outsiders. Over the last fifteen years, the question of political self-government has received unprecedented public attention. This question can no longer be ignored. It surely did not escape the attention of Pope John Paul II who, during his visit at Fort Simpson in 1987, adopted the political and economic expectations of Canada's aboriginal peoples. Without any hesitation, he supported the first nations' claim for self-government and a land base that would ensure the economic development of present and future generations.[32]

The Amerindian revitalization that we have been describing has no other objective than to transform the native peoples into distinct and autonomous societies. There is no reason why this movement should not be seen as the realization of an old Hopi prophecy uttered in the middle of the nineteenth century: "Our Indian people are in the midnight and we will come out of our midnight into the day to be world leaders. This change will start when the eagle has landed on the moon." Unfortunately, no one understood this business about an eagle landing on the moon. But in the 1960s, when the first space ship landed on the moon, the astronauts radioed back to earth "The Eagle has landed." That week, the first Indian Alcohol and Drug Abuse program was set up. Because of its holistic approach, this program is often identified as the beginning of the Amerindian cultural renaissance.[33] Since the early 1960s, the Amerindians have been truly committed to restoring the sacred and vital circle of the aboriginal peoples.

II. The Amerindian Nations of Canada: An Overview

1. An ethnic, cultural and juridical reality

The preceding reflection on the Amerindian renaissance inevitably raises questions about the Amerindian reality itself. Who are the peoples we have called Indians since the fifteenth century? What is their contemporary situation? We will now answer these questions by concentrating directly on the Canadian situation. What follows faithfully reflects the life of the majority of native persons who shared with us their vision of Christ.

In Canada, the Amerindian reality continues to be a kind of mysterious country inside a country, an object of abstract curiosity for the majority of Canadians, and a tourist attraction for the rest. In 1954, the famous writer Hugh MacLennan described the French and English Canadians, the two founding nations of Canada, as two solitudes who were never able to meet. But what about the peoples who were living in the vast areas of what is now Canada thousands of years before the arrival of the first Europeans? Can we speak of a true encounter between these aboriginal peoples and those who arrived later? In fact, it is only since the early 1960s that the Amerindians have really been able to take their place on the Canadian public stage as a socio-cultural reality which can no longer be ignored. This complex Amerindian reality is composed of three important factors: the tribal or ethnic factor, the cultural factor, and the legal or political factor. We cannot ignore these factors, even though the perspective of this research is strictly theological.

The ethnic factor

The Amerindian reality is, first of all, a diversified ethnic reality, composed of a great variety of nations, peoples, tribes and cultural subgroups. Throughout North America, native peoples define themselves as members of particular ethnic groups with specific names. The differences between these ethnic groups can be compared to those existing between the different European peoples and nations. The names given to these native peoples by the European discoverers have their traditional equivalent by which the different native nations now prefer to be called. For example, the Mohawks call themselves Hau-de-no-sau-nee (the People of the Longhouse) and the Slavy Indians call themselves Dene.

There are at present 53 Amerindian languages from 11 linguistic families, as distinct and different as the Latin, German and Slavic languages in Europe. Seven of these linguistic families can be found in British Columbia where the majority of native languages are spoken. Of the 53 languages, eight are on the verge of extinction. Twenty-nine are deteriorating rapidly because the majority of speakers are advanced in age. Thirteen are considered moderately endangered, that is they have from 1,000 to 5,000 speakers per language. If the present trend of language loss continues, only Cree, Ojibway and Inuktitut, each with over 5,000 speakers, have a good chance of survival well into the twenty-first century.[34] Most native groups know that language, the means of communication and the vehicle of ideas and belief, is a vital aspect of their culture. Even though English or French has gradually become the language of communication among them, the different native groups in Canada have increased their efforts to save their own languages.[35] Since 1984, the first nations have developed a native language policy which emphasizes their desire to remain distinct peoples.

The cultural factor

The Amerindian reality is also a very complex cultural reality. We refer here to the cultural differences which exist among the different native groups in Canada as the result of a twofold acculturation process. First, we have the different cultural exchanges between the native groups themselves. This movement is creating a pan-Indian identity often adopted by those who are involved in politics and by persons who have lost contact with their own cultural group. Secondly, there is also the forced acculturation of all native groups by the North American and western civilization. Consequently in each native group or tribe we meet persons who have adopted a very western lifestyle and also others who hold to the traditional ways. One may also meet persons with a professional and academic formation, who continue nonetheless to practise ancestral spirituality and rituals. Medicine persons can be found in the urban centres as well as on the reserves. Often the daily life of these traditional persons is little different from the daily life of other Canadians.[36]

The first reaction of non-Amerindians to this situation is astonishment. It destroys their traditional perception of the Indian. In fact, for most Westerners, the word "culture" is so closely related to economic, industrial and technological progress, that they find it difficult to believe that a "civilized" Indian is still an Indian. For many others, on the contrary, the concept of Indian culture remains tied to the image of the "noble savage," the noble child of nature. Both perceptions of the native reality seem to imply a static understanding of Indian cultures. They tend to keep the Amerindians imprisoned in a past from which they are not allowed to escape. For many Westerners it is difficult to perceive the Amerindian reality as a truly contemporary phenomenon. Underneath these common perceptions of the Amerindians we detect the usual paternalistic attitudes which have dominated the ethnocentric relationships of western society with the aboriginal peoples.[37]

Therefore it is important to insist on the fact that Amerindian cultures are contemporary cultures, that they are able to adapt to modern life, and to offer their members the basic values they need to survive in the modern world.[38] Western society does not have the right to keep the Amerindians imprisoned in an idealistic cultural past. We can no longer declare that Indian cultures definitely belong to the past and that the only way to see what is left of them is to visit museums or watch the ethnic shows which we include in our national celebrations! Indian cultures represent several thousand years of extended and changing life experience. They continue to mark profoundly the overall Canadian reality and, therefore, they cannot be ignored in any debates on the future of Canada.

The political factor

The Amerindian reality is also a complex political and legal reality. In Canada, it is not always easy to know who is Indian and who is not. Dictionaries do not provide the answer to this question. Dictionaries may define Indians (Amerindians) as the original population of the Americas, Eskimos (Inuit) as the inhabitants of the Arctic territories (American and Greenland), and the Métis as persons of mixed races. Canadian legislators have come up with more technical and legal definitions. In Section 35-2 of the 1982 Canadian Constitution, the term "Aboriginal peoples of Canada" includes the Indian, Inuit and Métis Peoples of Canada. This term, the equivalent of the more commonly used terms native people or native peoples, has three related meanings. First, it refers to those contemporary societies that trace their historical ancestry, at least in part, to those societies that existed in Canada prior to the arrival and settlement of Europeans. Second, it refers to the members of these societies. Finally, it refers to persons who, although not currently members of these societies, can trace their biological ancestry through at least one line to individuals who belonged to them.[39]

According to the 1981 Canadian census, 491,460 individuals or about two percent of the Canadian population identified themselves as members of this collectivity (367,810 Indians, 98,260 Métis, 25,370 Inuit). In the 1991 census, 1,002,675 people reported having aboriginal origins, either as their only ancestry or in combination with other origins. This is an increase of 41 per cent from 1986 when 711,720 people reported aboriginal origins. Within the general category of Indians, the Canadian government maintains a precise juridical distinction between the "Status or Registered Indians" and the "Non-Status Indians."[40] The term "Status or Registered Indians" refers to those who are governed by *The Indian Act*, created in 1868 and substantially revised in 1951. According to this law, which is seen by many as one of the worst types of colonial legislation, the Canadian government maintains almost total control, by means of its Department of Indian and Northern Affairs, over these registered Indians. This power is based on the *Constitutional Law of 1867* by which the Canadian Federation was created.[41] The non-status Indians, who are not governed by *The Indian Act*, can, therefore, not claim the rights and privileges stemming from this law. Only since the repatriation of the Canadian Constitution in 1982 do the Métis peoples have certain ancestral rights.

It is important to note that the demographic information provided by *Statistics Canada* is often limited to the status Indians. Shortly after the beginning of the Canadian Confederation (1867), the total number of native people was approximately 102,000. According to the 1931 census, reviewed by Sametz[42,] the total native population of Canada was estimated to be between 105,000 and 121,900 in 1881, between 127,900 and 106,600 in 1901, and between 105,500 and 113,800 in 1911. Over the next seventy years (to 1941) the Indian population fluctuated between that level and about 122,000, which represented from 2.5 to 1.1 per cent of the total Canadian population. Not until 1941 did the Indian population begin to show a pattern of sustained growth and not until 1966 did the Indian population of Canada again reach the size it had been just prior to European contact. Between 1967 and 1981, the number of status Indians increased by 36% (an average of 2.6% per annum), in comparison with an 18% increase of the total Canadian population. It is estimated that there will be approximately 531,700 status Indians in Canada by the year 2001. However, the majority of anthropologists estimate that about 5% of the total Canadian population (about 1 million) now has ancestral origins.[43]

2. A fragile social situation

Notwithstanding their cultural revitalization, the social situation of the Amerindian populations in Canada remains extremely fragile. Many native communities are broken by successive waves of violence. Their social and psychological conditions are worse than those in any other segment of Canadian society.

Statistics demonstrate, for example, that in the areas of child protection, infant mortality, education, unemployment, criminality, alcohol and substance abuse, violent deaths and suicides, the native situation is disastrous and shows little improvement. In 1987, 70% of the Indian population living on the reserves was institutionally dependent on the government. It is estimated that in 1990, 337,000 of the 510,905 Indian men, women and children needed social assistance, while 90% of the adults were underemployed or without employment. The life expectancy of the adult native population is eight years less than that of other Canadians. The number of native infant mortalities is twice that of the rest of Canada (17.2 compared to 7.9 per 1,000 infants). The number of violent native deaths is more than three times the national average (157 compared to 54.3 per 1,000). About 35% (the worst record in the entire world) of native deaths are the result of accidents and violence. During the 1980s, many native communities were devastated by epidemics of suicide, especially among their young. The native suicide rate is three times the national average among adults and seven times the national average among youth (15 to 24 years). Amerindians represent 10% of the Canadian prison inmates. On the Indian reserves, 30% of the houses are overpopulated, 40% without a central heating system, and 47% are deteriorated or beyond repair. About 45% of the native population (national average 17%) is functionally illiterate.[44]

We cannot assess this situation without referring in a particular way to the social condition of native women and children. A remarkable study on native women, published in 1987, concluded: "One thing is clear—that to be born poor, Indian and female is to be a member of the most disadvantaged minority in Canada today, a citizen minus. It is to be victimized and utterly powerless and to be, by government decree, without legal recourse of any kind."[45] Among other things, this study refers to the discrimination against native women who, through their marriage with a non-native man, lose their official Indian status. This law, which was changed only in 1985, also applied to the children resulting from these marriages. Other studies reveal that native women are often victims of violence in their own reserve communities. Until recently, their voices were practically unheard in the dominant society. But native women are rapidly emerging as a source of energy and inspiration within contemporary society.[46]

Another study, published by Patrick Johnston in 1983 for The Canadian Council on Social Devopment, offers a poignant picture of the tragic situation of many native children.[47] The study deals with the highly disproportionate representation of native children in the Child Welfare System across Canada and with the dramatic implications that the existing welfare policies in most Canadian provinces and territories have for native families. From the mid-1960s to the early 1980s, about 15,000 native children were taken away from their families by social workers, often for no other reason than to offer them better life conditions. In most cases, the adopted parents were white and urban. The children were placed in homes far away from their own community. The strongest demand for native children came from the United States, where private agencies were making a profit by finding children for middle-class couples who were ready to pay up to $4,000 for a child. By 1980, this policy was perceived as a national tragedy. It caused enormous cultural, psychological and emotional trauma among the children and it discredited the traditional role of the native (extended) family as the basic unit of the Amerindian communities. The Indian and Métis children were totally submerged in another culture, and their native identity soon disappeared. They became a lost generation. Hundreds of adopted children have now found their way back to the communities where they were born. But nobody knows how many native children were permanently damaged as a result of the Canadian adoption policies. The child welfare system, like the residential school system, has left a permanent legacy of pain and cultural confusion in the lives of many native adults.[48]

The history behind all these statistics is rather disconcerting. It is the history of an oppressed people trying to cope with the disastrous consequences of many years of forced acculturation. The aggressive character of this cultural phenomenon is not always evident. In fact, today we meet many Amerindians who have become Christians and who have benefited from western school systems, medical services and political or juridical institutions. Everything is not necessarily negative in the acculturation process.[49] But these success stories cannot hide the final toll of disaster of the western civilizing mission in North America. In fact, we must recognize that most of the violence in the native communities can be interpreted as the dramatic reaction by which the Amerindians manifest their opposition to the western politics of assimilation, and to the western obsession with having all peoples conform to its viewpoint and ways of thinking. According to an almost fatal logic, western society's negative image of the Indian is reinforced by the Indians' negative reaction to our foreign interventions in their communities.[50] The internal violence of the native communities does not tragically illustrate the Indians' incapacity to adapt to the western lifestyle, but the limits of our own cultural systems and their universal pretensions.

Unfortunately, the media have made most Canadians familiar with only this negative side of the Amerindian reality. They end up believing that the Indians are the members of a "culture of poverty" or, even worse, that they have no culture at all. It is therefore important to remind ourselves that the basic differences between the aboriginal and the other Canadian peoples is not a matter of pathologies! These differences are truly cultural differences deeply rooted in the past. We must be aware that the traumas which affect and kill Indians today are not primarily physical or psychological, but cultural. They are largely the result of what Doctor Wolfgang Jilek has called a situation of "anomic depression," which causes the socio-cultural disintegration of individuals and the cultural confusion of their communities. The term "anomy" (borrowed from Durkheim) has been adopted here to describe the socio-cultural dynamics implied in this syndrome that affects a considerable number of Amerindians. These persons constantly find themselves in conflicting situations with respect to the dominant society by which they have been placed in a position of almost total dependence. They have become "irresponsible," powerless and desperate.[51]

3. A difficult coexistence

The 1970s have been described as a crucial period for Canada's first nations. That is when they reversed the social, economic and political condition of non-existence produced by the process of signing treaties in the nineteenth century. From the famous inquiry conducted by Judge Thomas Berger on the construction of a pipeline in the valley of the MacKenzie River (North West Territories) early in the 1970s to the enshrining of aboriginal rights in the Canadian Constitution of 1983, the first nations have become a powerful reality which can no longer be ignored in negotiations on the political and economic future of Canada.[52] Almost everywhere in Canada, Amerindians have intensified their land claims as well as their political, social and economic demands. Beyond the inevitable tensions caused by this new scenario, we are facing a point of no return: the Indians' desire and right to control their own future. In fact, what the first nations want to achieve closely resembles the political and cultural aspirations of the Province of Quebec since the 1960s. Both the first nations and Quebec speak of distinct societies, political self-determination, control of their economic development, and the respect for their cultural identity. Therefore, it was by a strange irony of fate that a native person and member of the Manitoban Parliament, Elijah Harper (Cree Indian), put an end to the so-called Meech Lake Accord that recognized Quebec as a distinct society, and that it was the people of Quebec who suffered most from the heat of the Indian Summer in 1990, when the Oka crisis brought the Mohawk Indians and the white population in the Montreal area into conflict.

It should be noted, however, that the Canadian landscape has witnessed more than one native crisis over the last twenty years. The Oka crisis received more media attention, but cannot be isolated from the other native protests.[53] Even though a certain number of contemporary studies continue to reveal the persistence of positive attitudes vis-à-vis the Indians among the majority of Canadians,[54] the Oka crisis points to the existence of latent forms of racism, the result of the gradual marginalization of the Indian population. There have not been that many real encounters between the Amerindians and the other Canadian peoples. The massive migration of the Amerindians to the cities has not changed the picture. Amerindians move to the cities, not to shake hands with the white population, but out of desperate economic needs (overpopulated Indian reserves, unemployment, inadequate medical care, and so on). This forced migration results in the creation of new ghettos instead of fostering positive rapports between the Amerindians and other city dwellers. The urbanization of Canada's Indians is a complex phenomenon with dramatic consequences in terms of human adaptation, the loss of cultural identity, and the cost of social welfare.[55]

In view of the present political and economic situation of Canada, the situation of the first nations will likely not improve, at least in the near future. The fact that, since 1960, the Indians (Status Indians) have been administered by the Department of Indian and *Northern Affairs* (a curious combination indeed) indicates that the fate of the Indians is dominated by Canada's economic interests and by the exploitation of its rich, northern resources. This is clearly illustrated, for example, by the present conflict between the Government of the Province of Quebec and the Cree Indians about the hydroelectric megaproject of Poste-de-la-Baleine. It is also interesting to note, in this context, that the English- and French-speaking populations of Canada are usually described as its two "founding nations." The Canadian federation has developed itself without and even *despite* the aboriginal peoples. The majority of Canada's two founding peoples live in its nine provinces where all the major political and economic decisions are made along an east-west axis (Montreal, Ottawa, Toronto, Winnipeg, Edmonton, Calgary, Vancouver). The Canadian North does not have provinces, only *territories* (the Yukon and the North West Territories). We may well conclude that what matters here, when Canada is considered in terms of its south-north axis, is the exploitation of the forests, mines, oil and natural gas of these territories, rather than the well-being of the peoples living in these territories.[56]

Conclusion

All the data presented in this first chapter concerning the Amerindian reality of Canada indicate that one of the most important challenges in the years to come will be the recognition of the basic rights of Canada's first nations. It was our purpose to show that this is not just a political, social or juridical challenge, but a spiritual and cultural adventure. Are we ready to assume this challenge? Are we ready to recognize that, notwithstanding their remarkable renaissance, the Amerindians are a people who have been dispossessed of their land, their social, political and juridical institutions, their languages, and their children? The only thing that the western, Euro-Canadian society was unable to take away from the Indians was their ancestral spirituality. It is to this central aspect of the Amerindian reality that we will turn in the next chapter.

CHAPTER II

The Amerindian Religious Experience: Past and Present

I. The Amerindian Religious Experience

1. A millennial spiritual heritage

Although the Amerindian renaissance described in the previous chapter has many ramifications, it remains basically a spiritual movement. One of the immediate consequences of this rebirth is the awareness that ancestral spirituality is alive and well in contemporary native North America. There is much more to Indian religion than what the ritual artifacts we see in the museums indicate, or the descriptions in the early writings of the missionaries and the explorers suggest. American and European anthropologists and, also to some extent the Christian churches of North America, have taken an interest in the contemporary manifestations of this ancestral spirituality. In their traditional, as in their updated expressions, the Amerindian religions represent a unique aspect of the North American religious and cultural landscape.[1] In the next chapter we will see how these religions have reacted to contact with Christianity. But to enable the reader to appreciate this phenomenon truly, we will first complete our presentation of the Amerindian reality by offering a summary analysis of Amerindian religious experience and theology.

The first observation that must be made concerns the variety of forms in which this religious experience expresses itself. Just as the Amerindian reality is composed of a great variety of ethnic groups, so too the Amerindian religious experience is not a homogeneous phenomenon. Notwithstanding the scarcity of written sources about the origins of the Amerindian religious experience, archaeological and anthropological research is able to demonstrate that many cultural transactions took place between the different aboriginal peoples of the Americas well before the arrival of the first Europeans. Therefore, we cannot interpret the Indian religions as a static and uniform reality which started moving and changing only after contact with western civilization and Christianity.[2]

Anthropologists agree on the Asian origin of the first inhabitants of the Americas. But the date of their first appearance and the chronology of the successive waves of migration over a long period of time continue to challenge scientific research. More and more sophisticated archaeological research tends to situate the arrival of the first Paleo-Siberians (the real discoverers of the New World) around 10,000 to 50,000 B.C.E., perhaps even earlier, but there is no consensus among the scholars on this question. It is the prevailing view that the migrations of humans from Asia did not happen all at once but over many thousands of years and in many waves. These early Indians seem to have travelled in small family units and bands over ice-free corridors. The complete dispersal of these early peoples over the Americas, from Alaska to Tierra del Fuego, probably took centuries or even millennia. It is also probable that later migrations to the New World by Eskimos, Aleuts and Athapascans using wooden dugouts and skin boats occurred after the final submersion of Beringia. By 8000 B.C.E. (end of the Ice Age), native peoples can be found in all parts of the Americas.[3] The common Asian origin of all these peoples suggests that from the outset they shared a uniform circumpolar or circumboreal culture with more or less similar characteristics: hunting taboos, animal ceremonialism, belief in spirits and shamanism. Some scholars speak of a kind of Pacific religious substratum because of the parallels they find among the totem poles of the Northwest Coast Indians, the shamanic poles of Siberia, and the ceremonial poles in the cultures of the South Pacific, and even among the Maori of New Zealand.[4] At the end of this long period of migration, this common religious stratum gradually diversified into two contrasting religious systems: the old hunting religions and the new horticultural religions. Each system developed its own myths, beliefs, symbols and rituals according to the law of fidelity to the origins (tradition and cultural continuity) and to the law of adaptation to the new geographical and historical conditions (cultural discontinuity and acculturation).[5]

The Amerindian religions are therefore excellent examples of so-called primitive, primal or tribal religions which have managed to remain living religions. They represent a millennial religious experience which occupies a specific place among the great religious traditions of the world. In the course of history, this spiritual heritage has developed and diversified in relationship with the various geographical and ecological conditions of the Americas. This evolution has produced a wide spectrum of religious traditions which clearly demonstrate the Indians' remarkable ability to cope with cultural changes and deprivation provoked by intertribal contacts and the confrontation with the western world. They have done this by borrowing from the non-Indian world with pragmatic and cautious selectivity what they needed for the survival and further development of their cultures.[6]

This flexibility may be explained by the fact that the Amerindian religions have no historical founder and dogmatic content. They are the result of oral traditions, handed down by the communities themselves (tribe, clan) from generation to generation. The native religions, which are quite charismatic in nature, leave much room for personal experience, dreams and visions, especially during long periods of social, economic and political crisis. In these situations native prophets and spiritual leaders produced new rituals and ceremonies which allowed the community to maintain the meaning of life despite the inevitable transformations of its environment.

In the next chapter we will show how the Indian desire for cultural survival inspired the great nineteenth-century movements of religious restoration which were often very syncretic.

2. An inner reality

The Amerindian religions are not to be viewed as institutionalized religions. They present themselves, basically, as a not-easily-accessible inner reality which is first experienced on the level of tribe, clan and extended family. In fact, it would be better to speak here of a *spiritual journey* and a *religious process*, rather than a religion, because of the experiential relationship the native person has with the supreme being and the spiritual world. Notwithstanding the great variety of beliefs, myths and rituals by which it expresses itself socially, the Amerindian religious experience has some basic characteristics which can be found among the majority of the native groups. These characteristics are the benchmarks of the Amerindian spiritual universe.

Among these characteristics, the first to be noted is the intimate relationship between the religious dimension and all other dimensions of Amerindian life. What we call "Amerindian religion" does not constitute a separate sector of reality (as is now the case for the Christian religion in western, secularized society) which is experienced privately and then applied to the public life. This religion constitutes the most profound and intimate dimension of all native life. The Amerindians therefore cannot imagine their relationship with God as though it is separated from all other relationships which constitute the social fabric of personal and community life. Their religious experience is both very sacramental and deeply mystical.

Strictly speaking, Amerindians do not believe in God. They know God as an intrinsic dimension of all their relations. All the living beings of the universe are mystically related to each other and receive their substance from God or from the Great Mystery, their vital centre and source of energy. The Amerindians experience their relationship with the Great Mystery in and through their latent awareness of the intimate links which exist between the human being, all other living beings of the universe, and the earth itself. They know that all these living beings depend on one another. They also know that an intimate link exists between the visible universe and the invisible spiritual powers that belong to the sphere of the Great Mystery. In the spiritual universe of the Amerindians, there is no clear separation between the visible and the invisible world, between earth and heaven, between the living and the dead, between past, present and future generations. The Amerindian religious experience is the source of profound solidarity between the individuals, the community, the cosmos, the spiritual powers and the Great Mystery.[7] A typical illustration of this solidarity can be found in the formula *Mitakuye oyas'in* (All my relations) by which the Lakota and other native groups conclude their religious rituals, prayers and public speeches.[8] While in the Christian prayer formulas the term *Amen* accentuates the importance of the one who speaks, the term *Mitakuye oyas'in* (and its variations) links the individual with the communion of saints who confirm the truth of the speaker and offer spiritual support. The Amerindian religious experience thus reflects a very particular worldview which is quite different from the western (Judeo-Christian) worldview which maintains a radical separation and distinction between God as supreme being and the universe as created by, but separated from God.

There is an intimate connection between the Amerindian religious experience and the native enculturation process. Native enculturation or cultural education is basically experiential. The Amerindian education means learning-by-doing. In native religion, as in all other aspects of native life, the process is more important than the content. This does not mean, however, that the Amerindians are incapable of developing a truly Amerindian theology or of producing highly complex systems of thinking. The Amerindian cultures have produced theological and philosophical modes of thinking. But it is important to note that the written or theoretical expressions of these theologies and philosophies continue to bear the influence of the oral traditions and the experiential approach to life. In addition to the holistic nature of this religious experience we should also note a specific understanding of time, space, language and all the material elements used in the ritual expressions of the experience.

The *spoken word* always has precedence over the written word. The word is perceived as a sacred reality produced by the breath of life within the centre of the human person. Language is not seen as some kind of external element, separated from the human person. The word is an intimate aspect of the human being, the very expression of its vital thrust. Within Amerindian cultures, *time* is, likewise, not conceived, in the first place, as the material measurement *(chronos)* of successive events, but as the intensity *(kairos)* of the events themselves. Time tends to be experienced as cyclical, spiral and rhythmic rather than as linear and progress-oriented. The *elements* (earth, rocks, plants, trees, water, fire), which are used in the rituals, are not material objects but living beings whose spiritual power is tied to the place they come from. The very gathering of these elements is an important dimension of the Amerindian rituals.[9]

These few general observations illustrate the central place of religion within the life of the Amerindians who truly consider themselves spiritual people. Indian life is a spiritual journey. As in all religions, this spiritual journey finds its expression in beliefs, myths and rituals. But the link with the land remains primordial. Therefore, Amerindian religion is often described as a religion or metaphysics of nature.[10] This description is correct as long as we do not lose sight of the holistic character of the Amerindian religious experience. The rituals and the ceremonies remain, of course, the more visible and accessible dimension of this spirituality.[11] But the Amerindian experience of the Great Mystery is more than a ritual affair. Amerindian ancestral spirituality, as we have noted, must be understood as a global or holistic journey. This journey is constituted by personal visions and experiences of the Great Mystery, rather than by beliefs, doctrines and rituals. It is, above all, *a state of consciousness* of the concrete but incomprehensible presence of the Great Mystery, the source of the energy of everything that is.

3. The basic characteristics of the Amerindian religious experience

Until now, we have deliberately avoided looking at the Amerindian religions from the point of view of the questions which normally constitute the starting point of religious investigations: What is your religion? What are your beliefs? How do you understand and name the Absolute Being? Valuable as they are, such questions focus on the content rather than on the process of the religious experience. The fact that we have preferred to present the Amerindian religions primarily as religious experiences is decisive for the basic orientation of this study on the Amerindian vision of Christ. We are not concerned here with a comparative study between the Amerindian and Christian doctrines or rituals, but with the mysterious presence of Christ in the Amerindian spiritual process.

This particular approach demands that we outline the basic characteristics of this religious experience. It also takes into consideration the fact that there are not that many Amerindian theological publications. Our own access to the spiritual universe of the Amerindians largely depended on our participation in their religious ceremonies and rituals while we were planning and preparing this study.

What is most characteristic of the Amerindian religious experience is its *sacramental* (concrete) and *mystical* (relational) quality. In fact, the concrete universe in which the Amerindians make their spiritual journey is already perceived as a sacred or mystical reality. We should therefore also insist on the *existential* dimension of this experience. Although in the course of history native religions have produced a certain protology (myths of origin, creation or emergence) and a certain eschatology (the ultimate destiny of the Amerindian soul and spirit), they are based on the present possibility of significantly situating oneself in a spiritual universe where everything is interrelated.

Given this particular configuration of the Amerindian religious experience, most native groups share a certain number of important insights, most of which are acquired through personal or collective experiences. These insights (systems of knowledge) resemble what the Christian tradition designates as the essence of mysticism: *Cognitio experimentalis* (experiential knowledge). They concern, above all, the spiritual powers which belong to the sphere of the Great Mystery and enter into the human circles of life. They also concern the particular gifts of spiritual persons (shamans, healers, prophets, dreamers) and their function within the community. They deal with the cosmic harmony which exists among all living beings in the universe, with the fragility of human existence, and with the healing process and practices.

We must insist here on the *performative* aspect of the Amerindian religions and on the *immediate* aspect of the oral traditions which assure their continuity by various techniques which valorize extensively the personal contributions of all the members of the community. In fact, it is the people who assume direct responsibility for the transmission of oral traditions, ancestral wisdom and culture. While western civilization depends a great deal on the invention of printing—and Christianity is perceived by the Amerindians as a "religion of the book" (the Bible)—the survival of the Amerindian religions largely depends on the willingness of community members to participate in their ongoing realization. The fact that we now find more and more published studies on Amerindian religions does not change this situation. Moreover, these literary sources may well contribute to the gradual depersonalization of Amerindian religious experience and to its transformation into a theoretical or abstract system.[12] There is no question here of opposing the advantages of the written cultures (of the so-called civilized or advanced peoples) to the oral cultures of so-called illiterate and primitive peoples, but of being aware of the particular dynamics involved in the Amerindian religious experience. This experience maintains a strong link between its informative and performative dimensions. One learns through participation!

This last observation applies to Amerindians as well as to non-Amerindians who want to know more about ancestral spirituality. In the field of spirituality there is no substitute for personal experience.[13] Objective and theoretical approaches do not suffice. Personal initiation is a must. It is interesting to note, in this context, that a certain number of anthropologists are now convinced that the lack of studies of the Amerindian religious experience, for example among the Athapascan peoples, is not related to the linguistic incompetency of the anthropologists, but to their inability to enter into the spiritual universe of the Amerindians. There is a fundamental difference in enculturation between the majority of anthropologists and the native peoples. Generally speaking, anthropologists are not familiar with the same ways of learning as native peoples (for example, through dreams and visions). This explains the difficulties they experience in trying to enter into the cognitive process that constitutes the basis of the Amerindian religions and determines their uniqueness.[14]

Between 1983 and 1987, we were able to participate in a series of intercultural encounters set up by Cree Indians of Alberta with the purpose of introducing non-Amerindians to the experiential mode of Amerindian spirituality.[15] These meetings were based on the conviction, so often expressed by the elders and the native spiritual leaders, that the same Spirit is at work among Amerindians and non-Amerindians in a creative and innovative way. The Amerindian religious experience, with all its ascetical and mystical orientations, its dreams and visions, its personal and collective rituals, is nothing but a sustained and repeated effort to connect with the Spirit in order to receive the vision which determines one's unique place in a universe where all things are interrelated.

II. Amerindian Theology

1. The Great Mystery *(Wakan Tanka)*

The fact that Amerindian religions give high priority to experiential learning, practice and ritual does not mean that they are less theological or philosophical than institutionalized religions. Our previous analysis of the Amerindian religious experience indicates that over the centuries the aboriginal peoples have developed an extraordinary awareness of the sacred. We will now continue this presentation by concentrating directly on the speculative dimension of this experience. Hartley Burr Alexander found himself obliged to write in 1953 that the concentration of research on the Indian rituals seemed to forget that the first nations of North America had developed complex systems of highly theological and philosophical thinking.[16] One may think here, for example, of the extraordinary metaphysics surrounding the sun dance of the Plain Indians.[17] The Indian vision of the Great Mystery and the Indian interpretations of nature are the sources of human wisdom and of an ethics of responsibility whose importance is increasingly recognized by the West as it struggles with an ecological crisis which illustrates the limits of its own philosophical systems.[18] In the pages that follow we will concentrate on the three dimensions of the Amerindian theology which will support or further research on the Amerindian visions of Christ: God (the Great Mystery), the cosmos and the ethos. Before we present these three elements, a short note on the formation of the Amerindian traditions.

It is a well-known fact that most religious systems are composed of a high tradition, represented by the elite, the experts and the priests, and a low tradition, represented by the people who reflect on religion by practising it. The elite is always concerned with the coherence of the system, while the people are more interested in its visible expressions. This dynamic also characterizes the Amerindian religions. In many native groups we find a sort of religious elite or hierarchy, often composed of shamans, healers, prophets, dreamers and wise persons, whose religious mission seems well-defined. Sometimes we also find secret religious societies whose initiated members are more directly involved in the exact interpretation and the transmission of the religious traditions. But in any Amerindian religious complex there is always a close link between these spiritual persons and the community.[19] While in the institutionalized religions the hierarchy is perceived as a group of persons set apart from the community, in the Amerindian religions these spiritual persons do not constitute a group as such. They exercise their religious function while fully participating in all the other tasks of community life. Even though the special gifts of these persons are recognized by the community, one rarely meets "professionals," "experts" or "technicians" of Amerindian spirituality. This does not mean, however, that we can entirely eliminate the distinction between the high tradition (elite) and the low tradition (people).[20] We must recognize that our presentation of Amerindian theology, especially of the Amerindian vision of God, largely depends on the authorized interpretations of spiritual persons (the keepers of the tradition) who have, recently, started sharing their knowledge with the western world.[21]

One of the main functions of each religion is to name the supreme being and to produce a coherent vision of the spiritual powers in the universe. How do the Amerindians exercise this function? What are the Indian names of the supreme being? Where and how do the Amerindians experience their living God? The experiential and existential orientation of the Amerindian religions immediately suggests that this God experience occurs in the ordinary elements of daily life. The supreme being is not first perceived and experienced as the origin (protology) and the end (eschatology) of the world, but as the foundation of everything that is, here and now. It is perceived as the very centre of each living being and as a *presence* in the universe. We can truly experience the supreme being once we have found our right place in the universe and once we have developed right relationships. This God experience is basically a matter of internal and external harmony, because the entire universe is perceived as a sacred reality filled with spiritual powers.

Because of this particular approach to the Great Mystery it was often assumed that the Amerindians did not have the concept of a supreme being. As a matter of fact, according to the evolutionistic perspective of the nineteenth century, influenced by the animistic doctrine of Edward Tylor, "primitive religions" and "monotheism" were mutually exclusive concepts.[22] The early anthropologists seemed convinced that religions necessarily moved from their initial nature cult to pantheism, dualism, and, finally, to monotheism. Most scholars now admit that the traditional Amerindian religions were indeed structured around the concept of a supreme being even before contact with Christianity. However, we should also be aware of the fact that it is not easy to express the Amerindian God-experience with the western concepts of polytheism and monotheism. Amerindian theology represents a kind of theism that situates itself in between these two mutually exclusive concepts. In fact, the only western concept which might be able to express this experience adequately is that of "pan-en-theism," borrowed from Christian mysticism. God is everywhere and, at the same time, above everything. God is not only the Other, but the Non-Other *(Non Aliud)*, the Incomparable One. This is why the oldest names of God, like the Lakota name *Wakan Tanka*, are polysynthetic and all-inclusive concepts which are hard to translate into western languages.[23] In certain Amerindian cultures, like the Dine (Navajo), the supreme being had no proper name. It was celebrated as the Great Invisible Power, universally present in nature, which simply refused to be named and defined.[24] Most Indian tribes were opposed to anthropomorphic representations of the supreme being. But many used terms such as "Grandfather" when they addressed the supreme being. According to Vine Deloria, this term never served as the basis for the development of a theological doctrine concerning the complex relationship between God and the created world as in Christian doctrine. The Amerindians were not interested, as such, in a personal relationship with God. Instead, they perceived the supreme being as an indiscernable and indefinable presence.[25] But they knew, at the same time, that the supreme being constituted their own substance. A contemporary native spiritual woman expresses this very well. Her witness reflects the *Deus (est) intimior intimo meo* of Saint Augustine: "The Great Spirit was closer to my ancestors than their own bones, and prayer was as natural as breath."[26]

This is the reason why we have adopted here the term *Wakan Tanka* of the Lakota people to present the Amerindian understanding of God. This divine name is older than the names Great Spirit, Gitchi-Manitou or Creator which have been influenced by Christianity. What does *Wakan Tanka* mean? The word *Wakan* is often translated by saint or sacred. *Wakan Tanka*, therefore, means the Great Holy Being. In his book, *Sacred Pipe*, Joseph Epes Brown, quoting Black Elk, writes: "We should understand well that all things are the work of the Great Spirit. We should know that He is within all things: the trees, the grasses, the rivers, the mountains, and all the fourlegged animals, and the winged peoples; and even more important, we should understand that He is above all these things and peoples. When we do understand all this deeply in our hearts, then we will fear, and love, and know the Great Spirit, and then we will be and act and live as he intends."[27]

This quotation refers to one of the deepest mysteries of *Wakan Tanka*. The supreme being is present in a certain way in all the elements of the universe, but he is, at the same time, a totally distinct reality. According to the Lakota, *Wakan Tanka* has the unique quality of being, at the same time, one and everything. William Stolzman writes: "Most medicine men view *Wakan Tanka* as a distinct, single person, who is the Great Grandfather over all. He is the most powerful Other who lives above the heavens. Each *taku wakan kin* is personally distinct from him and is freely and personally empowered by *Wakan Tanka* to be truly free and personal. One medicine man indicated that he thought of *Wakan Tanka* as the whole which is greater than the *taku wakan kin* parts. When the spirits do a healing, it is *Wakan Tanka* who is thanked because all that which is *wakan* originates from Him and is an expression of his power and life. Concentrating on *wakan* power he considered the individual spirits as merely particular figures through whom *Wakan Tanka* communicates his power to men."[28]

Wakan Tanka is thus many-in-one (see the western concept of pan-entheism). Everything that is *wakan* (sanctified, holy) in this world is ultimately related to *Wakan Tanka*: the mysterious power above eveything. But this mysterious power is more than the union of all things.

It is now common for many native groups to designate the supreme being by the term Great Spirit. But as in the case of *Wakan Tanka,* it is unclear that this term designates a personalized being. William Powers, one of the experts on the Oglala religion, writes: "This term *(Wakan Tanka)* has become the conventional gloss for God. Although singular in form, *Wakantanka* is collective in meaning. *Wakantanka* is not personified, but aspects of it are. These aspects are often personified or manifested in the sun, moon, sky, earth, winds, lightning, thunder, and other natural phenomena. Man exists as an integral part of nature, not as one wishing to control its vicissitudes, but as one wanting to live in harmony with it. Man is innately powerless and cries out to be pitied when confronted with danger, famine, and the unexplainable. When an Oglala is in need of supernatural help, he asserts his powerlessness by intoning *Wakantanka unsimala ye* (*Wakantanka*, pity me). Man's relationship to nature is always *unsike* (pitiable). By crying out to *Wakantanka* he at once addresses the sum total of supernatural help at his disposal. *Wakantanka* may also be addressed in the metaphor of kinship. Thus an Oglala says '*Ho Tunkasila Wakantanka...*' (Ho, Grandfather *Wakantanka*). Here *Grandfather* is used to appeal to an aspect of *Wakantanka* independent of any manifestation; *Father* is used to appeal to an aspect of *Wakantanka* which is capable of being manifested, such as the sun. The same metaphor of kinship is used to differentiate between the potentiality of the earth to grow things (*unci* 'grandmother') and the actual manifest produce of the earth (*maka ina* mother earth)."[29] Joseph Brown is of the opinion that kinship titles such as Father or Grandfather, when applied to *Wakan Tanka*, are considered by spiritual persons to have a symbolic meaning. The term Father refers to *Wakan Tanka* as a real being, while the term Grandfather refers to its unlimited and unqualified essence.

Paul Steinmetz writes that contemporary Lakota see *Wakan Tanka* as a personal transcendent God, as Creator and Provider, who rewards the good and punishes the evil. Most believe in the Christian doctrine of the Trinity and claim that even before the Europeans came they believed in the same God as the Christians. Early research on the Lakota religion seemed to confirm that the original meaning of *Wakan Tanka* was not a single, distinct being, but the totality of being. It is only under the influence of Christianity that the Lakota understanding of the supreme being has become more personified. Steinmetz adds a particular dimension to the interpretation of *Wakan Tanka* by stressing the difference between implicit and explicit monotheism. According to him, explicit monotheism is a conceptual form of knowledge that cannot be present on a merely symbolic level. It is achieved only by reducing symbols to concepts through a process of philosophical reflection. Such a process is characteristic of western thinking. In the religious experience of the so-called primitive peoples, dominated by symbolic modes of thinking, we find only implicit types of monotheism.[30]

What precedes clearly illustrates the tensions between the high and the low tradition within the Amerindian religions as far as their understanding of God is concerned, especially since they came into contact with Christianity. In order to avoid being perceived as animistic, the high tradition will focus on the transcendent and supernatural nature of the supreme being, while the low tradition, especially on the level of ritual and religious practice, is not afraid to relate to the many spiritual powers which are manifestations of the Great Mystery. It is therefore very difficult to grasp the Amerindian understanding of the exact relationship between the Great Mystery and these spiritual powers.

Finally, the Amerindian view of God can be compared with the Hindu understanding of God. In both cases, the supreme being is perceived as impersonal, because it is supra-personal. God is the totally Other, but its (her, his) otherness cannot be placed outside us. It is the task of the human person to interiorize the otherness of the supreme being. One could apply to the concept of *Wakan Tanka* what Jacques Dupuis says about Hindu mysticism and, more specifically, about the Hindu mysticism of the *advaita* (the principle of non duality): "In the light of the mysticism of *advaita*, does not a tripersonal communion with God seem a propaedeutic to be transcended, that one may be lost at last, beyond all distinctions, in the divine mystery? The question is a plausible one, even in the context of Christian tradition. The concept of person—an analogical one—is a fragile thing, as applied to God. If, furthermore, the Father is the unfathomable trinitarian Source beyond the Spirit and the Word, have we not the right to ask whether there is in turn a Beyond-the-Father? Is not the insurmountable Abyss beyond all personhood? Certain Christian mystics have thought so and have spoken of the Superessence of the Deity, beyond the three Persons."[31] The term *Wakan Tanka*, it seems to us, implies such an understanding of God.

The Amerindians are convinced that no human person can achieve anything in life without supernatural assistance. They search for this assistance in rituals such as the Vision Quest (individual quest for spiritual power), which allow the human person to relate to powers which transcend humanity. The aim of all this, as we have noted above, is not to establish a personal relationship with the supreme being, but to become attentive to its presence, when and where it manifests itself, and to look for the spiritual powers which it puts at the disposal of the humans. The Amerindians encounter God on the road of daily life and, especially, in nature. They do not divinize nature, but visualize it as the manifestation of the supreme being who is the Spirit of life of all creation.[32] The polysyncretic meaning of the experience of God corresponds to the polysyncretic meaning of the names given to the supreme being. This experience is more inclusive than exclusive. The Amerindians welcome all roads leading to the Great Mystery. We will see in the next chapter that this attitude has profoundly influenced their relationship with Christianity and their conversion to Christianity.

We will not dwell any further on the names the Amerindians give the supreme being. They reveal the great sense of mystery which has developed among them. In fact, what do we know about the power whose very name is Mystery? The more we advance in the experience of this Great Mystery, the more we see the limitations of all our divine names and titles. The name *Wakan Tanka*, given by the Lakota to the supreme being, itself sets the limits of any authentic experience of God. This term recalls the words of one of the greatest Christian theologians, Saint Anselm: the human spirit knows that God is, ultimately, a mystery that no human concept can adequately express *(Comprehendit incompre-hensibile esse),* because God is above all human comprehension *(Id quo majus cogitari nequit) (Monologion* 64; *Proslogion* 15).

2. A metaphysics of nature

There are major differences between the Amerindian and the western world-views. The Amerindians continue to perceive the universe as the habitat of spiritual powers associated with the Great Mystery and with the cycle of human existence. The Amerindian universe is a spiritual universe where there is no clear separation between all the living beings which compose it. The Amerindians maintain a mystical relationship with the animals, the herbs, the trees, the rocks, the water, the sky, and with all other "natural" elements. While the western and Christian worldviews see God as the absolute being who is at the beginning and at the end of the world, the Amerindians concentrate on the unlimited abundance of spiritual powers within the universe itself. These spiritual powers freely enter into the cycle of human existence. The main function of most native rituals, therefore, is not to establish new relationships with these powers, but to become more aware of their influences and the orientation they may give an individual's life. Ake Hultkrantz maintains, rightfully, that the native American view of nature is much more alive and filled with spiritual activity than the western view of nature.[33] Joseph Epes Brown speaks of a "metaphysics of nature" spelled out by each native group in great detail and in close relationship with its environment, notwithstanding the pressures of North American society and technological culture. This native mysticism is based on an intimate relationship with the land and on the interrelatedness of all living beings.[34]

This native worldview has caught the attention of the contemporary ecolog-ical movement. The ideological danger of this recuperation of Amerindian cosmology, especially in the counter-culture of the 1970s (see the works of Castaneda), must be noted. It has produced the new stereotype of the ecological Indian, while demythologizing the sacredness or the religious dimension of the native worldview. The rhetoric of Mother-Earth, which can be found in some of the literature produced by the American Indian Movement, may have contributed to this modern version of the *noble sauvage*.[35] It is therefore important to acknowl-edge the distinction between the Indians' modern life style and the persistence of their sacred and pre-modern worldview. Many Indians no longer want to live like their ancestors. They have adopted a modern lifestyle and manifest no desire to return to the primitive past as some overwrought ecological literature seems to suggest. Calvin Martin is right when he maintains that the native American worldview cannot simply be reduced to environmental ethics, and that it remains, basically, a spiritual way of life which cannot easily be appropriated by western people with a Cartesian mindset.[36] Ecology, as science, is a western phenomenon resulting from the contemporary natural sciences which seem unable to control the consequences of the industrial and technological evolution. The difference between this scientific ecology and the native worldview is the difference between rationality and religiosity. However, it is important to note that the ecological crisis is more and more perceived as a spiritual crisis.[37] In this sense, the native religious worldview may become a source of inspiration for the West. What matters here is not the so-called primitive lifestyle of the Indians, which belongs to the past, but the persistence of their *philosophia perennis* and of the essential values needed for the survival of our planet. We should welcome the fact, noted by many anthropologists, that this sacred worldview has survived the shock of western civilization. We will now present a few typical examples which clearly illustrate the contemporary vitality of native cosmology.

The animated universe

Among the Indians living in the Great American Desert, where conditions of life continue to be very harsh, the world is a beautiful but dangerous place to live. This world is perceived as an animated universe wherein the visible and the invisible elements interact in such a way that they form one indivisible and indistinguishable reality. The situation of humans in this universe is always *unsike* (pitiful) and extremely vulnerable. Humans enter into this universe as powerless beings. Without power, humans are nothing. But, when they seek and find their power, which is always spiritual power, everything becomes possible. The main purpose of human existence, therefore, is not "to be or not be," as a western Shakespeare would say, but to become a true personality (animated being) who lives in harmony with all the surrounding spiritual powers. This is only possible when human beings receive the breath of life (*Wakanskanskan*—What moves in a holy way) and decide to walk on the sacred path of life.[38] The Ojibway Indians share this Lakota view of life. They, too, maintain that "no man begins to be until he has received his vision."[39] Humans are bound to seek and to fulfil the vision by which they enter as moral beings (person-alities) into the order (relations) of the universe.

We can deduce from this sacred cosmology two significant implications. First, human life is understood in this context as participation and total immersion in a spiritual universe.[40] Life is, basically, a matter of communion and relationships. This communion is possible only when a human being appropriates the spiritual powers provided by the universe. Secondly, human life is not merely existence in a world where everything is subject to physical laws. It is the result of the imaginative capacity of the human spirit. At the most profound level, human beings are what they imagine themselves to be. Scott Momaday, a Kiowa Indian and well-known writer, speaks here of the "moral act of imagination" by which the Amerindians comprehend their relationship not only to the physical world but to the spiritual powers in that universe.[41] The secret of Amerindian life is the capacity to imagine oneself richly, as is suggested by the Momaday-inspired title of Christopher Vecsey's book on the mythic narratives of the native North American peoples: *Imagine Ourselves Richly*.[42] We can already foresee that this perception of the universe, so common among the Plain Indians and other native groups, nourishes a certain number of values which constitute the basis of the Amerindian ethos: a profound sense of the sacred, humility, personal discipline and solidarity.

A meaningful universe

From the Great American Desert we will now move to the spiritual universe of the Beaver or Duneza Indians of Northeastern British Columbia with the help of anthropologist Antonia Mills who has closely followed the socio-cultural and economic evolution of this people. The Beaver Indians are a typical example of a native group whose ancestral spirituality has been deeply influenced by Christianity (Catholics and Pentecostals), but whose worldview has remained very shamanistic. The universe of the Beaver Indians is a "meaningful universe." A meaningful universe, Antonia Mills writes, is one in which there is a supernatural order which affects the order of life in the natural realm. In this type of universe, accidents do not exist. Everything is penetrated by Spirit. Each event has a profound reason for happening. In everyday life, the Duneza function according to two kinds of road maps: the one tracing the roads from the village to the traplines and the hunting territories of each clan and family, and the one tracing the spirit trails. The entire community life of the Duneza is structured according to the complex relationships between the physical, visible world and the spiritual, invisible world. Dreams and visions remain the most important means of access to the meaningful, spiritual universe. Thus, when the child is about three years old, the elders may prepare it to go out into the bush for a vision quest to seek contact with its guardian spirit, usually a spirit animal. The spirit may give the child a song, special instructions or guidance. The elders may later assist the child to integrate this mystical experience into his or her life. The entire life of the Beaver Indians thus consists of learning to understand the implications of one's original vision which is often amplified by subsequent visions and dreams and by the use of a medicine bundle, the outward sign of the owner's contact with the spirit realm.

In such a prophetic and shamanic tradition, which jealously preserves the memory, knowledge and wisdom of its ancestors, the community openly recognizes that some persons (elders, prophets, dreamers, shamans) are better able to contact the spirit world than others. These persons are able to travel from the visible to the invisible world and to bring back important messages for the community. But the Duneza will always insist on the importance of the group rituals (feasts, dances, meals) which enable the entire community to stay on the trail of the spirits. During these rituals (Spirit Dance and Prophet Dance), the community remembers the songs of the ancestors and listens attentively to the exhortations of the elders. The Spirit and Prophet Dance ceremonials are both serious and joyful events. They help the Duneza to maintain the basic meaning of things while living in an ever-changing world.[43]

The question cannot be avoided: What happens to this spiritual vision of a meaningful universe when it is suddenly threatened by the economic power of the dominant society? Like many other native groups in North America, the Duneza Indians almost desperately fight for the preservation of the land base on which they carry out their traditional way of life.[44] In this context, one detects hints that the Duneza worldview has become almost apocalyptic. On the one hand, the Duneza believe that the world is going to end soon because too many people have forgotten, or never learned, to respect the spiritual powers needed to keep the world going. On the other hand, they also believe that the world and life will go on, if only on another plane. Their Vision Quest and shamanic experiences have demonstrated that it is easy to make the passage from the visible to the invisible world. Therefore, life cannot be simply imprisoned within the restricted boundaries of the physical world.

From their prophetic and shamanic tradition the Duneza have learned about the previous transformations of the world to which the Duneza ("the true people") were able to adapt. Why should they not be able to overcome, once again, the tribulations of the present times? The Duneza also believe that the children born today in a world deeply influenced by modern civilization are the reincarnation of former Duneza who lived many lives before the modern innovations arrived.[45] They believe that their worldview will be maintained through the succession of reincarnations that each person will experience. It is through the "recycling" of these specific Duneza personalities that the Beaver Indians hope to preserve their traditional culture and distinct identity. Their universe thus remains a meaningful universe. The value system related to this universe remains largely intact. It can easily be compared to that of the Indian tribes of the Great American Desert. Antonia Mills remarks, rightfully, that the persistence of this meaningful Duzena universe poses a real challenge to the Canadian endorsement of multiculturalism. While it is perfectly possible and acceptable to speak Polish, Flemish or Greek in Canada, in addition to the two official languages which are French and English, it seems more difficult for the dominant economic and industrial society to accept within its self-determined boundaries the persistence of cultural traditions which require a land base for their survival. It is obvious that the entire development of the Canadian North is based on a value system that has little in common with the Duneza meaningful universe.[46]

The worldviews which we discovered among the Teton Sioux and the Lakota of the Great Amerian Desert and among the Duneza Indians in British Columbia represent typical examples of the sacred cosmology shared by many native groups throughout North America. Generally speaking, the Amerindians were able to develop and to maintain a profound and tangible faith (knowledge, experience) in nature. This Indian approach to nature is met by many Euro-Canadian observers with a certain amount of scepticism. It escapes their scientific control and even their emotional comprehension. In fact, we are dealing here with experiences where the frontiers between what we call "nature" and the "supernatural" are practically non-existent and are constantly trespassed in the intimate consciousness of the Amerindians and in their interpretation of events.[47] What should we make, for example, of the prayers addressed by the Koyokan Indians in Alaska to the raven?[48] What do we think about the mystical link entertained by the Innu hunters from Quebec and Labrador with the spirit of the caribou which they capture with their songs and the sound of the drum?[49] What about the religious treatment by the Cree Indians of the bones of the animals they have killed, to pacify the spirit of these animals and to maintain good relationships with them?[50] What about all these Amerindians (often the very acculturated ones) who, everywhere in Canada, practise the vision quest, the traditional fast in an isolated area, to meet with their guardian spirit who is often an animal spirit?[51] The examples which illustrate, in a variety of ways, that the Amerindian environment is both natural and supernatural could be multiplied. Everything in this universe contains consciousness and spiritual power. Everything that happens in this universe is, potentially, a manifestation of this spiritual power. Everything accomplished by the Indians in this universe is influenced by their profound sense of the sacredness of all things, and they must, therefore, sometimes obey a complex code of ethics.

The preceding reflections on the persistence of the Amerindian sacred cosmology represent an enormous challenge from a cognitive point of view. No doubt, there is a specific way of looking at things with a native eye.[52] There is a specific Indian way of knowing reality which is quite different from the scientific approach to the universe, but not less important and valuable. The first thing to note here is that in the Amerindian theology the human being and the universe are inseparable realities. The Amerindians visualize their personal existence (microcosmos) as an integral part of the universe, and the universe (macrocosmos) as the organic extension of their own being. They will therefore establish close connections between the rhythms (cycles) of nature and human life.[53] The relationship of the Amerindians with the universe is never unilateral. We are dealing here with a mutual relationship and appropriation.[54] Therefore, Amerindian theology is not interested, primarily, in the secrets of nature as objects which we can submit to our scientific investigation. It considers nature as the mirror of the human being. Everything that nature teaches us concerns the fundamental relationships between the human being and the universe. Amerindian theology has not become the victim of the twofold reduction which characterizes western theology when it moved from its cosmocentric to its anthropocentric vision of reality.[55]

In his study of the Ojibway from Ontario and Manitoba, Irving Hallowell demonstrated that the Amerindian worldview also postulates a particular vision of the human person which is quite different from the western concept of the human being. The Ojibway categories of thinking always included the possibility of animation in, and communication with, the totality of the surrounding universe.[56] Other anthropologists, especially those who have a subjective experience of the Amerindian modes of thinking, confirm the validity and the unique character of the Amerindian cognitive systems. Their studies reveal, for example, that the

Amerindians knew about the importance and the relevance of dreams well before the Freudian psychologists![57] These anthropologists have tried to offer a positive definition of the native cognitive experience because they know full well that it is not enough to speak of a pre-scientific approach to reality. They confirm that we are confronted here with a level of knowledge which remains the source of tremendous spiritual power. The purpose of this knowledge is not to master the universe, but to favour the constant transformation of the human being in harmony with the universe.

In his classical study on the Naskapi hunters, Frans Speck has identified this type of knowledge as the work of the active soul *(Mistapeo)* of the human person —a life-orientating power manifesting itself in dreams.[58] Adrian Tanner describes the knowledge acquired by the Mistassini Cree hunters in Quebec as a spiritual knowledge which can be compared to the scientific knowledge of contemporary ecologists.[59] Robert Bunge observed that the Teton Sioux, when performing the sweat lodge ritual, know that cold water poured on very hot stones has the scientific effect of producing steam. But this is only one level of reality and knowledge to which the Indians add another dimension. They also perceive the release of the visible cloud of steam as the release of Spirit. We speak here of a mutual investment of the visible, physical order and the invisible, spiritual order which is apprehended by the imaginative faculty of the Indian mind.[60] Jean-Guy Goulet, in his anthropological studies on the Dene-Tha of northwestern Alberta, identifies this type of knowledge as a religious experience which does not consist of mere "beliefs" but of the true knowledge of things, the knowledge which only a strong mind can develop. In other words, among the Dene-Tha, those who possess this knowledge that comes through visions, dreams, songs, dances and rituals are not described as believers, but as those who really know.[61]

All these studies indicate, convincingly, that the Amerindian worldview remains a tremendous source of personal and collective energy for the different native groups in their struggle to adapt to modern society and to maintain, at the same time, their cultural identity.[62] We will now consider the main values which come from the Amerindian wordview and from the Amerindian understanding of the Great Mystery.

3. The basic characteristics of the Amerindian ethos

The contemporary Amerindian renaissance clearly illustrates that the North American native peoples want to remain distinct societies and to preserve their traditional value systems. More and more native persons are determined to uphold their traditional values while adapting to the conditions and the institutions of modern society. In the field of economics, for example, they want to control the development of their own communities, but without adopting the image of the *homo economicus* projected by the neo-liberal system. In politics they may look for structures inspired by the traditional organization of their clans and tribes. In the social domain, inspiration comes from the wisdom of their elders. All this points to an important fact: the persistence of a set of traditional values which constitute what we can call the Amerindian ethos.

The application of the term "ethos" to the North American native world seems somewhat problematic. One may object to it by pointing to the great diversity among the different aboriginal nations. Given this diversity, can we attribute a common ethos to all these nations and peoples? To answer this question, we must consider the destructive elements of the acculturation process to which most Indian tribes have been subjected since contact with the Europeans. Many tribes have lost important aspects of their traditional culture and are now searching to reconstruct their identity. They may do so by borrowing elements from other native peoples. In fact, this is one of the basic dynamics involved in the pan-Indian movement since the beginning of the twentieth century.[63] We use the term "ethos" to refer to the conscious effort made by many Indian nations to reconstruct a data base of common values from which each native group can borrow elements to reaffirm its own identity. The differences between the various Indian nations are maintained, while they share a common ethos which greatly benefits the tribes that have suffered most from the acculturation process.

When we analyze the content of this Amerindian ethos it is not enough to enumerate simply the common characteristics of the Amerindian psychology such as, for example, courage, individual freedom, sharing, generosity, flexibility, practical knowledge, humour and piety.[64] We must consider the fact that each tribe may have different ways of educating its own members (the enculturation process) and face the important question: What does it mean to be a human person and how does an individual become one in the various Amerindian cultures? We find the immediate response to this question in the title of the book which contains the Amerindian photographs taken by the famous artist, Edward S. Curtis, at the turn of this century: *In a Sacred Manner We Live*.[65] Our previous presentation of the Amerindian vision of the Great Mystery and of the cosmos shows that the North American native peoples continue to view life as a sacred reality, even though we must admit with Joseph Epes Brown that many Amerindians have adopted a secular lifestyle and that their spirituality may be fragmented as a result.[66]

At the very basis of Amerindian psychology and attitudes we find a particular understanding of the human person which is different from western anthropology. English dictionaries define man as "an adult male human being as distinguished from a woman," or as "a human being regardless of sex or age, considered as a representative of mankind." They may define person as "an individual human being," or as "a being characterized by consciousness, rationality and a moral sense." This person is not an animal or a divine being. The Amerindian ethos, on the contrary, does not focus on the differences between all these entities but on their relations which are sacred. The human being is connected with all the sacred powers of the universe. The Indian ethos is the result of this awareness and practical knowledge. Native spirituality, therefore, is a celebration of life and

communion with the sources of life, while Amerindian ethics is the art of maintaining all the vital forces of the universe in balance.[67]

One of the most difficult aspects of Amerindian theology concerns its vision
of evil. We can limit ourselves here to only a few basic observations on this issue.
Before contact with Christianity, it seems that Amerindians did not have the
concept of sin and that they had not developed a theological doctrine to deal with
the existence of evil within a universe viewed as sacred *(wakan)*. Vine Deloria
maintains that their traditional spirituality was constructed around a positive
understanding of creation.[68] However, we must observe that the term *wakan* is
usually translated in English as holy, mysterious, or magic, never or seldom as
good.[69] This seems to indicate that the traditional Indian considered evil as a basic
aspect of his or her universe and as a possible manifestation of the Great Mystery
itself which was simultaneously viewed as good and evil. William Powers maintains that, for the Oglala, the universe is composed of a limited amount of energy
and that both goodness and evil are aspects of that energy.[70] Some Indian groups
attribute the origin of evil to mysterious powers which are part of the Great
Mystery. In the absence of a theological doctrine that explained the origin and the
nature of evil (which is characteristic of Christianity), traditional Amerindian
spirituality seemed to adopt a rather practical approach to all the adversities of
existence. There was no basic distinction between the profane and the sacred.
Thus we may conclude that there is a certain amount of fatalism involved in the
Amerindian ethos (evil is a necessary dimension of existence), while the art of
living consists in maintaining the manifestations of evil (caused by spiritual
powers or humans) within certain, acceptable and tolerable limits. What counts,
ultimately, is harmony: the internal harmony of each living being and the harmony
of the universe.

Now that we have defined the Amerindian ethos as a coherent (pan-Indian)
system of values, we will briefly highlight some of these particular values,
especially those that came into almost direct confrontation with western civilization.[71]

The contemporary Amerindian ethos is primarily based on the conviction that
the Indians have won a moral victory in their long confrontation with western
civilization. Many peoples have been victims of long occupations by foreign
powers. Many have disappeared from the surface of the earth. The Amerindians
have survived. They have undergone more political, socio-cultural, economic and
religious oppression than many other peoples, but they maintained their identity.
The Amerindian desire and aptitudes for survival, Harold Turner maintains, have
no parallel in the world of tribal peoples.[72] The North American native peoples are
not about to give up this struggle for survival. The young generations especially
are inspired by this moral victory. It has become the source of a new creativity
which stands in sharp contrast with the former attitudes of defeat, powerlessness
and despair. Who could have imagined only a few years ago that the new Museum
of Civilization in Hull would be the creation of a Cree architect from Alberta

(Douglas Cardinal) whose architectural designs were inspired by the elders of his people? Who could have foreseen the tremendous explosion of Anishnabe art (paintings) in Ontario, obviously inspired by the traditional Midewiwin society and by the age-old rock paintings and sacred birch bark scrolls?[73] Is it not significant that the great ballet produced by the conductor and composer John Kim Bell (a Mohawk) is entitled: *In the Land of Spirits*?[74] The Amerindian universe remains a spiritual universe.

The Amerindian ethos is also characterized by the conviction that the North American native peoples have been able to maintain a unique expression of the human experience that belongs to the great spiritual traditions of humankind. Amerindian spirituality, as we have shown, is a close-to-the-earth mysticism which offers a spectrum of unlimited relations. Contemporary Amerindians are more and more assuming the responsibility of keeping alive this spirituality which is a primordial experience that many other peoples have lost but which is of great importance for the harmonious and total development of the human person. It is interesting to note, in this context, that certain Indian symbols, such as the tree of life, were perceived by Carl Jung as archetypes of human consciousness, capable of expressing the most fundamental aspects of human existence, exactly because they confront us with the basic questions of life and death, with the cycles of nature, the mysteries of goodness and evil, order and disorder, and with the question of the origin and the ultimate destiny of everything that is.[75]

The Amerindian ethos, as we have already noticed, also contains the instinctive awareness that the North American native peoples have mastered the art of survival in a unique way. Thomas Berry observes that historians acquainted with the great cultural developments of humankind consider this instinct of survival as a quality of peoples who live close to the earth. These peoples do not draw their energies from their social or political achievements, but from the spiritual quality of their existence.[76]

In fact, a centuries-old experience has allowed the Amerindians to develop a profound communion with the archetypal world of the collective conscious of humankind in their dreams, visions and rituals. This experience continues to develop itself because the development of the Amerindian person enhances the value of the intuitive and visionary capacities of the human mind, while the West continues to stress the rational side of the mind and the phenomenological ego. Must we not recognize that the native capacity to connect with the deepest level of the human ego and the human psyche has allowed the North American native peoples to absorb the shock of western civilization and to adapt successfully to the modern era?

While this remains fundamentally true, we must however avoid idealizing the present conditions in which most native groups live. These conditions are surely not "romantic." We cannot underestimate the deep conflict between their world-vision and that of the dominant, western society. Notwithstanding all the native spiritual resources mentioned above, Amerindian survival remains an ongoing challenge. The values which continue to give life and energy to the Amerindians are not those which animate the dominant society and the American middle-class with its obsession with scientific progress and the mastery of nature, its exaggerated desire of material possessions and money, its superficial optimism, calculated humanism and a democratic idealism that welcomes others (ethnic minorities, immigrants, and so on) only to the extent that they are willing to integrate themselves into the dominant system.[77]

No event better illustrates the depth of this conflict than the famous inquiry, presided over by Justice Thomas R. Berger, on the construction of the MacKenzie Valley pipeline, following the discovery of natural gas in Prudhoe Bay (North West Territories) in 1968.[78] Gibson Winter has rightfully observed that the conflict between the major oil companies such as *Arctic Gas*, supported by the federal government of Canada, and the indigenous communities of the North West Territories was a conflict between radically different interpretations of human life, community and nature.[79] The Berger Inquiry ultimately demonstrated that the distances which continued to separate the indigenous peoples of the Canadian North and the rest of Canada were not simply geographical but cultural.

In fact, we are confronted here with the radical difference between what Gibson Winter calls the root metaphors or paradigms of historical development and the technological outlook of the western world. At the very centre of the conflict are two totally different visions of historical development. The dominant society and the industrial world function according to a technological understanding of development which is mechanistic, linear, rationally calculated, controlled and manipulated. The native communities, on the contrary, continue to dwell within an organic world of interdependence, communal participation, and respect for the sacredness of the universe.

The conflict between these two root paradigms illustrates, once again, that the aboriginal and other peoples of North America are involved in a truly spiritual adventure. This adventure, however, has important social and political implications. Ultimately, it concerns the occupation, ownership, and use of the immense territories (North America) which have become the common home of the aboriginal peoples and those who came after them. Over the centuries, the aboriginal peoples have developed a unique type of relationship with the land. This relationship constitutes the foundation of their spirituality. With respect to this native spirituality, the West is now forced to recognize that, notwithstanding its Judeo-Christian foundations (the Old Testament creation narratives), its true symbols are power (oppression), progress, conquest and individualism.

Conclusion

In this chapter we presented an overview of Amerindian spirituality without considering its encounter with Christianity. We felt that it was important to consider first this centuries-old spiritual heritage in itself and to insist on the contemporary importance of the ongoing "Indian presence" in the western hemisphere. Thomas Berry rightly observed that the Amerindians as well as the other peoples who now live in North America have not yet seen all the implications of this "Indian presence" for the further development of civilization in the western hemisphere. We insist once again, in concluding this chapter, that Amerindian spirituality is a very concrete spirituality because of its closeness to the earth. This fact is not sufficiently acknowledged. Because of an almost unilateral insistence on rituals in Amerindian studies, the extraordinary social, scientific and technological contributions of the Indian peoples have long been overlooked. For example, as far as medicine is concerned, many modern medications depend on the discoveries of the pre-Columbian Indians. In politics, one may note that the Constitution of the United States of America is largely dependent on the traditional structure of the Mohawk Confederacy. This is why we developed a comprehensive view of the most important aspects of the Amerindian reality in this chapter and in the one preceding it. We will now examine how this complex reality continued to develop in contact with Christianity. This is the basic purpose of the next chapter where we will present the main features of the mission of the Christian churches in native North America as well as the reaction of the Amerindian peoples to this missionary intrusion.

CHAPTER III

Amerindian Responses
to Christianity

I. Assessment of Historical Confrontation

1. New approach to mission

In his impressive study on the Christian missionary epic in Canada, John Webster Grant writes: "To think of the encounter between Christianity and the Indians of Canada is almost inevitably to conjure up a picture of dominant missionaries gathering Indians around them, collecting them into villages, and forcing on them a strange religion and an alien culture. This picture captures an element of painful reality, but is unfair not only to the missionaries but to the Indians: recognizing only the former as actors, it reduces the latter to the role of passive recipients. Since the Indians were under no direct compulsion to embrace Christianity, there could have been no native Christian communities unless they had voluntarily converted themselves. To round out the story, therefore, we need to consider how the Indians responded to Christianity, what they made of it, and how they used it to reshape their lives and societies."[1] It is quite obvious that the *active participation* of the Indians in the Christian missions not only allowed numerous generations of missionaries to survive in the hostile territories of North America, but that it also contributed to the survival of Christianity itself. The implantation of the church in Indian territory is not the result of pure chance or the exclusive initiative of the missionaries, but of the active participation of countless Amerindians who often assumed the responsibility for transmitting the Christian faith once the missionaries left their tribes.[2] It is the purpose of this chapter to examine how this active participation of the North American Indians in the Christian missionary epic has produced specific native forms of Christianity. We will first illustrate this with some typical examples from the past and the present, and then propose a theological interpretation with the help of the term *incultura-tion*.

It is important to note that this method represents a rather new approach to the history of Christian missions in North America.[3] Most of the time, history is written from the point of view of the conquerors and the victors, seldom from the point of view of the losers! Since the Christian missionary epic in North America was not just a spiritual enterprise but also a cultural conquest,[4] with the victory going to the Christian West, it is easy to understand why classical historiography focused almost exclusively on the missionaries, the churches and western culture. In fact, the peoples of North America, dubbed "Indians" by Christopher Columbus and "savages" by Jacques Cartier, were looked upon, throughout the political, cultural and religious conquest of their lands, as lacking the usual marks of civilization—literature, law, government, art, commerce, agricultural and, in particular, religion.[5] The discovery of the Indians stirred a real theological debate in Renaissance Europe. Pope Alexander VI felt obliged to produce a papal bull in 1493, only one year after Columbus' first voyage, to declare that the peoples of the Americas, who "being in peace, and, as reported going unclothed and not eating flesh," were truly human beings, and therefore capable of being civilized and Christianized.[6] Yet, the classification of these newly discovered peoples within the human family did not happen at once as is illustrated by the famous debate of Valladolid (1550-1551) opposing Juan Ginés Sepulvedo and Bartholomé de las Casas, and by the early ethnographic studies of José de Acosta and Joseph François Lafiteau. Pope Alexander's bull nevertheless set the stage for the twofold orientation of the Christian missionary epic in the Americas.[7] This missionary epic will be, inseparably, civilizational and Christian. "Civilize to save" was the credo of the great majority of missionaries in North America, whether Catholic or Protestant.[8] Henri Maurier's thesis that the spread of the Christian message has always been realized within a framework of imperialist state expansion, with European missionaries imposing, in an aggressive manner, a veritable change of civilization on the non-civilized peoples of other continents, is just as true in North America as it is elsewhere—perhaps even truer.[9] Even though the question of priorities (civilization first, evangelization later?) often sparked intense debates, especially in the Protestant churches,[10] the ambiguous and ambivalent link between mission and colonialism was seldom questioned. In the writings of the great Protestant and Catholic nineteenth-century missionaries, who planted their church in western Canada, one finds an ongoing insistence on the four elements which constituted the foundations of their missionary enterprise: agriculture, education, morality and civilization.[11] This twofold orientation of the Christian mission extended well into the twentieth century, because missionaries were convinced that the Indians had practically no chance of surviving as distinct peoples. Therefore, it was in the best interest of the Indians (and of the churches) to prepare them for their assimilation into Euro-Canadian society.

Given this context, it is rather easy to understand that the missionaries and the early historians paid little attention to the participation of the Indians themselves in the promotion of Christianity. They were no more than "savages" to be civilized and "pagans" to be converted. Among the missionaries of the nineteenth century there are not that many who, like Bishop Alexandre Taché (1823-1894), recognized that "The Indians [in this instance the Montagnais] were able, by the light of reason alone, to achieve true knowledge of God and without giving in to the gross absurdities which kept the most civilized peoples of Antiquity captive. They believed in one God, the Creator, Provider and Protector of everything, the One who remunerates virtue and who punishes evil, the eternal God whose providential care covers everything (...) This notion of divinity appears to me as the most exact one to be found among peoples deprived from the immense benefits of revelation. Our savages found this understanding of God in the contemplation of nature."[12] One should not forget that the church that was sown among the aboriginal peoples of North America was the unequal society spoken of by Popes Leo XIII and Pius X, who drew a radical distinction between hierarchy and faithful. This church, since the Council of Trent, in line with this dualist clergy-laity schema, had tended to stress almost exclusively the role of the ordained minister in the transmission of revelation and the church's sacramental system.[13] In a church thus structured on dualistic lines, the Amerindians were in some way doubly "marginalized" or "excommunicated." They were considered children, persons hardly to be counted on. In the missionary imagination of the nineteenth century, the church was frequently visualized as a great family, with the bishop and missionaries as the parents, and the white Catholics as the elder children supporting their lesser brethren (the Indians) "by their work, example and devotion, and thus contributing to the happiness of their old parents [bishops and missionaries] and to that of the family as a whole [Christendom], as well as to their own good [the advantages of Christian life and civilization]."[14] The exclusion of the Indians from active church life was reinforced by the colonialist attitudes, evinced from the outset by most missionaries. "How could hordes of formerly cruel and barbarous men be counted on to build up the Body of Christ?" asked Bishop Taché (1823-1894). "What," asked Bishop Vital Grandin (1829-1902), "can be done with the poor savages among whom the missionaries live," in a church whose universal mission had been entrusted to the civilized peoples of Europe?

The women and men who set out three and a half centuries ago to establish the church in Canada and most of those following thereafter could hardly have imagined the Amerindian renaissance of the second half of the twentieth century and its implications for the internal life of the church. It is exactly this Amerindian renaissance which invites us to make the journey the other way around and to start reinterpreting the history of the Christian missions in North America in order to understand better the conversion of the Indians to Christianity and the impact of the gospel on their spiritual life.

2. The Amerindian reception of Christianity

The theological interpretation of the contemporary religious situation of the North American native peoples depends largely on the results of modern historiography, in particular of ethnohistory.[15] For example, it is impossible to understand that the Amerindians became Christians but that Christianity was unable to change drastically their religious worldview, without considering the results of this modern, historical research. This research indicates that we can no longer limit ourselves to the study of the development of Christian institutions in North America, but that we must adopt an intercultural hermeneutics of the historical encounter between the missionaries' western worldview and that of the Indians. In many cases, such a study is difficult and complex because of the scarcity of written sources and because most of the sources are tinged with the ethnocentric vision of the early reporters of the Amerindian reality.[16] Even in the areas where we have significant sources, such as the *Jesuit Relations* for New France, contemporary historical research demonstrates that the encounter or confrontation between Christianity and the Amerindians was, from the outset, a matter of cultural transactions, adaptations and transformations in which the native communities played a significant and decisive role. This was not always acknowledged by earlier historians.

From the sixteenth century on, Europeans came in North America not to "discover a new world," but to impose their own world and worldview on the aboriginal peoples. This adventure was marked, especially in New France, by complex interactions between Christianity and the Amerindians. It forced the missionaries to make a constant effort to understand and to interpret the traditional Amerindian religions whose existence had been, at first, simply ignored or misunderstood. It required gradual negotiations and accommodations, as soon as it was understood that the Indian soul was not a *tabula rasa* on which one could easily print faith in the Christian God.[17] The early missionaries rapidly understood that the Amerindian response to Christianity was a highly qualified response with many theological presuppositions and implications. It is impossible, in the context of this research on the Amerindian Christ, to reconstruct the dialogue that took place in the early days of the conquest of North America between Christianity and the Amerindian religions. We will limit ourselves to a short classification of the Indian responses to the missionary intrusion by drawing on Harold Turner's anthropological considerations concerning the Christian missions in native North America, and on the conclusions of Cornelius Jaenen's historical analysis of the missions of New France in the seventeenth and eighteenth centuries.

Harold Turner has made an interesting effort to sum up the most relevant features of the Amerindian-Christian encounter in six propositions. They may help us to understand the complexity of the contemporary Amerindian situation better. He proposes that:

1. the Amerindian peoples were a fine race and

2. made as good an initial response to the Christian faith as any other tribal people;

3. their subsequent treatment by the whites was as bad as anywhere else, but

4. their survival qualities have been unexcelled in the tribal world;

5. they have been the object of Christian missions for a period as long as that of any other people in modern times, and yet

6. the overall Christian results are among the least impressive of all mission labours.[18]

At first sight, this interpretation looks severe, given the enormous sacrifices made by many generations of missionaries for the implantation of the Christian churches in native North America. But it forces us to make a clear distinction, in estimating the results of the Christian mission (see the second part of this chapter), between what the missionaries wanted to achieve and the types of Christianity developed by the aboriginal peoples themselves. This interpretation also forces us to recognize that the initial response of the Indians to Christianity cannot be reduced to a simple yes or no.

This is confirmed by the historical research of Cornelius Jaenen who, basing himself on the Jesuit *Relations*, has made an attempt to classify the dominant types of responses to the French missionary intrusion in the seventeenth and eighteenth centuries.[19] His study shows, first, that evangelization was a European intrusion into native societies in which the spiritual values were diffused throughout the entire cultural system. The evangelization of the Amerindians was therefore impossible without challenging their entire socio-cultural life and, therefore, the conversion of the Amerindians to Christianity was much more than a superficial change of their personal, religious convictions. Jaenen's study also demonstrates that this evangelization was intimately related to French trade, military commitments and cultural assumptions. The native peoples had to respond to a very contextualized theology which was embedded in a radically different social organization. In fact, their conversion implied such a cultural transformation that they were not ready to accept the Christian faith without measuring its advantages and inconveniences.

Given this global, political and religious context, some Amerindians said no and others said yes to Christianity. Their negative responses ranged from aggressive hostility to derisive rejection without overt aggressiveness, and from manifest disinterest or indifference to the assertion of the existence of a dichotomous universe. The hostile aggressivity was often caused by the classical competition between the spiritual power of the shamans and the Catholic priests, while the derisive rejection of Christianity was characteristic of the southern tribes which had a more institutionalized form of religion, and of the Algonkian bands where the women were very influential. The Algonkians considered themselves superior to the male-biased French culture. The manifest disinterest or indifference of the Amerindians, after a period of initial enthusiasm, was often the result of the "bad example" of the French colonists. The dualistic rejection was rooted in a dualistic vision of the world according to which there was a different present and a different hereafter for the Amerindians and the Europeans. Each culture, therefore, had to preserve its own belief system and social practices.

On the other hand, it cannot be denied that the French Catholic missions also enjoyed a good measure of success. Just as one can identify four categories of negative responses, so it is possible to distinguish four types of positive responses: dual acceptance, religious dimorphism, syncretism and full conversion. Dual acceptance was based on the tolerance that was characteristic of native societies. One could give an external assent to the new religion while keeping one's own inner thoughts and convictions. Religious dimorphism is understood as the simultaneous assent to the traditional Amerindian religion and Christianity, and to their respective, internal structures. Amerindians were able to call upon each religion as circumstances and concrete needs dictated. Syncretism is distinguished from religious dimorphism by the way in which it fuses the two belief systems to form a third, new reality. This syncretism, as we will show later in this chapter, has often allowed the native cultures and beliefs to survive under the protective coloration of the religion of the intruders, whether Catholic or Protestant. Finally, a good number of Amerindians were fully converted by the missionaries. They abandoned their "sinful past" and a culture which, in the eyes of the missionaries, was contrary to God's design. Cornelius Jaenen is inclined to believe that the state of religious dimorphism more adequately represents the real conversion experience of most Amerindians, while syncretism refers more to societal accommodation than to individual change.

This wide spectrum of native attitudes towards Christianity, which existed not only in New France but in many other parts of North America, suggests that the term "conversion" did not have the same meaning for the Indians as it did for the missionaries. We may assume that, generally speaking, the Indians welcomed the missionaries as prayerful men and women. They understood Christianity to be a new way of praying which had come to them not to replace but to enrich their own prayer life. If so, we could ask ourselves with Grant whether the Amerindian yes to Christianity was indeed not a sort of no, given the astonishing survival of the traditional, native religions.[20] It is important to note that the more developed, organized native societies offered more resistance to Christianity than the tribes which found themselves in a precarious socio-political and economic situation. In many parts of Canada, the missionaries undertook evangelization at the very time when the cultural world of many native groups was seriously threatened if not already destroyed by the powerful colonists. In those concrete circumstances, Christianity was all the more perceived as a "religion of salvation" offering to the Indians what was necessary for their survival. However, this does not mean that the Amerindians should be regarded as "rice Christians" or that there were no authentic conversions. Each authentic conversion to Christ is a mystery accomplished in the intimate conscience of a person, while being, at the same time, a complex process marked by the cultural situation of that person. Therefore, we observe with Grant that the most formidable obstacle to the acceptance of Christianity, namely its close association with western cultures, constituted also its chief attraction.[21] It is not always easy to separate the "benefits of western civilization" from the "eternal blessings" promised by the church! In fact, we should note that many native conversions to Christianity took place during the *"Moon of Wintertime"'* (the title of Grant's book), when the ancestral spirits had ceased to perform their expected functions satisfactorily and the angel choirs (sent by the church) promised to fill the spiritual vacuum!

Thus we are always brought back to the central question of the relationship between Christianity and the traditional, Amerindian religious experience. The studies we have quoted confirm that the reception of Christianity by the Amerindians should not be understood as a rebellion against their own religion. These studies also suggest that some Amerindians may have opted for Christianity because of its superior qualities and because of the lure of western civilization which was an integral part of the missionary epic. Finally, we must recognize that the reception of Christianity by a large number of Amerindians (their yes) was indeed a sublime form of the rejection of Christianity, at least in its western, cultural expressions. *Their yes was also a no!* This is the reason why any critical study of the encounter between Christianity and North American native peoples must examine not only what the churches have given to the Amerindians, but also what the Indians did with and to Christianity. In the following pages we will concentrate directly on this question by showing that one of the most interesting, but the least expected, results of the missionary epic in native North America is the formation of specific Amerindian expressions of Christianity, inside and outside the official boundaries of the churches.

II. Amerindian Assimilations of Christianity

1. The syncretic and prophetic movements

John Webster Grant succinctly summarizes the missionary epic in Canada by stating: "If the measure of success is that most Indians have become Christian, the measure of failure is that Christianity has not become Indian."[22] This conclusion is obvious when we look at this missionary epic from the vantage point of the churches. Notwithstanding large numbers of native conversions, truly native churches have not yet seen the light of day. It is as if no cultural transfers ever took place between the Amerindian cultures and the Christian faith. The Christian faith has remained deeply embedded within the closely guarded frontiers of western culture. It was generously welcomed by the Amerindians. But we have reached the point of asking ourselves whether the churches have welcomed the Amerindians' readiness to integrate the Christian message in their own cultural universe.

Grant's conclusion is less self-evident when we look upon the same missionary epic from the vantage point of the Amerindians. As we have suggested earlier, contemporary ethno-history demonstrates that the Amerindians ought to be considered co-actors in this missionary epic and that they were able to develop native forms of Christianity in the absence of the official, Amerindian churches. This historical research suggests that many cultural transfers did occur between the Amerindian cultures, the traditional native religious experience, and Christianity. While it remains true that religion is the most conservative dimension of the Amerindian cultures and that it radically resists social transformations, native religion is capable of adapting to new historical and ecological conditions. Indeed native religion became a decisive factor in the Amerindians' reaction to the social and cultural upheavals caused by western civilization. From the very beginning of the missionary epic, this situation has activated several religious movements which represent different types of interactions between Christianity and native cultures: the syncretic and prophetic process, the nativistic movement, and the independent churches.

The syncretic process: Abenaki Catholicism

One of the earliest examples of syncretism is the type of Catholicism which developed in the seventeenth century among the Abenaki peoples of the Kennebec river (present-day Quebec, Maine and New Brunswick). This example illustrates what was going on in many parts of North America when Christianity came into contact with the aboriginal peoples. Abenaki Catholicism is a curious mixture of the religion imported by the Jesuits and Abenaki mythology. According to Kenneth Morrison, who draws his information from the Jesuit *Relations* and from the myths, legends and folklore of the Abenaki oral traditions, this syncretism illustrates the type of interaction which certain native groups initiated in order to reconstruct their communities and to redefine the meaning of their life when they found themselves on the brink of social and cultural disintegration.[23] The Jesuit *Relations* offer a detailed account of the Abenaki conversion to Catholicism. The Abenaki did not react to the missionary intrusion of the Jesuits and the implantation of the church by setting in motion a "nativistic" movement or by returning to their traditions and by rejecting the world of the white people. Unlike the Innu (Montagnais), their northern Algonkian-speaking neighbours, they did not practise religious dualism or dimorphism. Instead, Abenaki Catholicism represents a *syncretic intensification and a revitalization of their traditional religious life*, especially of the mythology which founded their world vision and their cultural identity.

Morrison's study demonstrates that, like many other Indian nations, the Abenaki responded to the imported religion in a very critical way and deliberately transformed some of it to serve their cultural survival. Morrison maintains that we can no longer support the traditional anthropological and missionary thesis that the Abenaki, along with other sub-Arctic Algonkian peoples, were extremely religious "individualists" who accepted Catholicism once their own religion had become defective. Current interdisciplinary research in history, anthropology and theology focuses, on the contrary, on the *social dimension* of the Abenaki reception of Catholicism.

The critical and conservative response of the Abenaki to the missionary intrusion managed to produce the type of Catholicism they needed for their cultural survival until the present day. One of the more dramatic and interesting aspects of this syncretic process (in the context of this study on the Amerindian visions of Christ) is the extraordinary survival of *Gluskabe*, the central figure of Abenaki mythology.[24] Abenaki mythology does not describe the creation of the world itself. Instead, it concentrates on a world where the humans and the animals were essentially alike. Among all the mythological beings, *Gluskabe* stands out as the one whose acts made the world hospitable for the Abenaki people. Morrison maintains that the most dramatic evidence of Abenaki responses to Catholicism and of their overall reponse to Euro-American contact can probably be found in the accounts of *Gluskabe*. One Abenaki myth states that, though the Great Spirit was responsible for the creation of the world, he needed *Gluskabe*'s advice about its ultimate arrangement. Another myth describes the basic equality between *Gluskabe* and Christ. In fact, *Gluskabe* seemed to have been perceived as a kind of Amerindian Christ who prepared his people for the coming of Catholicism and western civilization. *Gluskabe* was just like Jesus. They were both sent into the world to improve the peoples' understanding of right and wrong and they both had similar missions for human well-being. When departing from this world, *Gluskabe* invited his people to remain faithful to their traditional God (the Great Spirit), but admitted at the same time the primacy of the Christian God. There is a widespread belief in *Gluskabe*'s continued existence and in his promise to return at some future time of need. These different myths confirm that the Abenaki always believed in the basic compatibility of their traditional beliefs and Catholicism.[25]

The prophetic movement

The Amerindians have always manifested an intense desire to survive and a great capacity to adapt to the radical transformation of their environment. These attitudes have inspired the movements of religious revitalization and restoration, especially the prophetic movement, which have characterized Amerindian reality since it first made contact with Christianity and western culture. *Prophetism* must have been part of Amerindian culture since the beginning. Throughout the entire history of humankind we observe the emergence of prophets in different cultural and religious contexts. They seem to be in charge of the basic needs of their communities and responsible for their reconstruction. But in the case of the Amerindians, we have almost no information on prophetism before contact with western culture. Since the sixteenth century, however, we possess detailed information on Amerindian prophetic movements. In his classical study on the Seneca, Anthony Wallace demonstrates the basic link between these movements and the acculturation process which threatened the cultural survival of the Indian peoples.[26] Even more than syncretism, the prophetic movement is a typically Amerindian answer, composed of traditional and Christian elements, to the missionary intrusion and to the pressures of western civilization. But the prophetic movement is political, nativistic, militant, and even millenaristic. Without a doubt this movement, which was extremely powerful in the nineteenth century, directly or indirectly prepared the Amerindian renaissance we are witnessing today.

One of the first great Amerindian prophets was Neolin, known as the Delaware Prophet, who was very active during the second half of the eighteenth century in Pennsylvania and Ohio where he proclaimed his message about the Master of Life, the Great Spirit. Neolin was very much preoccupied with the loss of Amerindian land, the adoption of Euro-American customs, the devastation caused by alcoholism, and the abandonment of the traditions. Like many other prophets or dreamers who followed him, he helped his people to interpret its situation in a spiritual manner, using the religious symbols of death and rebirth. He established a direct link between the misery of his people and the corruption of the Indian soul, and proposed a radical return to ancestral traditions. His nativistic message allowed for no compromise. Neolin had a direct influence on Pontiac, the famous Ottawa chief, and on the policies of nearly twenty tribes from Lake Ontario to the Mississippi River. But his spiritual message was not always appreciated and understood by the great warriors: the regaining of Indian lands was intimately linked to the recovery of lost innocence. This theme will remain an important dimension of the Indian prophetic movement.[27]

We are not sure whether Neolin ever met Handsome Lake (Gamo Dai Lo), the great Seneca prophet, shaman and sachem of the Six Nations of the Iroquois (1735-1815), who received the first of several visions in 1799, after having suffered personally from the destructive implications of western civilization. But both prophets faced the same socio-cultural situation when they saw their peoples' loss of land and pride following the Revolutionary War. But Handsome Lake's "Good Word" (gaiwiio) and central message differs considerably from that of the nativistic and cultic prophets. The cultic prophets claimed that renewal would come only when the people returned to their traditional rituals and sacrifices, while the nativistic prophets proclaimed that the white people would be destroyed when the native people rejected their influences and returned to the old ways. Handsome Lake was a kind of ethical-eschatological prophet. The teachings of Handsome Lake and of his half-brother, Edward Cornplanter, aimed at the reform of the Longhouse religion. The early messages which the prophet received condemned the corruptions of Iroquois culture (for example, alcohol, witchcraft, abortion, the neglect or abuse of children, women and the elderly). At the same time, the prophet warned against some aspects of western civilization such as private property and the cruelty towards farm animals, and emphasized the reform of the communal rituals of thanksgiving centred on the agricultural cycle. Handsome Lake did not link the Amerindian restoration to the disappearance of the white race, but prepared his people to live in a world more and more dominated by Euro-American civilization. Unlike the biblical prophets, his message was not accompanied by a desacralization of nature, but maintained the traditional link (cosmic harmony) with the spiritual powers in the universe. His eschatological and ethical teachings were rooted in the idea that the holy was both a transcendent being and an immanent presence and power. The present-day Longhouse or Handsome Lake religion, while basing itself on the teachings of the prophet, includes shamanic practices, agricultural ceremonies, and political meetings such as the Six Nations Conference. The "Code of Handsome Lake" forms the basis of a cultural reform which tolerates external (non-Indian) elements while, at the same time, eliminating all elements (native and non-native) that threaten the well-being of the community.[28]

Among the prophetic movements which emerged among the native peoples in the nineteenth century, the *Ghost Dance* is one of the strongest revitalization movements with a messianic and millenaristic connotation. Strictly speaking, there have been only two *Ghost Dances*, the 1870 *Ghost Dance*, introduced on the Walker Lake Reservation in Nevada by the Northern Paiute Indian, Wodziwob (1844-1918?), and the 1890 *Ghost Dance*, inspired by the prophet Wovoka (1856-1932) on the Pine Ridge Reservation in South Dakota. The 1890 *Ghost Dance* was followed by the so-called *Ghost Dance Uprising*, which resulted in the arrest and the assassination of the famous Lakota leader Sitting Bull and of his son Crow Foot on December 15, 1890, at Standing Rock (North Dakota), and in the massacre at Wounded Knee, December 29, 1890. But even after these tragic events, which put an end to the armed resistance of the Plains Indians, *Ghost Dances* continued among the Shoshoni Indians on the Wind River Reservation (Wyoming) and among the Dakota Indians in Canada until the mid-1950s.[29]

The messianic *Ghost Dance* has mobilized thousands of Plains Indians because of its spiritual and moral message and its socio-political implications. But anthropologists and historians disagree on the real driving force of the movement. Are we dealing here with a strictly religious phenomenon or with a movement of socio-cultural adaptation among the Plains Indians, once their traditional life had collapsed with the extinction of the buffalo in 1883? The *Ghost Dance* movement is surely rooted in the prophetic visions of Wodziwob who predicted the restoration of the old tribal life, and in the eschatological visions of Wovoka who announced the imminent coming of a new world where the living would be guided by a celestial spirit (Jesus) and be reunited with the deceased in a state of eternal happiness. Wovoka was welcomed by his contemporaries as the Messiah, even though, according to James Mooney, he claimed to be only a prophet.[30]

The prophetic movement initiated by Wodziwob and Wovoka is part of a long tradition of religious acculturation which has marked the native reality since it made contact with Christianity and western civilization. We find here the same concern for the restoration of the traditional values as in the ethical-religious program of Neolin who can be considered as the model of native American prophetism. But this native American prophetism was also influenced by Christianity, even when, in the case of the *Ghost Dance*, the ritual is profoundly shamanistic.[31] Native American prophetism implies an understanding of the Supreme Being and an ethical program that bears many resemblances to the Judeo-Christian tradition. The ideology of the *Ghost Dance* also contains a linear eschatology (future liberation, retribution, new earth) which is different from the traditional native eschatology.[32] It is also suggested that the famous *Ghost Dance shirts*, which were supposed to make the Indians invulnerable, were directly influenced by the Mormons, while the teachings of Wovoka could be compared to the Presbyterian interpretations of the Bible and of the story of Jesus (pietism).[33]

Throughout the nineteenth century, many Euro-Canadian observers mentioned the existence of prophets among the Indians of British Columbia and the Dene in northwestern Canada. These prophets (men and women) often reported that they had visited the land of the Creator and the spirits from which they had returned with a spiritual message for their peoples. This phenomenon deeply affected the Protestant *Church Missionary Society* as well as the Congregation of the Oblates of Mary Immaculate, a missionary order, which had assumed responsibility for the Catholic missions throughout northern and western Canada.

In Canada the emergence of native prophets is situated within a large nativistic and syncretic movement which has both religious and socio-political causes. Native Canadian prophetism can be interpreted as religious and political resistance to the cultural imperialism of the Christian missions. The spiritual revolt (ceremony of the return of the traditional God-Spirit), which occurred in 1877 among the Tsimshian Indians in the famous Anglican mission of Metlakatla, challenged the missionary system and the oppressive leadership of William Duncan.[34] On the Catholic side, the famous missionary-colonist, Adrien-Gabriel Morice (1859-1939), continually faced similar movements of spiritual resistance, especially from those tribes on which he was trying to impose the "Durieu System" of total, spiritual acculturation, created by Pierre-Paul Durieu (1830-1899), Bishop of New Westminster, "the Apostle of British Columbia."[35] In certain cases, the newly converted Indians returned to their traditional belief systems because they were disappointed with the Christian understanding of the Sacred (the Supernatural) and with the Christian sacramental system for communicating with God. They considered their own rituals superior to the sacraments of the church and their own doctrines more solid than the Christian dogmas. In other cases, the Amerindians felt obliged to create new rituals (syncretism) or to modify their traditional ones, in order to compete with the superior religious "techniques" of the white missionaries. The development of the *Prophet* or *Ghost Dance* among the Duneza Indians, and the millenarism of the Carrier Indians, their southern neighbours, represent this type of reaction.[36]

The prophets and the Christian shamans who appear almost everywhere in the Canadian north during the nineteenth century[37] were a real threat for the Christian missions because they proposed a new religious experience which combined the most attractive elements of Christianity and their traditional religion. But the anthropologist and the historian disagree, once again, on the significance of this phenomenon, especially among the Dene Indians. Martha McCarthy is convinced that we are dealing here with a truly syncretic movement (religious revitalization) which allowed the shamans to recuperate part of the prestige and the power which they had lost after the arrival of the missionaries.[38] But most of the time, the conflict seems limited to the individual struggle for spiritual power between the shaman and the priest, rather than the construction of a new type of Christian religion or independent church. Kerry Abel hesitates to speak about a religious revitalization movement or a cultural crisis. Instead she interprets the activities of the Dene prophets as a traditional cultural reaction to the ongoing pressures of daily life in the harsh conditions of northern Canada.[39] She situates Dene prophetism within the larger context of Dene spirituality which was able to withstand the pressures of Western culture.[40] According to her, the ongoing development of Dene prophetism shows that the Christian message was unable to reach the depth of the Dene psyche. While borrowing some elements from Christianity, the Dene prophets were able to demonstrate the superiority of their religious complex compared to the system proposed or imposed by the Christian churches.

2. The independent churches

Almost everywhere in the world Christian missionaries discover that, after the speedy implanting of the church in a non-western culture, the peoples belonging to that culture often respond to the proclamation of the gospel not only by becoming members of the missionary church, but by setting in motion new religious movements composed of aboriginal and Christian elements. This is another type of syncretic process which produces the so-called independent churches. Aylward Shorter has reported at least 5,000 independent churches in Africa alone.[41] This type of movement was never very successful in native North America. North American Christians, Harold Turner writes, probably know more about the independent churches of Africa than about the different transactions which took place between Christianity and the Inuit or Indian peoples.[42] However, it is in Canada and the United States of America that the three oldest examples of independent churches can be found: the Narangansett church of Charlestown (Rhode Island) has been in existence since 1740; the Religion of Handsome Lake developed among the Iroquois at the beginning of the nineteenth century; and the Yaqui church of Arizona and New Mexico became independent in the 1770s.

The history of the Yaqui church is most interesting and fascinating because of the complex interactions between their traditional shamanism, dances and music, and the Christian faith and liturgy. According to Edward Spicer, an expert on Yaqui history, the early Jesuit missionaries (seventeenth and eighteenth centuries) and Spanish culture had a tremendous impact on the Yaqui. But the Yaqui people often reinterpreted important aspects of Christianity (the figure of Jesus, the cult of the Virgin Mary and the feast of the dead) in light of their traditional mythology. The religious history of the Yaqui is thus marked by comings and goings between their traditional religion (especially during extended periods of missionary absence) and Christianity (especially during more recent periods of socio-cultural transformation). The Yaqui church remains an independent church and has never been officially recognized by the Roman Catholic church.[43]

The Peyote religion

Near the end of the nineteenth century, a new religious movement arose among the Plains Indians who had been confined to the reservations. This movement was the Peyote religion, which was to become the most significant and widespread pan-Indian religion in the twentieth century in the United States of America and Canada. Faced with opposition from the Indian Bureau and the Christian churches, the Peyote religion gradually adopted the Christian church model partly for defensive reasons and partly out of admiration. The Peyote religion is therefore the best example of a contemporary native independent church. The cult of the peyote, a small, spineless cactus having psychedelic properties, which grows in a limited area principally in northern Mexico and southern Texas, was known to the Aztecs. They considered this cactus (*Lophophora Williamsi*) as the "flesh of God." There has been a considerable lack of misunderstanding about the peyote which is often confused with the *Sophora Secundiflora* or the mescal bean or button, an extremely powerful intoxicant.

The Peyote cult remained very obscure until the middle of the nineteenth century, when the Mescalero Apaches acquired it from Indians in northern Mexico and used it to reinforce their traditional religious values. The Comanche and the Kiowa Indians, who adopted the cult in the 1870s, contributed to its diffusion in the United States at the time of the ghost dance movement. One of the leading exponents or "missionaries" of the Peyote religion was Quanah Parker (born c. 1840), the last great chief of the Apaches and a friend of Theodore Roosevelt. Another important figure in the early history of the Peyote cult was John Wilson (born in 1840), who was partly French, Delawara and Cado. Under the influence of these two men, the Peyote religion rapidly developed as a pan-Indian syncretic movement, first in New Mexico and Oklahoma. Between 1900 and 1910, it spread to Arizona, Iowa, Nebraska, Wisconsin and Wyoming where it stimulated the interest of well-educated and Christianized Indians and disturbed the Indian Bureau and the Christian churches.

The pan-Indian and syncretic nature of the Peyote religion has been documented by the well-known anthropologist, James Mooney, who took the initiative to protect legally this new religious movement by having it incorporated as a Christian church.[44] In fact, around 1918 the anti-peyote campaign had gathered considerable strength. The first *Native American Church* was founded in Oklahoma in 1918. The Winnebago Indians of Nebraska obtained their first charter in 1921 and created the *Peyote Church of Christ*. One year later, they adopted the name *Native American Church,* which became the official name for the Peyote religion throughout the United States. In 1950, the Peyotists obtained a national charter and became the *Native American Church of the United States*, and later, so as to include Canadian Peyotists, the *Native American Church of North America* (NAC of NA). This church does not necessarily represent all the Peyotists. It is a flexible organization which continues to play an important role in the legal recognition of Peyotism by constantly appealing to the *American Indian Religious Freedom Act* (1978) and against the *Drug Abuse Control Act* (1965). In the United States, peyote is still considered a narcotic substance forbidden by law. It can only be possessed and transported by *bona fide* members of the NAC of NA for religious purposes. In Canada, peyote is no longer on the list of forbidden drugs.[45]

Many scholars situate the origin and the development of the Peyote religion within the same socio-cultural context as the Ghost Dance and other prophetic movements. Vittorio Lanternari classifies the Peyote religion as a "religion of the oppressed."[46] Weston LaBarre speaks of a "crisis cult,"[47] while Anthony Wallace interprets it as a "revitalization movement"[48] and Ralph Linton as "nativism."[49] James Slotkin maintains that the strength of the movement is in its capacity to adapt to Euro-American culture (accommodation). David Alberly, on the contrary, links the Peyotism of the Navajo with their economic deprivation following the reduction of their herds by American law.[50] Christopher Vecsey, basing himself on the research of Omer Stewart and Ake Hultkrantz, as well as on the mythical stories concerning the origin of peyote, goes beyond all these "reductionist" interpretations in his analysis of the historical, experiential, ethical, ritual and theological dimensions of the movement. He considers the Peyote cult to be an authentic religion.[51] What follows is a synthesis of his conclusions.

Historically speaking, Peyotism, just like the other new religious movements, originated in a context of profound socio-cultural changes. This explains its syncretic nature. Peyotism remains a native American religion, but it also represents an *accumulative tradition* with a strong, Christian content. Peyotism, for example, reserves a central place for Christ, Christian symbols, biblical values and certain theological doctrines (sin, redemption). Questions can be raised, however, about the exact link and interaction between the aboriginal and Christian elements in the cult. Should we speak of "accumulation" or "integration"? Do the Christian elements constitute only a facade for the traditional native religion? Is Peyotism an example of religious dualism? Is Peyotism a typically Amerindian expression of Christianity?

There are no definite answers to these questions because of the basic differences between the western form of Christianity and the Peyote religion. Peyotism is basically experiential. It is a religion that, just like the vision quest and many other native rituals, concentrates on the personal experience of God. Traditionally, peyote was perceived as a spiritual power or as a sacrament with highly medical and nutritious properties that stimulates the visions needed for the development of an individual's spiritual life. Peyote remains experiential in nature, notwithstanding the fact that Parker and Wilson have developed its ethical and theological dimensions. From the ethical point of view, for example, they insist that peyote should not be sought for personal, mystical or shamanic experiences and advantages, but for the well-being of the community. Peyotism favours social transformation on the basis of love and peace among the peoples.

This explains the remarkable contribution of the Peyote religion to the pan-Indian movement in the twentieth century. Peyotism can be understood as an authentic Amerindian religion and as a Christian church. In adopting the model of a Christian church, Peyotism has not changed its experiential and sacramental outlook. Its theology has remained non-dogmatic, flexible and syncretic. Therefore, it is obvious that the relationship between traditional Amerindian religion and Christianity within Peyotism may vary considerably from one person to the other, or from one native group to the next. It is not uncommon that, within the same Peyote ritual, prayers to the Christian God, Jesus and the Virgin Mary are followed by prayers to the ancestral deities and spiritual beings.

The Peyote rituals and theology are based on the belief in the supernatural origin of the cactus. Peyote has always been perceived as a sacred plant revealed by the Creator to the Amerindians for their survival and development. The ethnolinguist, Sven Liljeblad, describes Peyotism as a monotheistic religion which maintains that the peyote was given to the Indians just like Christ was given to the white race. God has truly revealed himself in the peyote cactus which has become a sacrament of communion with him and with the spiritual universe. Peyote prayers are addressed to the Christian God as well as to Mother Earth, who is sometimes understood as a pantheistic symbol. Many Peyotists know and use the Bible in their ceremonies, even though the real strength of their faith derives from their personal (psychic) experience of the supernatural. Peyote ethics are a mixture of traditional native and Christian values. The peyote is perceived as a true medicine, pharmaceutically as well as spiritually.[52] While adopting the structures of a Christian church, the Peyote religion is able to offer to its approximately 250,000 members all the services of an organized religion. The visionary experience of peyote does not exist for its own sake. Peyotism is not a form of mysticism in which the contemplation of God is a goal in itself. The visionary experience of peyote has no other purpose than to confirm the healing power and the life-giving holiness of this spiritual substance provided by the Creator.

In his study of the Oglala Lakota of the Pine Ridge Reservation, Paul Steinmetz presents several witnesses who illustrate the profound interaction between Peyotism and Christianity. For example, one man reports that peyote is not a drug but a powerful means which turns the mind to the Great Spirit and to Jesus Christ. Another compares the seven stones in his drum, which are the seven Indian sacraments (the holy peyote, the dirt Half Moon, the fire, the water, corn, meat and fruits) to the seven sacraments of the Catholic church. He compares the thong of the rope on the top of his drum to the crown of thorns that Jesus wore. Peyotists easily affirm that everything in their traditional religion can already be found in the Bible. In the second part of this book we will offer a detailed analysis of this interaction. Drawing on his own experience, Steinmetz notes that such testimonies require many hours of meditation before they can be understood correctly.[53]

It may suffice here to say that these witnesses also accentuate the mystical and experiential aspect of the Peyote religion. They also confirm Hazel Hertzberg's opinion on the complex origin and development of Peyotism. We may therefore conclude that this new religious movement which was totally created by the Indians has managed to remain a truly Amerindian religion. It has become a source of pride for them and a means to establish a significant connection between their traditions and their new socio-cultural environment.[54]

The Body of Christ Independent Church

Steinmetz also presents a short analysis of the *Body of Christ Independent Church* on the Pine Ridge Reservation that broke off from the traditional Christian churches towards the end of the 1950s. Pentecostal in nature, this church is radically opposed to the traditional Lakota religion, yet it considers itself a truly Amerindian religion. This church rejects all traditional Lakota religious symbols as a means to true Lakota identity, but recognizes the importance of some Lakota cultural features such as the *tiospaye* or the extended family. Steinmetz reports that some Lakota became members of this church because they believed that Christ had more power than the Sacred Pipe. The *Body of Christ Independent Church* has an important contribution to make to the study of acculturation, since it shows that Christianity can be a dynamic force in the life of full-blooded Lakota who are acculturated in all areas of life except religious symbolism. The *Body of Christ Independent Church* seems able to fulfil the cultural needs of its members through a deep religious experience of commitment to Christ.[55]

3. Contemporary religious dimorphism

The preceding presentation of Peyotism and the other new religious movements brings us to a fundamental fact about the religious situation of many Amerindians today. Many, if not most, Ameridians have in effect become Christian (Catholic or Protestant). They received the Christian faith from the missionaries, and learned the basic elements with a view to integration into Euro-American society. Normally this should have led to a radical transformation of their culture and the gradual disappearance of their aboriginal religion. However, many missionaries discovered that the contrary was true once they settled in their aboriginal "missionary territory."

Augustin Joseph Brabant, a diocesan priest of Flemish origin, noted in 1880 that six years of intense missionary activity among the Nootka of Vancouver Island had not eliminated their "superstitious practices."[56] But how could one expect rudimentary catechetical instruction to eliminate age-old traditions which were the cornerstone of that people's communal life in that short time? In 1931, Pierre Duchaussois remarked that evangelization over half a century had at last managed to get rid of "directly barbaric and satanic practices," but that various other "superstitions" were only gradually giving way.[57] Fifty years later, Quebec anthropologist Jacques Rousseau came to the conclusion that aboriginal religion was far from being exterminated, despite missionary efforts and governmental laws.[58] On the contrary, he noted the existence of a veritable religious *dualism* among Amerindians: the coexistence of two religions (the aboriginal and the Christian), which, in the life of individuals and that of the tribes, ran parallel without any real integration.

Rousseau's view has received support from numerous observers of indigenous life in various regions of Canada. Adrian Tanner showed in 1978 that the Cree of Mistassini in Quebec switched from the Anglican religion to their indigenous one with the change of the seasons.[59] From May to August, the Cree are to be found at the trading post of Mistassini searching for part-time jobs: their social life is then entirely organized around the Anglican church; they practise the Anglican religion (prayers, sacraments and so on) just like Anglicans elsewhere in the world. But, when autumn comes, they leave Mistassini and make for their hunting grounds. Their life is then entirely conditioned by their ancestral religion, which provides them with a vision of the world, rituals and prayers which are suitable for people who live by hunting and fishing, in profound communion with nature. After ten years of sharing the life of the Cree Indians in northwestern Alberta, the famous Oblate missionary, Roger Vandersteene, was invited by his parishioners to a religious ceremony *(wikkokewin)* in honour of the dead. Until then the missionary had been unaware of the existence of this ritual, held each year in the forest far away from the village, despite his enculturated life style and almost perfect knowledge of the Cree language. On his arrival at the place where the ritual was held, he was surprised to see almost all his Catholic parishioners taking part in the ceremony along with the Protestants of the village, whereas, back home, there was hardly any contact at all between the two groups. Vandersteene watched an imposing ceremony that lasted all night long, in which the Cree brought into play all the elements of their traditional religion (the sacred pipe, drums, dances, song and sacrifices). Even after the feast, he found it hard to believe that such a ritual was still possible.[60]

R. Vanderburgh, in the biography of Patronella Johnson, points out that this religious dualism or dimorphism is taken for granted by many Amerindians and does not seem to give rise to any major problem.[61] Christopher Vecsey observed the same attitude among the Anishnabe in Ontario and Manitoba.[62] Even among the Innu in Quebec, most of whom are devout Catholics, this dualism is not viewed as a contradiction or as a source of conflict, but as a mutual enrichment of their religious practices.[63]

The well-documented research of anthropologist Jean-Guy Goulet among the Dene-Tha of northwestern Alberta confirms this fact. His personal relationship with some Dene-Tha prophets suggests furthermore that we are dealing here with a widespread phenomenon among the native peoples in Canada. It is interesting to

Dene Tha Prophet Alexis Seniantha
Assumption, Alberta
Photo: Jean-Guy Goulet

note that young Dene describe their traditional practices and beliefs as "supersti-tions," when they are using the English language, while being aware of the fact that in their own Dene language the term "superstition" corresponds to the expression *dene wonlin edadihi* which means "a person who knows an animal." This expression, obviously, refers to persons who know the true nature of things because of the spiritual power they receive from their animal guardian spirit.[64] Goulet's research and field experience illustrate that the Dene-Tha are able to integrate key elements of Christianity into their traditional religious complex without modifying the worldview in a significant way. In the next section of this chapter (theological interpretation) we will therefore ask ourselves whether the terms "religious dualism" or "religious dimorphism" adequately describe this situation. Would it not be better to speak of "religious integration" at least in the case of the Dene Tha who represent the so-called high tradition in their aboriginal religion: the shamans, the prophets, the dreamers and other spiritual leaders? It appears to us that this interpretation applies to the case of the Dene prophet and shaman Alexis Seniantha (born in 1908) who belongs to an important prophetic tradition which developed in the nineteenth century.[65] Alexis Seniantha's personal vision or initial dream, as documented by Paul Hernou and Jean-Guy Goulet, situates itself on the intersection between two religious traditions (aboriginal and Christian). In the Dene Tha tradition, prophets or dreamers are viewed as persons with a "strong mind" who are able to travel from this world (*ndahdigeh*, "our land") to the other world (*ech'udigeh* or *yake*, "heaven," or *Ndahxota digeh*, "the land of God"). After he experienced his vision in 1928, Alexis Seniantha returned to his people, transformed in the image of the Son of God. Alexis Seniantha can be considered a truly "Christian" prophet whose religious experience has remained profoundly aboriginal. It is, therefore, different in many ways from the religious experience of the missionaries who brought the Christian faith to his people.[66]

We must also consider the fact that this religious dualism or integration has recently been viewed as an important phenomenon in the ongoing negotiations concerning the territorial rights of some native groups. Some of these groups, like the Gitksan-Wet'suwet'en in British Columbia, defend their title to the land on the basis that they have kept their spiritual relation with the land intact. In arguing the case before the Supreme Court of British Columbia (Delgam Uukw versus the Queen) they presented specifically religious arguments. The Gitksan-Wet'suwet'en demonstrated that they had never surrendered their title to the land *and* that they had never ceased to practise their traditional religion despite the fact that they had become Christian (Catholic or Pentecostal). Their "religious dualism" has been scientifically documented by anthropologist Tonia Mills. It strongly contests the argument of the government that the Gitksan-Wet'suewet'en had become citizens and Christians like other Canadians, and that, therefore, they should abstain from appealing to their traditional religion (dreams, spiritual links with the animals, reincarnation and so on) when they are in court. The Canadian judicial systems (British and French) do not seem to tolerate any type of argument that does not fit within the Euro-American cultural sphere, even though the Supreme Court of Canada has rendered two important judgments (*Sparrow versus the Queen,* May 31, 1990; *Quebec versus Sioui,* May 24, 1990) in favour of the recognition of ancestral rights (territorial and religious) wherever these rights were not given up by the native peoples.[67] Therefore, on March 8, 1991, the Honourable Chief Justice Allan McEachern of the Supreme Court of British Columbia judged that the Gitksan-Wet'suwet'en had lost the title to their traditional land.

The simultaneous practice of two different religious systems is a widespread phenomenon, not only in Canada but also in the United States of America and other parts of the world where indigenous peoples have embraced Christianity in the context of colonialism. This phenomenon has often been interpreted as an example of cultural adaptation or as a transitory phase within the acculturation process leading, unavoidably, to the disappearance of the aboriginal religions. The extraordinary survival of these religions contradicts this theory. But it confronts us, once again, with the meaning of the conversion of the Amerindians to Christianity. How can one justify this simultaneous belonging to two religious systems which have practised mutual exclusion in the course of history? How can we explain that Anishnabe native medicine men can now also be ordained deacons in the Roman Catholic church?[68] Why is it that we now meet non-native Roman

Catholic priests who participate in traditional native rituals? I myself have had the privilege of participating in various rituals since 1983.[69]

Native American conversions to Christianity must not be understood as an individual matter but as a *social* phenomenon. To explain the rise of religious dualism it is therefore insufficient to maintain, with the majority of anthropologists, that Christianity among the Amerindians is nothing more than a thin veneer covering a deep layer of native beliefs, or to maintain, with the majority of missionaries, that their native converts are strong and authentic Christians whose faith is (unfortunately) still tainted with old, sometimes silly, superstitions. These two interpretations ignore, to some extent, that aboriginal religion and Christianity are two religious systems with different social functions within the native communities, and that they may respond to different needs. Even though Christian faith constitutes a fundamental and exclusive option (one does not believe in two religions at the same time!), it is nevertheless possible to participate concurrently in two religious systems and to call upon their services according to the concrete circumstances of life. What Adrian Tanner has to say, concerning the double belonging of the Mistassini Cree Indians to the Anglican church and to their traditional religious complex, has also been observed by William Powers among the Oglala Lakota on the Pine Ridge Reservation in South Dakota.[70] After analyzing the social, political, economic and religious motivations of the conversion of the Lakota to Christianity, Powers proposes a structural and functional model to explain their simultaneous participation in the Christian and aboriginal religion. His sociological approach, enriched with historical and anthropological observations, allows him to conclude that on the Pine Ridge Reservation (the second largest reservation in the United States) the two religious systems coexist without mutual compenetration, despite the fact that some native shamans use Christian symbols in their rituals and that Catholic priests introduce native symbols in their liturgies.

Powers' analysis seems to confirm that the aboriginal religions continue to constitute the main factor of social integration in many native communities,[71] while Christianity has been adopted by many Amerindians to assure their survival in the larger Euro-American society. What happened on the Pine Ridge Reservation towards the end of the nineteenth century probably repeated itself in many parts of the United States and Canada. Notwithstanding the fact that Christianity was in direct competition with the aboriginal religions and that the missionaries really wanted to civilize the Indians (cultural transformation), the Christian churches were often the only sanctuaries where the Amerindians found refuge against the oppressive forces of western society. This explains the survival of the aboriginal religions in the shadow of the Christian churches whose social functions became vital within native communities which had become partially dysfunctional. Especially at the time of the *ghost dance* movement, many Amerindians rapidly understood that, in the eyes of civil and military authorities, the only good Indian was a Christian Indian!

But we are allowed to ask ourselves if this type of sociological analysis Powers proposes suffices to account for the complex historical encounter between Christianity and the native world. Does it explain religious dualism? The wide spectrum of examples which we have presented in this chapter shows that the traditional native religions continue to respond very well to the basic needs of peoples for whom contact with the sacred is part of daily life. Therefore, one may question whether these people have adopted Christianity merely for social, political or economic reasons in view of the collapse of their traditional societies. It cannot be denied that Christianity offered the Oglala and other native groups a *social structure* which permitted them to relate to the dominant society. But one must also recognize that the adoption of Christianity by the Amerindians involved truly theological discussions and significant religious interactions. Powers seems to recognize this fact when he writes that the native Oglala religious leaders were not only ritual practitioners but also philosophers who, unnoticed by the priests, argued among themselves and their adepts about the efficacy of the white man's God and the Christian ministers, comparing them to *Wakan Tanka* and to their own religious functions.[72] Therefore, Steinmetz's judgment that Powers is treating the whole process of inculturation very superficially and that he does not understand the significance of the presence of Christianity among the Lakota is too radical.[73]

All the data presented in this chapter led almost inevitably to the conclusion that the Amerindian reception of Christianity is truly theological. Therefore, we must analyze this reception and all its implications in a truly theological fashion. This can be done by applying the new theological term "inculturation" to the native North American world, and by focusing on the central meaning of the Christic mystery in the historical encounter of Christianity with the Amerindian peoples.

III. Towards a Theological Interpretation

1. Religion and culture

The different religious movements presented in this chapter illustrate the complexity of the Amerindian-Christian encounter. The North American native peoples have responded to the missionary action of the Christian churches with religious and cultural creativity. Their answer presents itself as a unique and original answer that transcends the expectations of the missionaries and the objectives of their churches. But it suggests that the gospel has profoundly penetrated the Amerindian soil. We can therefore slightly modify Grant's statement which we adopted at the beginning of this chapter. Instead of stating that the Amerindians have become Christian, but that Christianity never became Indian, it would be more exact to say that the Amerindians have not become Christian *like us* and that they have not spontaneously joined our western churches. After their conversion they managed to create their own expressions of Christianity on the fringe of the official churches and often in opposition to them. They often reinterpreted the Christian faith from the cultural vantage point of their own religious experience. Some have turned their back on the church while others commit themselves to the Amerindian renewal of their Christian communities. All these tendencies represent a wide spectrum of cultural and religious developments which need to be interpreted theologically.

The complexity of this evolution is clearly illustrated by Steinmetz's study on the religious identity of the Lakota on the Pine Ridge Reservation. In this native group the interaction of the sacred pipe, the Bible and Peyote has produced a large variety of religious developments which affect the relationship between Christianity and the aboriginal religion. We will present a detailed analysis of this situation in Chapter V.[74]

It is quite obvious that a complete analysis of the Amerindian response to the Christian missionary intrusion would require an anthropological and theological approach which transcends the limits of this book. What we propose is a more modest analysis which uses the theological concept of inculturation and concentrates on the *christological dimension* of Amerindian-Christian interactions. This interpretation is based on the conviction that we cannot reduce the missionary activity of the church to sociological, anthropological or ecclesiastical strategies alone. The mission of the church is understood to be at the service of the mystery of Jesus, the Christ, who gave his life for the salvation of the world. Through the church's mission, Christ himself reveals his mysterious presence among the peoples who welcome his gospel. Therefore this study looks for the signs of Christ's presence in the different religious movements which we have presented. It is not our intention to "recuperate" the religious creativity of the Amerindians for the sake of the Christian churches which are struggling for their own survival in native North America. This book simply wants to discover the hidden face of the Amerindian Christ.

Nonetheless, we have to recognize that this christological interpretation must take into consideration what anthropology and the other sciences have to say about the evolution of Amerindian culture. We agree with Kenneth Morrison that we must draw on the findings of several disciplines because "religion is closely bound up with metaphysical, cognitive, psychological, and social realms of meaning,"[75] and with Sergei Kan who insists on the importance of anthropology for an exact understanding of Christianity's impact on Amerindian culture.[76] Theology alone cannot do the job! Nevertheless, it is the task of theology to propose a truly theological interpretation of what is, after all, not just an historical phenomenon but a mysterious reality.

From the anthropological point of view, all the movements which we have presented in the first part of this book lead to the conclusion that North American Indian cultures have managed to survive within a larger society which intended to assimilate them. This fact has an enormous impact on the evolution of the social sciences and on socio-cultural anthropology. From now on, we should not concentrate, primarily, on the mechanisms by which various minorities are assimilated by the dominant society, but on the process which permits these minorities to propose alternative visions to the vision of this dominant society. There is no doubt that, in the case of the Amerindians, this process is a profoundly spiritual one. The North American native peoples are perhaps the best illustration of Paul Tillich's statement that "religion is the substance of culture; culture is the form of religion."[77]

It is, therefore, impossible to ignore the present state of discussion on the relationship between religion and culture. Over the last fifty years, the Christian churches have participated in this debate more and more.[78] Yet, we may ask ourselves with Karl Rahner whether they have really seized the opportunity to let themselves be transformed by the non-western cultures where they have built their homes.[79] How do they visualize their "universal" mission today? How do they understand the relationship between the gospel, Christian faith, and various cultures? How do they participate in cross-cultural dialogue?

Since the 1950s a new missionary vocabulary which expresses the church's increasing awareness about the cultural implications of its mission has appeared. Many of the terms it uses are borrowed from anthropology: adaptation, accommodation, localization, indigenization, acculturation, enculturation, contextualization. These terms represent a common missionary problematic and methodology. To become truly universal and supra-regional, the church must adapt itself to the different cultures of its members, implant itself locally to form truly indigenous communities, speak the cultural language of its members and construct itself from the grassroots up. We will show a little further on that the term "inculturation" is closely associated with these notions, but that it cannot be reduced to them. We intend to show that, at its deepest level of meaning, the term "inculturation" does not designate a new missionary method, but a new vision of the church's evangelizing mission, *centred on the Christic mystery.* We emphasize this despite the fact that in the official documents of the churches and in the contemporary missionary literature the content of inculturation remains more ecclesiological than christological.

Despite the efforts to renew itself, the theology of mission remains a church-centred theology. The missionary discourse continues to be structured from the vantage point of the churches which proclaim the gospel rather than from the vantage point of the people who receive it. This explains why the missionary churches have paid so little attention to the religious movements which appeared among the Amerindians. Yet, over the last few years, these "new religious movements" have become an important field of theological investigation. Theologian Carl Starkloff rightly states that we can no longer consider them a sort of "exotic" phenomenon which only occasionally stimulates the curiosity of theologians.[80] The fact that we find more than 5,000 independent churches in Africa, and that religious syncretism is a universal phenomenon indicates that we are dealing with a central issue in the missionary epic of the Christian churches. Anthropologist Arnold Turner, who stated in 1973 that the missionary results among the

Amerindians are among the least impressive of all missionary efforts, now invites us to pay attention to these new religious movements.[81] They are indeed the unexpected result of the type of evangelization that aimed at the radical conversion of the Indians to Christianity, and at their gradual assimilation into the Euro-American society. As stated above, we now ought to examine the mechanisms which have enabled the aboriginal cultures to survive inside and outside the churches.

From a theological point of view, our christological interpretation must also acknowledge the present state of discussion on the relationship between the Christian faith and culture, keeping in mind that the Christian theology of culture is still very fragmentary. The examination of the current literature on this issue, as Robert Schreiter has shown,[82] leads to many questions for which we do not yet have satisfactory answers: What must be the starting point of a Christian theology of culture, Christian faith or culture? Is the gospel message truly "supra-cultural"? Do we have an adequate method for the interpretation of culture? Should we insist on cultural identity (continuity) or on cultural transformation (discontinuity)? Is there some philosophical summit from which we can assess the different methods of cultural analysis without giving in to relativism? Can all cultures be evangelized? Are non-western Christians able to change the European-centred church? Is there room for cultural pluralism within the church itself?

The fact that these questions are raised by a growing number of anthropologists and theologians is significant. We are witnessing the transition from a missionary church-centred vision to a vision centred on the various peoples who form the universal church. We now understand that the church's mission is not finished with the proclamation of the gospel to a people and with their integration into a dogmatic system whose boundaries are fixed once and for all. We understand that the *religious creativity* of those who welcome and receive the gospel is an intrinsic dimension of the missionary expansion of the church. We try to understand what happens in the life of a person or of a people when the gospel becomes part of their culture.

Therefore, we insist on the fact that the theological interpretation and reconstruction of the evangelizing process must consider the various historical, ethnological and religious elements which shape the response of a people to the proclamation of the gospel and to the implantation of the church. The great variety of Amerindian responses which we have presented in this chapter calls for a *contextualized* theological interpretation.

2. The socio-cultural context

To grasp the originality of the native American response to the gospel we would like to focus briefly on the three main cultural elements which have determined the historical encounter of Christianity with the Amerindians.

The impact of colonialism

In the first place one should not forget, writes Sergei Kan, that the encounter between the Christian missionaries and the Amerindians was only one aspect of the relationship between the colonizers and the colonized.[83] In many parts of North America the mission stations were often the outposts of the colonial expansion of the European empires and represented the settlement of whites in native territory. In the western part of the United States, for example, the famous Flemish missionary, Pieter Jan De Smet (1801-1873), played a major role in the pacification of the Indian tribes and in their negotiations with the civil and military authorities.[84] In western Canada, Catholic missionaries like Father Albert Lacombe (1827-1916) or Gabriel Breynat (1867-1954) facilitated the signature of the treaties which turned the Indians into totally dependent peoples.[85] But even more important was the overall civilizing aspect of the Christian missions. Often, the missionaries were the first to contribute to the acculturation process by introducing new ways of thinking and doing in the native communities.

Another highly significant factor in the cultural evolution of the native peoples concerns the transformation of the church itself: the transition from the "itinerant" missionary life to the permanent mission stations. In certain regions, this came about only towards the beginning of the present century or even later. It marks an important change in missionary concepts and strategies. There was an early period during which the itinerant missionaries lived in close contact with the Amerindians and were almost totally dependent on them for transport, food and shelter. Then followed a period during which the church was established through the creation of permanent mission stations (with a church, presbytery, convent, residential school, clinic and so on) on which the Indians gradually came to depend for their survival.

We should immediately note that this evolution did not produce what it was expected to produce, namely the development of truly indigenous communities which would soon be able to function according to "the three-self formula," conceived by the Protestant missiologists Henry Venn (1796-1873) and Rufus Anderson (1796-1880), and become self-supporting, self-governing and self-propagating churches.[86] This evolution did not take place. The Amerindian churches have remained "missionary" churches, marked by a great amount of apathy and passivity, despite contemporary efforts at renewal. There is no doubt that remnants of ecclesial colonialism continue to influence the Amerindian communities, if by "ecclesial colonialism" we understand the urge of missionaries to impose the model of "mother church" upon the native communities, rather than giving the people the freedom to shape their own churches in response to the gospel.

This also raises the important question concerning the native perceptions of the Christian God and of Christ himself. How can the "God of the oppressors" become a liberating God for them?[87] How can the gospel become "good news" for those who try to reverse centuries of political, economic, cultural and religious oppression? These questions surely invite the Christian churches to join the Indians in the reinterpretation and reappropriation of their own religious traditions.

It is not inappropriate to compare the cultural and religious situation of the Amerindians with that of many Asian or African peoples. After having been "discovered" by others, these peoples must now rediscover themselves. After having been involved, sometimes in spite of themselves, in the political wars and the religious conflicts of the white colonizers, they now want to become the artisans of their own history. This often implies the "rediscovery" of their ancestral religion and its integration in their new political and cultural projects. This is a difficult task indeed, because of the collective amnesia that affects them following years of oppression and dependency. Vincent Cosmao managed to show that the loss or suppression of the aboriginal religions was a decisive factor in the social collapse of the exploited peoples. The churches, whether in collusion or competition with them, arrived with the merchants, soldiers and colonists. The churches played a role in disturbing local religious traditions and structures. Now, they have a new duty to perform. By paying respectful attention to the surviving aboriginal religions and by trying to understand them, the churches can help the native peoples to reinterpret their religious traditions amid the growing pressures of western society and technological culture.[88]

As elsewhere in the Third and Fourth World, change, development and liberation have become key notions among the North American native peoples. They represent the cultural dynamism which aims at the restoration of the oppressed and at the transformation of the attitudes of the church towards them.[89] This new dynamic deeply affects the traditional relationship between the churches and the aboriginal peoples who often perceive the church as being on the side of the colonizers, notwithstanding the support given by the church to their present struggle for self-determination. In fact, the global colonial context makes it hard for the Christian churches to transform their assimilationist strategies into partnership with the native peoples.[90] In preparing this book on the Amerindian Christ, we found it, therefore, important to consult as many native persons as possible and to let them speak for themselves.[91]

An encounter between two universes of meaning

Notwithstanding the impact of western civilization on the aboriginal societies of North America, the encounter between Christianity and the Amerindians is also a spiritual adventure. We are dealing with the encounter between two universes of meaning which influence each other. This is the second factor that we must consider. This mutual influence situates itself between two extremes: the analysis which concludes that the adoption of Christianity by the Amerindians unavoidably leads to the decline or to the gradual disappearance of their traditional religion, and the analysis which considers the traditional religion as a primitive system which escapes the influence of Christianity. In fact, these two interpretations, which form the basis of certain anthropological interpretations of the Amerindians' religious dualism, are not sufficiently sensitive to the real nature of the Amerindian-Christian encounter. Our own presentation of this historical encounter has revealed that the Amerindian attitudes to Christianity are not a matter of yes or no, and that the early missionaries understood that the Indian soul was not a *tabula rasa* on which they could freely impose their Christian understanding of God. The Amerindian conversions to Christianity are a very delicate issue which cannot be adequately understood without considering the interiorization of the values implied in the encounter between the Amerindian spiritual universe and the missionaries' Christian ideology.

Throughout history we meet missionaries who have made a tremendous effort to adapt to the local culture in order to facilitate the implantation of the church among the Amerindians. We also meet Amerindians who found important elements in Christianity which confirmed their world vision and enhanced their spiritual life. Conversion to Christianity does not necessarily lead to the decline of the aboriginal religions, while exposure to western civilization does not necessarily mean the extinction of native culture. It is more appropriate, in this context, to speak of mutual influences and transformations. Therefore, it is also inappropriate to describe this process as syncretism, unless one carefully specifies what this term means.[92]

In a remarkable study of the evangelization of the Tupi-Guarani in Brazil and Paraguay by the Jesuits, Judith Shapiro offers an interesting example of an intercultural encounter with lasting and unforeseen implications. The early accounts of this missionary epic show that those who attempted to spread Christianity among the Tupi-Guarani sought to translate their message into a language their potential converts could understand. They found many elements in the culture of this people which were compatible with the Catholic religion. They even thought that these elements were remnants of the early evangelization by Saint Thomas who, according to their beliefs, had passed through South America, introducing the Amerindians to the gospel. The Guarani, on the contrary, were deeply impressed by the power and resources of the Europeans. Calling the white men *Maira* or *Caraiba*, the term they used to designate their most powerful shamans, the Tupi-Guarani believed that the Europeans had received their power from their cultural hero, *Maira-Monan*. The early Jesuits used the name *Tupa*, a central figure from Tupian mythology, to designate the Christian God, but they hesitated to Christianize the "land without evil," the earthly paradise that constituted the very centre of the traditional religion of the Tupi-Guarani's who were known for their large-scale and far-ranging migrations. According to Tupi-Guarani belief, this "land without evil" was a place where crops grew by themselves, people spent their time feasting and dancing, and no one ever died. It was the permanent abode of the culture's hero and of the souls of exceptional individuals after their death. The missionaries considered the Tupi-Guarani permanent search for this paradise, under the guidance of their shamans, as a contradiction of the Christian doctrine of heaven and hell and as an obstacle to the creation of permanent settlements which would allow them to control the life of the Amerindians. These early missionary attitudes stand in sharp contrast to the contemporary situation of the Catholic church in Brazil where the *Conselho Indigenista Missionario* (CIMI) has taken the side of the oppressed Indians and has played a major role in fostering a pan-Indian movement in Brazil. Four centuries after the arrival of the first missionaries, it now appears that the native myth of the *land without evil* has become particularly suited to the church's own ideological needs and to the prophetic struggle for liberation in the name of Christ. On 22 April 1979, in the cathedral da Se in Sao Paolo, the first celebration took place of a mass entitled "The Mass of the Land Without Evil" *(Missa Da Terra sem Males)*. Set to native music drawn from various regions in South America, the mass is primarily the work of one of Brazil's most progressive bishops, Dom Pedro Casaldaliga. For the theology of liberation there is no heavenly paradise without justice and peace on earth. The Tupi-Guarani utopia, once rejected as a major obstacle to the Christian faith and to the evangelization of the Indians, has now become a potent symbol of the church's own conversion, the condition *sine qua non* for the effective evangelization of the South American indigenous peoples. Those who were viewed four centuries ago as a people without religion have now become the pioneers and the prophets of the theologies of liberation.[93]

The cultural situation of the actors

The contextual analysis of the missionary epic in native North America must consider a third cultural factor, namely the cultural situation of the persons who were directly involved in that epic. Evangelization must not be understood, in the first place, as the encounter between abstract systems of thinking or universes of meaning, but as the encounter between persons who represent these ideologies or visions. Mission always involves inter-cultural and interreligious communication. Thus it is possible to observe, as Sergei Kan has done in regard to the missionary epic of the orthodox church among the Tlinglit, that certain types of native Christianity are largely influenced by native "missionaries" (preachers, catechists) who freely use their own symbols to spread the Christian faith among the members of their tribes.[94] It also becomes clear that certain prophetic movements or syncretism are the work of shamans and native spiritual leaders who were systematically excluded from the Christian communities.

In fact, the entire missionary epic among the Amerindians can almost be summarized as a struggle for power between the shaman and the Christian minister. Certain native cultures were more prepared than others to accept the spiritual innovations and social transformations implied in their evangelization. They got involved in a truly inter-cultural communication with the Christian missionaries. But, usually, the encounter between Christianity and native North Americans was marked by a ferocious battle between the shamans and the priests for the control of the spiritual destiny of the people. This observation can be drawn from most historical studies of the implantation of the churches among the Amerindian peoples.[95] Among the Tupi-Guarani, as we have seen, the conflict rapidly focused on the spiritual power of the shamans and the priests. It must be observed that the priests or the Christian ministers were part of religious systems which gave them practically full power over the spiritual destiny of the people. In the early stages of the missionary epic they were often perceived by the Amerindians as "super-shamans." The priests will gradually replace the shamans in the ongoing confrontation between Christianity and the aboriginal religions. They will exercise the same functions as the shamans, and will often become, willy-nilly, ministers of the native religions they were supposed to eliminate. At the same time, the priests often exploited their new status as "super-shamans" to impose the Christian religion on the Amerindians, without the collaboration of the shamans and native religious leaders who had been guiding the spiritual journey of their people before the arrival of Christianity. Since Christianity was considered to be the only true religion, the shamans were often described as charlatans or even agents of the devil.[96]

Because of this major conflict at the start of the missionary epic in native North America, the dialogue between Christianity and the aboriginal religions will remain a difficult and fragile enterprise. We observe today, for example, that many native spiritual resources, rejected by the Christian churches, have now become major elements in the spiritual revitalization of the Amerindian peoples. Likewise, we observe that within many native Christian communities these same resources are now welcomed for the renewal of the church itself. Many native persons, especially the elders, find it difficult to accept that the "paganism" formerly rejected by the Christian church, now finds favour with its leaders and missionaries. However, we also observe the emergence of a new type of cultural and religious actor in native North America: native persons who are striving, sometimes very discretely, for the integration of Christianity and their traditional religion, and Christian ministers who are truly moved by Amerindian spirituality. These are the actors whom the Christian churches need to make the passage from their traditional "missionary" perspective to that of intercultural and interreligious dialogue.

3. The theological dimension

The simultaneous or successive participation of many native persons in two different religious systems, one Christian and one traditional, is one of the most fascinating dimensions of the Amerindian reality. This phenomenon is so overwhelming that William Powers does not hesitate to speak of a truly Amerindian "ecumenism" whose values are adopted by many tribes and even by many white persons, for example in Europe, who want to support the first nations of North America in the struggle for their basic rights.[97] This phenomenon has caught the attention of anthropologists who raise questions about whether it is truly the work of the Amerindians themselves, and of theologians who look at its implications for the internal renewal of the Christian church.[98] Even more fascinating is the fact that a growing number of native persons try to go beyond this religious "dualism" in their efforts to *integrate* Christian faith and their culture. We will present some of the results of these efforts in the second part of this book.

The inculturation of the gospel in native North America

The contemporary religious situation of many native persons indicates that the gospel is deeply rooted in the Amerindian soil. Therefore we cannot limit ourselves to an anthropological analysis of this situation. In the midst of the complexity of the inter-cultural reactions which anthropology and social sciences attempt to unravel, a mystery is unfolding that can only be perceived with the eyes of faith. It is the mystery of Christ's presence among the North American peoples to whom the gospel has been proclaimed by the missionary churches. To really account for this mystery, we make use of the new theological concept, *inculturation*. Inculturation is a concept that, by virtue of its two components, signifies a process that is vital for the Christian faith, but, also extremely complex. Its prefix, "in," reminds us of the demands of the incarnation of God in the person of Jesus; its root, "culture," asks us to take into account the richness and variety of human culture. This term had already been adopted by some Catholic missiologists, prior to the Second Vatican Council (1962-1965),[99] to indicate new directions in the understanding of the church's mission. Inculturation served as an alternative to terms such as accommodation and adaptation, and offered a more respectful approach to the cultural situation of those who welcome the gospel. But it is only since Vatican II that the term has received the attention of the church's leadership and theological community.[100]

While it has taken centuries for some theological concepts to become part of the teachings of the church, the term inculturation, on the contrary, has become an almost magical word in a very short period of time. It is our opinion that this term does not simply represent a new missionary strategy, but that it expresses *a new vision of the church's evangelizing mission*.[101] Beyond all missionary strategies, this term evokes the mysterious encounter between the gospel of Christ and peoples. The term "mystery" is imperative in this context, because inculturation, like the love between two persons, often remains undetected. The encounter between the gospel and peoples is much more than an ethnic, linguistic, geographical or social affair. It is basically a spiritual adventure that calls for the fundamental attitudes of listening, dialogue, research, active presence and careful discernment. It is also a complex anthropological and theological process, which is truly *christological* in its very core. Inculturation concerns the mystery of Christ, crucified and risen for the salvation of the world.

In the overall perspective of this book, we must insist on the fact that the proper subject or object of inculturation is neither the missionary, nor the church that sends him, but Christ himself. The role of the church must be acknowledged as the community that proclaims the gospel and verifies the result of its missionary enterprise. The church finds itself at the beginning and at the conclusion of the inculturation process. Its role can easily be compared to that of the sower in the little parable of the seed that grows all by itself while the sower sleeps (Mk 4:26-29).

Inculturation, in fact, is something that happens between the gospel itself (the seed) and the receiving culture (the soil). The role of the sower, the missionary church, remains very important, but is secondary with respect to the people who receive the gospel. The role of the receiving people or culture is primordial. It is "on its own," the parable says, that the land produces fruit. Each culture produces its own results when confronted with the gospel. But the main role, in this process, belongs to the gospel itself. Jesus, the Christ, is himself the main actor in the inculturation process, because he IS the Word proclaimed by the church and received by peoples. He IS the way, the truth and the light.

Each authentic inculturation can therefore be understood as a sort of "reactualization," in time and space, of the unique mystery of God's incarnation (becoming human) in the person of Jesus. It is because Jesus (the Son of God) enculturated himself, once and for all, in one particular culture (Hebr 9:26), that his word can do the same thing in each and every culture, as if each one were unique. The church that proclaims the word to all nations (Mt 28:19), therefore, has the task of verifying how each nation responds to this proclamation and, eventually, integrates itself in the universal communion of the disciples of Christ.

It is in the light of this mystery that we have tried to present the encounter between Christianity and the Amerindian cultures. This mystery accomplishes itself in the very midst of the acculturation, enculturation and transculturation process that is normally involved in any encounter between the cultural universe of the Christian church and the cultural universe of the peoples to whom it proclaims the gospel.

Therefore, the verification of the results of the inculturation of the gospel presupposes a great cultural sensitivity and a significant amount of theological courage. The history of the missionary epic of the church reveals that we are ready to welcome generously the fruits of our missionary efforts which faithfully reflect the theology and the structures of the (western) church, the one which has proclaimed the gospel throughout the world. But what about those unexpected fruits which the gospel also produces in the cultures of the peoples to whom it is proclaimed, the new fruits which do not necessarily correspond to our western theology and structures? We are dealing here with a theological and pastoral issue that the universal church cannot avoid: *the capacity and the courage to welcome responses to the gospel which, to the missionary who has sown its seeds in a foreign soil, are creative, unique, original and properly unheard of.* The mystery of inculturation is nothing other than the extraordinary power of the gospel (the living word of a living God) acting upon a culture from within and producing within that culture responses of faith which often exceed our expectations and predictions.

This mysterious action of the gospel within a given culture could be compared to the cultural situation of Jesus himself. Inculturation fits within the *logic of the incarnation and of the paschal mystery*. The story of Jesus is the story of a God who freely chose to become human by submitting himself totally to all the determinations of one particular human being within one particular culture in order that his word might be heard by all the peoples of the world. Likewise, the gospel wants to become a concrete and particular message for each people or group of persons to whom it is proclaimed. Is it not the fundamental mission of the church to make possible throughout history what was possible for God himself when he incarnated himself in the person of Jesus, the Son of Mary? Has Jesus of Nazareth truly become an Amerindian Christ?

The Christic mystery

To answer this question let us once again recall the statement made by Pope John Paul II during his 1984 visit to the Shrine of the Canadian Martyrs in Midland: "Thus the one faith is expressed in different ways. There can be no question of adulterating the Word of God or of emptying the Cross of its power, but rather of Christ animating the very centre of all cultures. Thus, not only is Christianity relevant to the Indian peoples, but *Christ, in the members of his Body, is himself Indian.*"[102]

By evoking the power of the word of God and the mystery of the cross, this prophetic statement reminds us that the theological foundation of this search for the Amerindian Christ is none other than the historical person of Jesus himself whom the native peoples of North America were able to encounter through the missionary activity of the church. The mystery of the ongoing encounter between Christ and these peoples is the reason why we understand inculturation as the inculturation of *Christ*, and not directly as the inculturation of the church.

We must keep in mind that Christianity (in all its cultural expressions) is inseparable from the concrete person of Jesus, confessed and recognized as the universal Christ or saviour. The singularity of this historical person cannot be denied. For the Amerindian peoples, Jesus of Nazareth remains the one of whom is written: "There is no other name under heaven given among mortals by which we must be saved" (Acts 4:12).

It is important to insist, once again, on the theological orientation of this search for the Amerindian Christ. Ours is not the perspective of the science of religions which sets out to analyze objectively all the implications of the historical encounter between Christianity and the Amerindians. Our theological perspective presupposes the confession of faith in Jesus as the universal Christ. This confession of faith is the very foundation of the church's universal mission and it determines the unique and absolute nature of Christianity. No one else insisted on the scandalous nature of this confession of faith more than the well-known theologian, Hans Urs von Balthasar. Balthasar's own answer to the question "Who is Christ for you?" may help us to clarify the theological orientation of this study on the Amerindian Christ:

Who is Christ for me?

He is the only person in the entire history of the world who dared to claim for himself what God had claimed in the Old Testament, and who, for this very reason, was considered a fool and a man possessed (Mk 3) and was crucified. In fact, it suits a wise person to be discreet, and a prophet may say: "The Word of God," but not "I tell you." Yet, God the Father has validated the truth of this claim by raising Jesus from the dead. Henceforth, the primordial centre of Christian dogma is set free: God is Love. The immanent Trinity has revealed itself in history as the orthopraxis of this God who has handed over his Son and abandoned him in the realm of dead. This is indeed the most sublime presentation of God: It is in him (according to Hegel) that coincides identity (God is all things, He is eternal life) and non-identity (God is dead to the extent that he identifies himself with the absence of God). God is so much alive, that he can permit himself to be dead.

No other religion or philosophical system has dared to think and to proclaim such a presentation of God, man and the world. This is why Christianity remains without analogy. Christianity is not based on an idea, but on a fact—Jesus, the Christ—that in the unity of the claim to be equal to God, the cross and the resurrection remains the atom that cannot be split. On this fact depends the possibility of considering each being as love and each existing being as worthy of our love—a viewpoint that the world itself (in all its expressions) could never have inspired in us.[103]

Since the beginning of Christianity, the singularity of the Christ event has constituted the very centre of the Christian faith. Yet, the entire history of Christianity illustrates very well that it is not easy to maintain the paradoxical link between Jesus, the unique historical incarnation of God, and the universal meaning of his salvific message.[104] Jacques Dupuis has convincingly demonstrated that the paradox of the particularity and the universality of Jesus Christ constitutes "the cardinal key question" of the Christian theology of religions.[105] Since the West has ceased to be the centre of the world, and Christianity has lost its connection with its traditional cultural foundations, this paradox has become almost unbearable. For a growing number of persons it has become more and more difficult to accept the exclusive link between God and the person of Jesus who belongs to another culture and to other times. Therefore, one should not be surprised that, throughout the history of Christianity, especially in the modern era, various attempts have been made to reduce the status of Jesus to that of a mere symbol that continues to inspire millions of persons in the search for the Ultimate, but that can no longer be considered as the only (ontological and constitutive) road towards God.[106]

The statement made by Pope John Paul II in Midland confronts us with the theological obligation to maintain the absolute particularity of Jesus of Nazareth. But, at the same time, it also contains a discreet invitation to develop a new theological discourse on the presence of Christ within cultures: *we must place Christ at the centre of each culture.* This is what this search for the Amerindian Christ is all about. For us, the issue is not to sever the indissoluble link between Jesus and the Christ, but to become more profoundly aware of the fact that the Christic mystery infinitely transcends the historical boundaries of the divine revelation contained in the person of Jesus and in the Christian movement of which he is the founder. For us, the issue is not to contest the unique mission of the Christian church, as sign or sacrament of Christ, but to become more profoundly aware of the fact that the Christian church has no absolute control over God's mysterious dealings with humankind and the world. It can be argued that this theological effort finds its source within scripture itself. The prologue of the fourth gospel, the christological hymns in Ephesians and Colossians, as well as many other texts, affirm the basic identity of the One in whom the world was created and the historical Jesus who died on the Cross for the salvation of this world.

It should be noted that only a *pneuma-christology* will eventually help us to see all the implications of the Christic mystery better. Only a trinitarian theology permits us to perceive more adequately the basic link and the necessary distinctions between the mission of Jesus, the mission of the church and the mission of the Spirit.[107] Walter Kasper rightly observed: "A Christology in a pneumatological perspective is therefore what best enables us to combine both the uniqueness and the universality of Jesus Christ. It can show how the Spirit, who is operative in Christ in his fullness, is at work in varying degrees everywhere in the history of mankind, and also how Jesus Christ is the goal and head of all humanity."[108]

We should not hesitate to place Pope John Paul's statement within this pneuma-christological perspective. The *Body that permits Christ to become truly Indian* cannot simply be identified with the frontier of the church that was planted in the Amerindian soil. This Body is constituted by the Amerindian culture itself. It is also the Body of dispossessed and suffering peoples. It is the sum total of everything that we have written about the Amerindian reality in the first part of this book.

When contemplating this complex Amerindian reality, we are also invited to expand our Christian confession of faith in Christ. While God has received a unique human face in the person of Jesus, he continues to reveal himself in many other ways throughout history. The total self-gift of God in the person of Jesus is indeed the very foundation of our hope that each human person will eventually see the Creator face to face. Jesus Christ is the very source of each human being's search for God, because in him this search has already reached its fulfilment. The death and resurrection of Jesus is also our death and resurrection (Rom 4:25). The unique mystery which has accomplished itself in Jesus Christ is made universally available through the gift of his Spirit to each human person and to the entire world. Distinctions of race, culture or religion should not be seen as obstacles to the ultimate fulfilment of this mystery but as the vehicles by which it unfolds. In the Christic mystery, the entire creation receives the centre toward which all the divine roads converge. Our search for the Indian Christ is therefore, ultimately, a search for the Christic centre of Amerindian culture.

Conclusion

In this chapter we have presented an overview of the historical encounter between Christianity and the Amerindian peoples. This encounter has not yet produced a truly native church, but it has given birth to a large variety of religious movements, often on the fringe of the Christian churches, which exemplify the inherent creativity of the Amerindian religious experience. We have avoided interpreting these movements as a failure of the missionary epic of the church. We do not consider them merely transitory phases on the road leading to the full participation of the Amerindian peoples in the Christian church. On the contrary, we want to understand these movements as unexpected but authentic signs of the hidden presence and action of Christ among the Amerindian peoples, which indicate that the gospel has become a powerful endogenous factor that continues to work on the Amerindian cultures from within. We have no way of knowing beforehand what the ultimate results of this powerful action will be. But, to the extent that the Amerindian cultures let the gospel work on them from within, they will allow us to discover the hidden face of the Amerindian Christ.

PART II

THE HIDDEN FACE
OF THE AMERINDIAN CHRIST

In the second part of this book we will analyse various forms of the inculturation of Christ in native North America. The main purpose of our journey is to discover the figure of the "Indian Christ" evoked by Pope John Paul II during his 1984 visit to Canada. We would like to show the unique beauty of this Christ figure as well as its dramatic contours and implications. For those Amerindians who shared with us their vision of Christ, this Christ figure is not an abstract reality. Even though for most of them the term "Indian Christ" was new and unexpected, the Christic mystery was really present in their life. All the testimonies in the second part of this book are therefore straightforward answers to the question: "But who do you say I am?" (Mk 8:29). What characterizes these answers in the first place is their contextual nature. They reveal a deep concern for the many problems faced by the native communities today: the development of the Amerindian identity within the multi-cultural Canadian society, the social collapse and reconstruction of the native communities, the struggle for political and economic self-determination, and, above all, the revival of traditional spirituality and its relationship to Christianity.

This complex reality constitutes the main *locus theologicus* (the theological milieu) in which the Indian Christ figure emerges today. We will see that the christology that is developing in native North America is a "negative" and "inchoate" christology. The Christ figure is deeply embedded in native North America, but the face of this Indian Christ remains hidden for many who set out to discover him, whether they are Christian Indians or traditionalists. Our own search for this Indian Christ will therefore be discreet and respectful. It is not our task, but the task of the native peoples themselves to unveil the face of their Indian Christ. It is not our task to transform their "negative" or "inchoate" christology into a positive and explicit discourse. Our task is primarily to mediate between the universal church and these particular peoples who, in the very midst of their struggle for self-determination, are also developing their own spirituality and theology.

In the second part of this book we hope to exercise this mediating role in four steps. We will first present a selection of testimonies which illustrate the kind of christology which is now developing among the Amerindians (Chapter IV). There are three basic themes in these testimonies which we will explore in the following chapters in relation to the figure of the Indian Christ: the Amerindian religious experience; the present struggle of Canada's first nations; and the Amerindian worldview. We will first concentrate on the most intimate aspect of the Amerindian christology, namely its religious dimension, by reflecting on the relationship between the sacred pipe and Christ and on the Amerindian contributions to interreligious dialogue (Chapter V). We will then present an overview of the present struggles of Canada's first nations. We will reflect on the soteriological dimension of the Amerindian christology and on the Amerindian contributions to liberation theology (Chapter VI). We will conclude this essay with the analysis of two important native rituals, the sun dance and the vision quest, which offer us unique access to the native American expressions of the universal Christ (Chapter VII).

CHAPTER IV

"Who do you say I am?"
(Mark 8:29)
Native people respond

Introduction

Since 1982 we have enjoyed the great hospitality of many Native American communities across Canada. We have been able to familiarize ourselves with the concrete aspects of native life in urban centres as well as in the remote villages of western and northern Canada. The "Amerindian reality" has ceased to be an abstract reality for us. This reality, henceforth, bears the name of all those who shared with us their daily preoccupations and expectations. It was always as a theologian who was eager to know the Amerindian reality from the inside that people welcomed me. Many of them became faithful companions in our common search for the Amerindian Christ.

This search is divided into two main periods. The first period (1982-1983) is marked by a profound preoccupation with the development of a truly Amerindian church and an Amerindian-Christian dialogue. The second period (1989-1991) is marked by a kind of christological "return to the centre."

This passage from ecclesiology to christology was mainly the result of our personal initiation into the religious and spiritual world of the Cree Indians in northwestern Alberta. Between 1983 and 1986 we made the *vision quest* four times. This ascetic and contemplative ritual, which includes a total fast of four nights and three days, gradually allowed us to contemplate the Amerindian reality from the inside.[1]

The different testimonies which we will present in this chapter follow this same pattern. It is as a *participant observer* of native reality that we have selected them. We have not tried to imprison them within the categories of western christology. These testimonies speak for themselves. In reporting them, we have tried as best we can to respect their content and their context.

I. Evocations of the Christ Figure

1. Among the Innu in Northern Quebec

The Innu or Montagnais Indians of the Lower North Shore of the Saint Lawrence River are almost all Catholic. From the very beginning of the Christian mission in North America they welcomed the missionaries as spiritual persons who brought them new ways of praying. The Innu language has no equivalent for the term "church." The Innu perceive the Catholic religion not primarily as an institution but as a spiritual reality. They now live in well-organized Christian communities with their own pastoral workers.

Since the 1970s, lay workers have held yearly sessions with their missionaries (priests and sisters) to reflect on important aspects of the Catholic religion. In June 1982, the theme of their pastoral and theological meeting was baptism. While attending this meeting, we were able to observe that the Innu continue to stress the importance of a personal relationship with the Creator. For them, the most important aspect of baptism is receiving a new name. Baptism has always been understood in continuity with their own traditional name-giving ceremony. The Innu continued to perform this ritual, even after they became Catholic, especially when the priest was not immediately available for Christian baptism.[2] Baptism adds a sort of "personal connotation" to the relationship of the Innu with their Creator. But where does Christ fit into this relationship?

In 1991, we invited the same Innu to reflect on their spiritual journey on the basis of three questions: (I) Who is the "Amerindian Christ" for you? (II) Is there room for Christ in your worldview? (III) What aspects of the gospel do you find most challenging today? These questions were discussed by the Innu during their pastoral session in Havre Saint-Pierre in June 1991. What follows is a synthesis of their answers.[3]

Who is the "Indian Christ" for you?

• Jesus came to save everybody, including the Montagnais Nation. He comes to all persons who open their heart to him. We recognize Jesus in each human face and in everything we accomplish. His ideals of charity, justice and love fascinate us and help us to change our behaviour. He is present in our joy and in our difficulties. Even though his word (the gospel) contains things we really do not understand, we recognize ourselves in many gospel scenes. For example, in the story of the storm on the lake . . .

• A universal friend, Jesus abolishes all frontiers. It is not a matter of race but of heart! Jesus meets us on the level of our heart. For us, Christ is Indian. He speaks and thinks in Montagnais when we address him in our own language.

• We are the children of God. God is our Power. God has given us a beautiful gift, his only Son. Myself, I would find it difficult to give one of my own children!

• Christ regenerates us to a new life. Our ancestors knew him already, but they preferred to speak of God instead, a providential and severe God. Christ is the centre of our life. He is with us in all the situations of our life. Christ becomes Amerindian in *our* way of being and living. I always thought that it was me who was going towards God, but, in Jesus, it is definitely God who comes towards me.

Is there room for Christ in your Amerindian worldview?

• Creation is good. Creation is the place where we discover Jesus. Jesus is the same as God the Creator and the Spirit.

• The old Montagnais used to tell us that, even though they did not know the God of Jesus Christ, they nevertheless addressed their prayers to him without knowing it. Even before the coming of Jesus, God had already revealed himself to the Amerindians. Before Jesus, there was no cross and no baptism, but God was already taking care of us.

What aspects of the gospel do you find more challenging today?

• What really questions us is his commandment of universal love and his preference for the littlest ones.

• Jesus does not make distinctions between persons. Look at his love for the sinful woman. He always comes toward us, even though we are lost to ourselves.

2. Christ in the land of the Anishnabe

The Anishnabe (literally: The People) who comprise one of the main native groups in Canada are better known as the Ojibwa (variations: Ojibway, Ochipwe, Chippewa), a name the Europeans originally gave to a small group of people who lived north of Sault Ste. Marie (Ontario). This name now applies to the Algonquin-speaking peoples of Ontario and Manitoba who live in a wide corridor, north of the Great Lakes, from Ottawa to Winnipeg, and also in the United States in Wisconsin, Minnesota, Michigan. On various occasions since 1982 we visited several Anishnabe communities in Ontario and became acquainted with their political, economic, cultural and religious situation.

In January 1991, we organized three meetings on the "Amerindian Christ" with the help of Eva Solomon, an Anishnabe Sister of Saint Joseph. The first meeting took place near the city of Dryden in the house of Elsie and Henry Chief who, together with some of their friends, were extremely interested in our christological research. Two other meetings took place in the parish hall of the Indian reserve near Fort Francis and in the small meeting hall of the Catholic Amerindians of Thunder Bay.

Approximately fifty individuals shared their vision of the Amerindian Christ with us and commented on his importance for their culture. It was an occasion for them to discuss freely the rather difficult question of the relationship between

Christianity and their traditional spirituality with a typical Amerindian blend of humour and seriousness. It should be noted that in many native communities this question constitutes a source of division.

It is not easy to present a faithful synthesis of these meetings. Most of the time, the Amerindian Christ was referred to in the context of intense discussions on the political, economic and socio-cultural situation of the native communities. In the report that follows, there is no direct answer to the question: "Who do you say I am?" These meetings with the Anishnabe illustrate in a unique way that for the majority of native peoples in Canada this question cannot be isolated from their spiritual and cultural journey and from their present struggle for aboriginal rights.[4]

A cultural and spiritual journey

The contemporary fascination that the Christ figure has for many native people is part of a complex journey, involving cultural, social and ecclesial elements. From the cultural viewpoint, many Amerindians have been separated from their traditional way of life because of their earlier education in residential schools or their immigration to Canadian cities. Many are now looking for elders and spiritual guides to reconstruct their native identity. From the social viewpoint, many native communities are broken by violence. Since we started this research in 1982, almost all the native families we met have been devastated by suicides and violent deaths, often as the result of alcohol and drug abuse. Everywhere, one can sense a profound desire for personal and collective healing. From the ecclesial viewpoint, many persons are concerned with the internal divisions of Christianity, with the increasingly dysfunctional orientation of their Christian community, and with the absence of dialogue between representatives of Christianity and traditional native spirituality. Many native persons feel alone and without real support in their personal effort to integrate the two religions.

In the lives of most native persons we met among the Anishnabe and elsewhere in Canada, the cultural, social and ecclesial factors form an indivisible reality. Each meeting brought together those who had never stopped practising their traditional spirituality, the Midewewin, and others who had almost completely lost their spiritual heritage. But almost all were proud to reconnect with their traditions and to get rid of the inferiority complex they had suffered from for so long.

Only a short while ago they had felt ashamed at being Indian. They had considered themselves second-class citizens. Powerless and dispossessed, they thought of themselves as the bottom level of an immense pyramid whose summit was totally dominated by the white race. Today, many are involved in developing self-sustaining native communities. They want to put an end to their situation of dependency on the government and other agencies. They speak with pride of their local projects. They are developing programs of mutual assistance with a solid spiritual basis. The elders and the medicine persons are rediscovering their traditional roles in the community.

Many Amerindians also appreciate the changing attitudes of the Christian churches with respect to their traditional spirituality. "In the past," Louise said, "the church condemned our religious traditions, while we are now permitted to use some of our Indian symbols in the liturgy. But many of us do not understand this radical change. They continue to ask themselves if it is possible to be Christian *and* Indian at the same time. Thus, an Amerindian Christ, what does that really mean?"

Comings and goings between their traditional spirituality and the Christian religion characterize the lives of many Anishnabe. Joseph represents a typical case: "From my parents and grandparents I received a very traditional education during my childhood. Then, I was sent to a residential school and became Catholic. Gradually, I lost contact with my culture. Once married, I became an alcoholic. My family sank gradually into misery. We lost the best years of our lives. But then, also, we started developing a spiritual thirst. It was our children who took the initiative. We knocked at the door of many churches. We were even thinking of becoming Mormons. Then, finally, we discovered that there were still medicine men in our area. We set out to find them. They have helped us a lot. We understood very rapidly that our traditional religion was very demanding, but that it was also a source of real energy. We managed to reconstruct our family life. During this long journey, we never ceased to read the Bible. I find in the Bible many things that resemble our traditional religion."

During the meeting at Fort Frances, a native woman told a somewhat different story: "Since my early childhood, I received a very Catholic education. I knew almost nothing about the Midewiwin. Then, as an adult, I became very sick. I spent several years in a hospital, even in a psychiatric institution. But then, at the very bottom of my misery, I had a dream: *Return to the Midewiwin, your traditional religion.* I set out to find our spiritual leaders and abandoned the Catholic church. But I was not happy. I always had the impression of missing something. Later, I met with a sister who convinced me to return to the Catholic church. I ceased to practise the Midewiwin. But, again, I felt constantly that I was missing something. It is only after seven years and many other dreams that I finally managed to bring together our traditional religion and the Catholic religion in my life. I received the help of two very old women in my village who had never ceased to practise the Midewiwin. They told me often that the Midewiwin and the Catholic religion are two ways which lead to the one and same God."

The search for the Amerindian Christ

The Bible and Christ hold an important place in the lives of many persons we met in the land of the Anishnabe. The testimonies quoted above show that the Catholic religion continues to play a crucial role in the reconstruction of their cultural identity. For many of them the issue is not a matter of choosing between their traditional religion and Christianity, but seeing how both religions can contribute to the revitalization of the Amerindian nations. In this particular context, the title "Amerindian Christ" refers, almost spontaneously, to the four following elements.

Christ and cultures

The term "culture" often came up in the discussions. Although this term seems to have a large political, social, economic and artistic content for most people, it remains closely linked to their traditional spirituality or religion. Therefore, the discussion often centred on the church. Some spoke of the historical and contemporary attitudes of the church towards the Amerindian culture, others for or against the contemporary strategies of cultural adaptation in the field of liturgy, catechetics and Catholic education. Some welcomed these changes as the long-awaited and official recognition, by the church, of their culture. Others, on the contrary, saw this as a kind of theft which might jeopardize the meaning of the traditional rituals. In other words, they did not like the way in which the church now "baptizes" the rituals which she has condemned in the past.

It was exactly this question of the meaning of the traditional native rituals which allowed the group to make the passage from ecclesiology to christology. Where does Christ situate himself with respect to these efforts of adaptation and innovation? Could it be that Christ was, or is already present, in these traditional rituals?

Elisabeth, an older woman, shared her story: "Two years ago, I participated for the first time in a sweat lodge ceremony. I was terribly afraid. I entered into a world which was totally unknown to me. My Catholic education had isolated me from our traditional religion. But during this ceremony I had an extraordinary vision. I saw a field covered with flowers. Each flower represented a particular people. I understood that all these peoples, with their different cultures, were the work of the same Creator. The Amerindian peoples were also represented in that field of flowers. And, in the middle of it, there was Christ. I understood that God had created that field for him and through him. The Lord has always been present among us. He is the very source of all the gifts we have received from the Creator. Christ himself constantly leads us back to our own traditions. I dare to think that our present revitalization is his very work."

Jimmy, a young factory worker, continued: "This very morning, I read again the beginning of the gospel of John. This is one of the texts I like most! In the beginning was the word. He was in the beginning of the world. He was there also when the Amerindians came into this world. He was with us throughout our entire history. Today, I enjoy a more expanded experience of God and a larger vision of Christ. I am discovering the true meaning of the word *catholic*. This means *universal* and *not exclusive*. We are now discovering that this includes everybody. Today, I understand in a better way that the word *Christ* is one title among others given by the early Christians to Jesus. All the peoples of the world are now invited to give other titles to him."

A Sister (Anishnabe) then recalled the profound meaning of the conversation between Jesus and the Samaritan woman near the well of Jacob (John 4): "For Jesus himself, the Samaritans were a foreign people. The well represented their traditions. Jesus was not afraid to revitalize himself by appealing to the Samaritans and their traditions. Why are we (the church) so afraid today about the spiritual and cultural resources of other peoples? How can we appreciate what these other peoples can offer us?"

Jesus and the Jewish people

The historical figure of Jesus was the second theme that caught the attention of the group. Most participants had a clear perception of the concrete aspects of the mystery of incarnation. When becoming human, God freely submitted himself to the concrete conditions, history and culture of the Jewish people. Jesus is thus visualized as the one who comes to purify and to complete the very tradition by which he himself is welcomed into the world and which he needs to reveal the humanity of God.

Beatrice expressed this very well: "Jesus was a truly traditional Jew. He was not a Christian! But he brought his people a new awareness about their religion. I wonder what Jesus would have said about our native religion if he had been an Indian?"

Henry added: "Personally, I have no problems at all with the teachings of Jesus. There is something basically Indian in everything he did. He teaches love, sharing, solidarity. He works for the liberation of his people. He shows us that we will be judged according to what we do to the most little ones among us. He practises himself everything he asks the others to do. There is a perfect correspondence between his words and deeds. For him, religion is, in the first place, a matter of life. It is easy for us to integrate into our own culture everything that Jesus said and the teachings of the Bible. Myself, I have always been inspired by men like (Jean) Vanier, who, walking in the footsteps of Jesus, invite us to be whole and to live in harmony with the entire creation. Vanier says that the greatest crime is not to be oneself! Jesus shows us that we have the freedom and the divine grace to become totally ourselves."

Jesus as healer and as model of humanity

In the third place, we discovered that the Anishnabe are fascinated by a particular dimension of Jesus' ministry: his gifts and attitudes as healer. This should come as no surprise to anyone because of the important role of medicine persons in native communities and because the Amerindian religions themselves are often referred to as "medicine." It is nevertheless important to note that the participants did more than simply compare the medical "techniques" of Jesus and those of their traditional shamans or healers. The Anishnabe, on the contrary, seem most impressed by the basic attitudes of Jesus with respect to those who suffer and seek his help. "Jesus is our brother" was a constant refrain throughout the discussions. Someone observed that Jesus' basic purpose was always to make the person a better person from all points of view. He was a real therapist. He is seen by many as the medicine man *par excellence* and as the most effective of all medicines.

At the same time, remarks about bad medicine (sorcery, magic and so on) were scattered throughout the discussion. Bad medicine continues to be feared by many Amerindians across Canada. Native medicine is perceived as a mysterious and ambiguous world, and it is a source of both admiration and fear. Jesus, the participants acknowledged, enters into this complex world as a unique figure in whom we can trust totally. He helps us to discern the good and the bad.

Tony, a medicine man, declared without any hesitation: "Jesus and the good Amerindian medicine men basically work in the same way. They adopt the same attitude vis-à-vis evil. Evil increases to the extent that we give it importance. Bad medicine is often a psychological affair. Jesus shows us what to do when we confront evil. He shows us that we should leave that to God. We can always trust him. He is never a loser. Above all, we should avoid blaming God for the evil things in our world. The most beautiful thing in life is to know God. Jesus, our brother, shows us that God is good."

Christ as the mysterious centre of the religions

In the fourth place, we moved from the historical Jesus to the Christ figure. The discussion again focused on the internal division of the Christian churches which established themselves in the land of the Anishnabe. These churches were warmly welcomed by most native peoples who have demonstrated a great sense of religious tolerance throughout history. But many Amerindians are now leaving the churches because of the divisions these institutions have created in their families and tribes.

Robert, a respected religious leader, told us: "Over the last couple of years, my family has knocked at the door of many churches. Finally, we decided to return to our traditional religion. We were looking for peace, harmony and humour! Christian churches are too serious. They never cease to fight amongst themselves. We found in our traditional religion time to express our faith in God and to laugh." Matthew, an elder, added: "The Christian churches must knock down their walls of Jericho. They would then be more able to help us find the inner peace and the cosmic harmony we need so much for our development as persons and as peoples."

The same man helped the group to make the transition from ecclesiology to christology. He invited people to be careful not to become the victims of what he called the different "belief systems." He described the ultimate encounter of all these systems as an historical and cosmic event—a holistic phenomenon: "I visualize this event very often. For me, the encounter between all the religions is not just a ritual affair. It is a search for what is fundamental in each religious experience." Another person took up this thought: "That is absolutely true. When Jesus tells us that there are many rooms in the house of his Father, our Amerindian traditions are included in that statement. Each room represents a different culture. I can therefore encounter the God of Jesus in my own culture as we experience it today."

Someone else reminded the group that the Bible teaches that the Spirit of God is given to all peoples, universally. Therefore, the meeting of the religions is necessary and unavoidable: "During the visit of Pope John Paul II to Fort Simpson (September 20, 1987), an immense rainbow suddenly appeared in the sky. The symbol of the universal circle of life." Finally, another person rounded out these diverse explorations of the Amerindian Christ figure: "There is truly a place for Christ in our (traditional) spirituality, because this spirituality is holistic. Christ is the Son of God. We, also, are children of God! Christ is present everywhere. He is the centre of all religions."

3. Christ among the urban Indians

One of the basic characteristics of the Amerindian reality in Canada, as we have already indicated in the first part of this essay, is the massive migration of Amerindians to the cities and urban centres. During the sixties, the Canadian government encouraged this movement, thinking that it would contribute to the integration of the Amerindians into the larger Canadian society. Things turned out quite differently. In many Canadian cities, the Indians now live in ghettos with substandard living conditions. Dispossessed of their ancestral lands, cut off from their traditional resources, and suddenly confronted with the enormous challenges of urban life, they struggle more than ever for the survival of their culture and spiritual heritage. In some Canadian cities the churches have created native parishes or centres which, together with the Friendship Centres (a native organization), assist the Amerindians in their struggles. But the disproportion between what these centres can achieve and the needs of the urban Indians is staggering. The social marginalization of the urban Indians is also mirrored in the churches which can offer only a limited service.[5] We must take this dramatic situation into consideration when listening to the following testimonies collected in the cities of Winnipeg, Toronto and Saskatoon.

Christ as community builder

Leo works as a native consultant in the "Family Centre" of Winnipeg, created by the United Church of Canada. He visualizes Christ, above all, as a community builder. One of the centre's objectives is the integration of the Bible, the teachings of Jesus and the traditional wisdom of the elders to help native people achieve an inner liberation. What does the "Indian Christ" mean in such a context? During a short meeting on March 12, 1991, Leo explained this title as follows:

The Indian Christ reveals himself, in the first place, in the brokenness and in the suffering of all the native people who are lost between two worlds: their traditional environment from which they were separated by the government and the churches, and western culture. The inner healing of these thousands of native persons must be the first objective of the churches.

The Indian Christ reveals himself also in the desire of those who want to establish a significant relationship between the teachings of Jesus and their culture.

The Indian Christ incarnates himself in the structural efforts to harmonize the institutional interests of the churches and the spiritual teachings of the elders.

Finally, on the level of personal prayer, it is always God or the Great Spirit who comes first in the life of many native people. The Great Spirit revealed himself to them well before the arrival of the Christian missionaries. For many native persons, Jesus has remained a stranger . . .

"For me, personally," Leo adds, "Christ is one of the greatest teachers. He is a real community builder and a remarkable healer. We can always consider him as an important resource for our personal development and the development of our communities. One of the greatest challenges for us is the encounter between our native traditions and Christianity. For many native people this challenge is a life-long struggle. Many go through a period of anger and reject Christianity. But they know that healing must come from within. When they return eventually to the churches, it is not, in the first place, for the services offered by these churches, but because of the healing they find in the gospel. In our centre we frequently organize Bible study sessions. These sessions, just like the teachings of the elders, play an important role in the healing of persons."

The Amerindian Christ: an abused person

We have known Mary for many years. Since the end of the 1970s, she had been a member of the team that organized the yearly "Summer Institutes for Christian Amerindian Leadership." For a while she was a member of the pastoral team of the Kateri Parish in Winnipeg. When we met her on March 13, 1991, she was working in the "North End Community Ministry" of the United Church of Canada. This dynamic centre answers the most basic needs of hundreds of urban Amerindians: food, clothing, children's aid and adult counselling. Mary works with children and adults who want to learn how to survive in their new urban environment. How and when can they appeal to the services of the government and the city? What role do the churches play in their life? Mary meets with many adults whose youth has been strongly influenced by the residential school system of the Canadian government and the Christian churches. She often hears about sexual, physical and cultural abuse. She hears about broken homes and families. Her daily ministry is a ministry of healing and reconciliation. We asked her the question: "Who is Christ for you?"

"For me, Christ is not a Spirit. He is a very concrete person. Jesus, himself, is an abused person. He is in the prisons. He is in the homes of the broken families. He travels with those who have no shelter or roof over their head. He is with all the victims of violence. Thus, my task is enormous: We must resurrect Christ in the life of our people. Because the history of Christ's suffering goes on, in a very real way, in the human suffering which I see every day.

"I like to work with children. One day, I asked them to draw a picture of God. One child came up with a picture of a baby in his mother's womb, in the middle of a teepee bathed in the light of a large and radiant sun. Another child drew the last supper of Jesus and his disciples. The supper was not held in a house but in a forest. There were many trees. A father was pouring water at the base of a tree. Another child drew a cross surrounded by the words: hope, love, God."

Our encounter with Mary was suddenly interrupted by the arrival of a young native woman. Mary, immediately asked her the question: "Who is Jesus for *you*?" The answer of the woman: "I see him as an angel or as a guardian spirit. He is very real, but invisible. Sometimes he is close, sometimes very far away."

Jesus would have been a good Indian

In Winnipeg we also met with a medicine man and spiritual guide whose life has been marked by pain and suffering. Separated from his family at an early age, he was first placed in a residential school and then adopted by a white, Catholic family. He quickly discovered that racism was real in Canada, and that the Christian churches had transformed the native people into "passive and submissive beings" so that they could easily be dominated by the political and economic powers. He remained Catholic for many years before turning to his traditional native religion.

One day, he understood (it happened during Mass) that God would continue to love him even though he abandoned the Catholic church. Catholicism had become for him the synonym of colonialism, materialism and fascism. He saw the church as a hierarchical institution, invented by humans, which had done lots of harm to the Amerindians. Jesus would not recognize himself in this church if he were to come back on earth!

We asked him the question: "But who is Jesus then for you?" His answer: "I believe that he is the Son of God. But I do not know who has invented the Trinity. I am convinced that Jesus would have been a good Indian! He prayed and fasted. Love was his central message. I also believe in the importance of interreligious dialogue. But it is difficult for the Christian churches to participate in that dialogue because of their dogmatic system and their limited understanding of God (white male). For the Amerindians, God is something different. He is the Great Mystery. There are many ways leading to him."

An official recognition of our religion

The (Amerindian) Kateri Parish in Winnipeg is a very dynamic and welcoming place where every night one can meet teams of native persons involved in the liturgy, catechetics, Bible study, and other activities. Many persons also come for counselling or, simply, to discuss the problems of daily life.

But despite all these activities, the parish is seen by many, above all, as a spiritual milieu where one can find inner peace.

As in many other places, the question of the relationship between Christianity and Amerindian spirituality is often on the agenda. In fact, the Pope's statement that Christ is Indian has been understood by many parish members as an official recognition of the Amerindian religion. One person said: "The church has finally understood that Christ is for all peoples, and that racism must come to an end. God is present in our lives. We are the temples of God. Catholicism must stop thinking that it is the only true religion. Religion, in the first place, is a matter of freedom and a spiritual journey." A native woman, educated in the traditional Catholic way, confided to us that, one day, she had asked a medicine man to find a name for her little girl so that the child could meet with the good spirits and ask them for help.

Another person deplored the opposition of Catholic-educated elders to the introduction of native symbols into the Catholic liturgy. "One year, on Easter morning," she says, "I assisted at a morning sunrise ceremony, presided by an Anglican priest. Suddenly, the death and resurrection of Jesus became very real for me. Since then, I have been reading the gospels. I like to visualize myself in the gospel scenes, for example, in the story of the boat on the stormy lake. I like to be close to Jesus when he suffers in the garden before his arrest. Jesus really became a brother to me."

Jesus: a very concrete being

A native woman remarked: "In the past, I was ashamed to tell the others that I was Catholic. To be Catholic meant to be racist and filled with prejudices. I was raised in a white milieu where the other children teased me because of the color of my skin. I was accepted by them only because I was good in sport! I suffered and was physically abused, because I was Indian.

"Despite my Catholic education, Jesus had practically no meaning for me. I considered the gospels as stories among others. After several years, I got involved in my parish. During Holy Week, when reading the story of the passion, I suddenly started crying. I suddenly understood that Jesus had suffered and given his life also for me. Since then, I do not like Holy Week. I always feel depressed and I anxiously wait for Easter Morning. Then, I get up early to contemplate the rising sun and to feel the new life. At Christmas, I feel the same way. I finally understood that we celebrate the birth of a real child."

We asked her the question: "Do you really believe that Christ is Indian?" Her answer: "I do not see Jesus as Indian. I rather see him as a human being who has suffered a lot for the sins of the world. This is the reason why I decided to get involved in the church. In the past, I saw the church as an institution to which I was obliged to belong. Today, I see it as a free and personal option. I am the church, the temple of God. It is in this sense that I renewed my baptismal vows as an adult. I feel that I am now liberated from my obligation to belong to the church.

"One day, I was asked to draw a picture of God. I drew a picture filled with animals, flowers and trees—all the elements of nature. For me, this is where we find God in the first place. I see him present in all living beings, because he is their creator. God is always close. I had to live forty years before I understood that, and before I accepted myself as an Indian woman."

4. The Wet'suw'eten Indians of British Columbia

The Wet'suw'eten are proud of their culture and their unique relationship to the land. Despite the fact that they have adopted Catholicism or other forms of Christian belief, they have never abandoned their ancestral beliefs and traditional rituals. They are the perfect illustration of the religious dualism described in the first part of this book. This religious dualism was a crucial argument when they defended their title to the land in the Supreme Court of British Columbia. For them, the dreams of the elders and the stories of their oral traditions are as important as the geographical maps of the white people! Here are some Wet'suw'eten answers to the question: "Who is the Amerindian Christ for you?"

• To me it means that there is only one God. And no matter who we are or what colour our skin is or what denomination we belong to as long as Christ is in me. Christ is Indian. There is room for Christ in our native spirituality. No matter what form you worship. As long as you believe with all your heart.

• It means that Christ is with us and with native people and with all nationalities all the time.

• There is room for Christ in my native spirituality because we are God's children.

• I think this means that it shouldn't matter what nation Christ is in, but who he really is as a person! I think it also means that we don't know what nation he is from and that as I said before it shouldn't matter. There is room for Christ in our native spirituality because I think that he belongs in all of our lives and hearts.

• Christ is Indian means to me that Christ could be every kind of human being he wants to be or just to be sure he can do anything, like he can be magic. He can cure people just by touching them.

• Bernie considers *Christ in America* to be a good book describing various appearances of Christ from Polynesia to the Americas. She does not agree that Christ is Indian. As her elder sister once put it: "We don't pray to another Indian!" Louise and Bernie say Christ is Indian because he thinks like an Indian. He does not judge. He takes people as they are and this is what traditional native people do.[6]

II. The Incarnation
of Christ Among the Cree Indians of Alberta:
An interview with Father Paul Hernou

Born in Bruges (Belgium) in 1940, Paul Hernou has been a missionary among the Cree of the Archdiocese of Grouard-McLennan in northwestern Alberta since 1966. He speaks the Cree language almost perfectly and has been initiated into the traditional religion of the Cree people. He counts several medicine men, elders and spiritual guides among his best friends. He became a sacred pipe holder (see Chapter V). He works as a priest in several very isolated native communities, spread over a territory that is as large as Belgium. We have visited Paul Hernou several times since 1982. We interviewed him on the topic of the Amerindian Christ in June 1991, in the presence of University of Calgary anthropologist Jean-Guy Goulet and his son Alexis. We reproduce here the main sequences of this interview.

AP. During his 1984 visit in Canada, Pope John Paul II declared that, in the members of his body, Christ himself is Indian. Over the last couple of months I have met with native persons across Canada to ask them what this statement means to them. Some said: "An Indian Christ! No way. Christ is universal." Others, on the contrary, welcome the Pope's statement as the confirmation of their culture, and also as an invitation for dialogue between their traditional spirituality and Christianity. In view of your missionary experience among the Cree, what importance do you give to this papal statement?

PH. It is, of course, a very beautiful declaration. But one may ask whether the Pope really knew about what he was saying! I had the advantage of starting my missionary experience with Father Roger Vandersteene who had really wanted to become an Indian with the Indians, somewhat like Father Damian, whom he admired very much, had become a leper with the lepers. Vandersteene learned their language and adopted their lifestyle and customs. Obviously, it is impossible for a white person to become Indian. We missionaries can only attempt to integrate ourselves in the Indian environment. In the same way, we also attempt to integrate Christ into that milieu, especially into the culture and the religion of the people.

While performing my ordinary duties as a priest (for example, in the field of the sacraments), I have also had the opportunity to participate in the traditional religious ceremonies of the Cree and I have observed that the Cree themselves have started to integrate Christ into these rituals. For example, in the ritual of the sacred pipe, Christ is often addressed as "our elder brother." Even the Virgin Mary, "our mother," and Saint Ann, "our grandmother," find a place in these rituals. Frank Cardinal, one of the elders who taught me a lot, often prays in this manner.

In 1984, the Dogrib Indians of the North West Territories prepared for the papal visit to Fort Simpson with an impressive sacrifice ceremony to the ancestors. The statues of the Virgin Mary and the Sacred Heart occupied a central place in this ritual. I do not understand the Dene language, but I am sure that the Dene also prayed to Christ during this ceremony. Last year I participated in a dance for the ancestors at Fox Lake in the Little Red River area (Cree Indians). On the main drum I saw a picture of the Virgin Mary. The songs started and ended with the sign of the cross.

Personally, I feel at ease with this effort to integrate Christ into native rituals. Did Jesus himself not adopt the most important ritual of his own religious tradition, the paschal meal, and transform it into the eucharist? The Cree Indians of this area have their own religious traditions, a set of rituals which are nothing but celebrations of life according to the seasons. Why could Christ not also incarnate himself in these rituals?

AP. Let us take, for example, the Dance of the Ancestors. Is this ritual not as important to the Cree as the celebrations of Holy Week to the Christians?

PH. One could easily compare the ritual of the dance of the ancestors with the Jewish paschal meal. We find here the same elements. The story of the tribe is told. There is a purification ceremony before entering into the presence of the Creator. Then follows a very special meal with a prayer of thanksgiving and other prayers. The ancestors, as well as all the good deeds of the Creator for his people, are remembered.

AP. A few years ago, René Jaouen, a missionary among the Giziga in northern Cameroon and professor at Saint Paul University in Ottawa, asked the question whether the history of the non-Christian peoples could be considered as their Old Testament ("L'histoire des peuples non-chrétiens peut-elle servir d'ancien testament?" Kerygma 20[1986], pp. 229-238). He writes that we must manage to navigate between two reefs: on the one hand, we cannot replace the Old Testament with the (Christian) pre-history of the other non-Christian peoples, because the situation of the Jewish people is absolutely unique with respect to Christianity and to the Christian understanding of salvation. On the other hand, we cannot reject the pre-history of the other peoples, because the Old Testament itself integrates the history of other peoples and their blessings into the holy history of Israel. Your comparison between the Jewish paschal meal and the Cree ritual of the ancestors suggests that you share the opinion of Jaouen and that, therefore, you believe that we are invited to discover how Christ is already at work in the pre-history of the Amerindians.

PH. That's correct. But I do not really like the term "inculturation." I prefer the term "incarnation." Christ incarnates himself in the history and the religious ceremonies of the Cree. This is the beginning of a new church. The Cree themselves are becoming a new "missionary" church. They are becoming the agents of

Purification Ceremony
Shrine of the Canadian Martyrs, Midland, September 15, 1984
Photo: Photo Features Ltd

their own evangelization, without denying their own history, their culture and religious traditions. This new missionary church is developing very rapidly. The young Cree, for example, are rediscovering the drum and the traditional songs.

AP. Over the last few years, I have met several missionaries who see this return to the ancestral traditions as a movement that competes with their own missionary work. One actually spoke of the "return to paganism." What do you think of that?

PH. First of all, I would avoid the term "return" to these traditions. In the area where I work, these traditions have always been there, despite the negative attitudes and the condemnations of the church in the past. These religious traditions never ceased to exist, despite the church. Therefore, it is impossible for the church to control this present movement. The church will never be able to stop the incarnation of Christ in the cultural and religious history of the Cree. When leaving this earth, Jesus gave us his Spirit. This Spirit of Christ is also at work among the Cree. Instead of opposing this religious revival of the Cree, the church would be better off getting involved in a true dialogue with the native religions, just like she tries to do with Buddhism and Hinduism.

AP. Have you perceived other signs of this incarnation of Christ among the Cree in the last few years?

PH. During the yearly pilgrimage of the Amerindians to Lake Saint Anne, near Edmonton, I saw how the Cree Indians were observing the Dene Indians when they were performing their rituals. The Dene always end their traditional songs with the sign of the cross. This is really their own way of expressing their faith in the presence of Christ, dead and risen, in their rituals. This is not a form of superficial syncretism, but the expression of a deep faith. Last year, I was able to observe a similar faith among the young Cree in John D'or Prairie and Trout Lake during their sacred pipe ceremony. The elders find it absolutely normal, for example, to introduce the saints of the Catholic church into their traditional prayers to the ancestors.

AP. Do you believe that the elders are still able to transmit their faith in Jesus Christ (Christ as incarnated in their traditions) to the younger generations? Almost everywhere in Canada, young native men and women, like other young Amerindians, seem to be turning their backs on the church.

PH. This often happens in communities where fundamentalist Christians have installed themselves. The fundamentalists radically reject native people's religious traditions and often create an atmosphere of confusion about the relationship between Christianity and the native religions. In such a context, it is difficult to speak of the incarnation of Christ among the Indians. In other communities, the situation is different. The young native people certainly do not remember everything they learned when attending Catholic religion class or catechetics, but they do possess a solid knowledge of the basic elements of Christianity. It is now their turn to start integrating these elements into their traditional ceremonies.

AP. To my knowledge, there is not one Christian church in Canada which has officially recognized the authenticity and the validity of the Amerindian religions. Such a recognition appears to me to be indispensable in view of the dialogue you are proposing. The major Christian churches seem to content themselves with introducing some native elements into their liturgies. Is the Amerindian-Christian dialogue really possible?

PH. The basic problem is the lack of knowledge of the native languages among many missionaries today. Without the knowledge of the native languages it is difficult to appreciate the richness and the beauty of the Indian rituals, the meaning of the prayers and the songs. One sees only the exterior aspects. It is obvious that dialogue must start on the local level. We cannot content ourselves with the Pope's statement that Christ is Indian. Our local bishop, for example, must simply start participating in the Cree rituals: the dance of the ancestors, the sacred pipe ceremony, the sweat lodge ritual, the healing rituals. Even though the bishop does not speak the native language, he could gradually familiarize himself with the religious life of the people. This is the first step toward religious dialogue. This is much more important than an official declaration. The fact, for example, that Pope John Paul II participated in 1984 in a native purification ritual with sweet grass was more significant for many Amerindians than his statement about the Indian Christ! This gesture was more important than his words. The fact that the pope was not the presider of this ritual but a simple participant was even more significant.

AP. Earlier in our conversation, you used the word syncretism. The church really seems to fear this phenomenon. What do you think about that?

PH. I think that on the level of the institutional church the word syncretism often serves as an alibi for not engaging ourselves in a renewal initiated by the people. The church is afraid to lose control over the religious destiny of the peoples she has welcomed into her ranks. She is observing the birth of a church in Christian communities which does not correspond to what she has foreseen and planned. But the history of the church shows that any attempt to control this movement results in dramatic failures. Pope John XXIII understood that. He opened the windows of the church. He knew that it was impossible to control the Spirit at work among the people of God.

AP. Father Roger Vandersteene has been an important influence on you. He was surely a remarkable missionary. In those days, almost all the missionaries learned the native languages. What distinguished Vandersteene from the others?

PH. The answer to your question was given to me by a Dene elder of Chateh. He told me that many missionaries learned the native languages to better impose their ideas on the Indians. Few of them learned the native languages to better under-stand the people or to understand how they prayed to God and expressed their faith in him.

AP. Do the Cree Indians of this area address themselves directly to Christ when they pray?

PH. They call Jesus "our elder brother," but in their traditional prayer and in the sacred pipe ceremony they address themselves mostly to the Creator or to the Great Spirit. Nevertheless, it was an elder, Frank Cardinal, who taught me to pray to "our elder brother," Jesus, when I was smoking the sacred pipe.

AP. How do you understand your present mission with respect to the Amerindian cultures?

PH. A few years ago, I was still convinced that it was important to introduce native elements into the Christian liturgy, as is done elsewhere in Canada. But I did not pursue this strategy of adaptation which is understood by some as an important step towards the creation of a native church. Today, I am more interested in finding out how Christ incarnates himself in the Amerindian cultures, and in how the people express this incarnation. It is exactly in this way that I understand the expression "Amerindian Christ." The Amerindian Christ is the total Christ who wants to be present in all aspects of native life, in politics as well as in Indian prayer. During the visit of Pope John Paul II to Fort Simpson in 1987, a represent-ative of the Canadian television (CBC) asked me whether this visit was a political or religious event. I answered him that for the Indians this event was inseparably religious, political, social and cultural. The Amerindians do not use these separate categories to describe an important event. This may help us to understand the true implications of the statement "Christ is Indian."

This Indian Christ is not just a spiritual being whom we address when we pray and who is thereafter put aside. He is the total Christ who, as I said earlier, is present in all aspects of native life. This being said, I nevertheless believe that it is urgent and important for the Christian churches to recognize officially the new expressions of native rituals which contain an explicit reference to Christ. Would it not be possible to recognize these prayers as authentic Catholic prayers?

AP. I have met Christian Amerindians and missionaries who would like to see an Amerindian rite in the Canadian church.

PH. This is not very realistic. There are so many differences between the native peoples in Canada from a religious and cultural point of view. For example, the symbol of water does not represent the same thing for the Amerindians of British Columbia and for the Cree in Alberta. Instead of speaking of a unique native rite, it is more important to discover how the different native peoples express their faith in God and in Christ from within their particular context. We must also consider the fact that this cultural diversity is not about to disappear. The different native cultures continue to be transmitted from generation to generation.

AP. What are the mechanisms of this transmission?

PH. This is more than simply a sociological or psychological affair. This is a spiritual process. Here, in this area, the transmission and the transformation of the Amerindian rituals is often the result of dreams by elders and other spiritual persons who, like some figures in the Bible, receive revelations about what they should do.

In each Amerindian nation, as in the Jewish people, there is always the phenomenon of "the little remnant." Its mission is to watch over the transmission and the development of the cultural and religious traditions. Father Vandersteene had already observed that phenomenon many years ago. That's why he found it so important to know the Cree language in order to communicate with the representatives of this "little remnant": the elders, the prophets, and the medicine men. Each culture has its high and low moments. A few years ago, most people thought that the native languages and cultures would disappear. Today, I observe that among the Cree this "little remnant" is becoming a real movement that attracts an increasing number of people.

Here, in this area, this movement does not imply a rejection of Christianity. During a meeting of elders from Guatemala, Mexico, the United States and Canada, which took place in Assumption (Alberta) in 1979, in which I was invited to participate, there were strong reactions against Christianity. Certain elders from the United States objected against my presence in their circle when they discovered that I was a Catholic priest. One of our own elders then stood up and said: Christ did not come only for the white race, but for all the peoples, including the Amerindians. We will continue to welcome him. The elder who spoke was Peter Otcheese, one of the most respected elders in Alberta, who received a vision during this meeting concerning the eventual encounter of Indian prayer, Catholic prayer and the prayer of the white people. (See Paul Hernou: "Même les oiseaux apportent des messages. Compte rendu d'une rencontre d'anciens tenue à l'Assomption du 12 au 15 août 1979," *Kerygma* 16[1982], pp. 110-122.)

AP. Yet, should we not recognize that there is a latent conflict between the Amerindians who maintain that Christ is universal and those who say that they do not need him and that their traditional religion suffices?

PH. That's true. But the church and the dominant Canadian society must understand that mutual respect and tolerance remain the most important values in the native communities. During the meeting in Assumption in 1979, Peter Otcheese was totally free to share his vision with the other elders. There were lots of tensions during this meeting, but also lots of humour. This is also typical of native communities.

AP. This would mean that elders like Peter Otcheese equally respect those who say no and those who say yes to Christ.

PH. These elders understood, a long time ago, that religion is something we cannot impose on other persons. They know that we can only speak out of our own experience. We can speak of Christ when we have experienced Christ in our life. Others may not share this experience, but they will respect it.

JGG. I would like to recapitulate a certain number of things that you have mentioned in this conversation and which appeal to me as an anthropologist. The fact, for example, that the symbol of water is different for the Amerindians of British Columbia and for the Cree in Alberta means that we must be ready to listen to the local cultural languages of the native peoples. I also saw Christian symbols on the drums of the Dene of northwestern Alberta among whom I lived. There is no doubt in my mind that Alexis Seniantha, one of their great prophets, is a truly Christian prophet who has a profound personal experience of Christ. The figures of Christ and Mary on the drums demonstrate that Christ is truly present among the Cree and the Dene. We find here signs indicating that Christ is also present in a world which is very different from the world of the majority of the Christian missionaries and bishops who work among the Indians. I believe that it is legitimate to interpret the dreams of certain elders as a language or word of God, rather than to describe them as purely psychological phenomena. These dreams are gifts of God. These elders are walking on a different road than the institutional church. In our traditional Catholic education we were told to forget our dreams. To take our dreams seriously was superstition and, therefore, sinful! All the experiences you spoke about show that Christ continues to incarnate himself in a world which is very different from the world in which the institutional church finds itself and in which the great majority of priests and missionaries function. Therefore, we must ask ourselves whether these missionaries are able to share their experience of Christ with the Amerindians, and *vice versa*. The central problem is the problem of communication between different cultures.

PH. I believe that this communication is possible on the level of the language of the heart. This is the language we gradually learn to speak when we participate in the native religious ceremonies. Rational language does not work here.

JGG. We observe this phenomenon in other fields too. The Dene, for example, even those who are Christian, believe in reincarnation. This reflects a very different understanding of life in general and of what happens after death. It implies a different ethic. Consequently, to be Christian in this cultural environment is not the same thing that being Christian is for us.

PH. One must therefore insist again on respect for the other. We judge others too rapidly without knowing them. Our judgments often reflect a lack of knowledge and experience. It is possible to observe others and to compare their world with ours, without judging them. My personal experience of Christ is different from the experience of the Dene prophet. I belong to a different cultural world. But, maybe one day, I will also be able to enjoy a truly Amerindian experience of Christ, if I continue to listen to the Indian world and to respect the spiritual journey of the Indian peoples.

AP. It seems to me that we can conclude this conversation by recognizing that, even at the end of the twentieth century, Christianity is still confronting a great variety of worldviews which continue to develop despite the impact of western civilization. We have not yet seen most of the implications of the incarnation of Christ in these different worldviews. Must the church convert them? Is she ready to welcome them as milieux in which Christ is authentically incarnated? Would this not be the greatest missionary challenge of all time?

III. Contemplations of the Christ Figure

1. Jesus: the most powerful medicine

In February 1991, we met with Dominic Eshkakogan, medicine man and ordained Catholic deacon at the Anishnabe Spiritual Centre in Espanola (Ontario). During the visit of Pope John Paul II at the sanctuary of the Canadian Martyrs in Midland (September 15, 1984), Dominic participated as medicine man in the purification ceremony just before the eucharistic celebration where he assisted the Pope as Deacon. He shared his vision of Christ with us:

"We have always understood the Pope's declaration as a confirmation of our native spirituality. Native people have never developed an 'organized' or 'structured' religion with, for example, a priesthood and religious orders. But we have developed, over the centuries, *a spiritual way of life*. Above all, our religion is a way of life centred on the mystery of the Creator. Creation, for us, is not understood as the activity of God at the beginning of the world, but as the permanent manifestation of God's creative power. Even though many things can be explained scientifically, it is the Creator who holds everything together. He is the source of all new life.

"The cycles of nature show us that creation is an ongoing regeneration. This is why our spirituality is, basically, a spirituality of thanksgiving. We also ask God to give us an open spirit so that we may see what we need to live in harmony with him and with all the other living beings. This is the prayer that I address to God when I leave my house to collect the medicine herbs. This prayer is also part of our hunting rituals. Traditionally, the native hunters left the heart of the animals they had killed in the forest. The heart contains the spirit of the animal. We leave the spirit of the animal in the forest, because this spirit belongs to God. All our traditional rituals manifest a great respect for life that is given to us by the Creator.

"This explains why we address our prayer mostly to the Creator. It is only recently that we address our prayer also to Jesus. The Anishnabe call Jesus 'Jesus-Nosse' (Jesus-Father). Our prayer is always a coming and going between 'the One who has the Son' (the Father) and 'the One who is the Son' (Jesus). All our blessings are done in the name of the Father, the Son, and the one we call the 'Good Spirit.' Jesus has an important place in our prayers. He belongs to the world of the Creator, of the Grandfathers or the Guardian Spirits (in the plural)! But we are not polytheists. 'Many Spirits' does not mean 'many Gods.' There is only one God. But this one God is at the same time unique and the totality of the spirits of all living beings. Because he is the one who creates everything, constantly.

"However, I must recognize that it is not easy to integrate the physical or historical Jesus into the traditions of our people. Jesus did not come among us physically. He came among us by his word. The way in which this word was presented to us in the past creates obstacles for the integration of Christianity and the traditional teachings of the Anishnabe. It was said in the past that all our traditions were bad. The church is now ready to recognize that. But the heart of our people is filled with confusion. We, Anishnabe, think with our heart. The integration of the traditional Anishnabe teachings is a long and arduous road.

"We have never ceased to practise our traditional rituals. The old missionaries knew that very well. For example, my grandmother was both a medicine woman and a very devout Catholic. She knew very well the medicine power of the plants. She practised a special ritual for the purification of the women after childbirth. It is with her help that I became a medicine man. She initiated me into our traditional medicine.

"Jesus has a very specific place in my healing ceremonies and prayers. He said: 'When two or three are gathered in my name, I will be among them.' Also: 'Everything you will ask in my name to the Father will be given to you.' It is in this way, according to me, that Jesus enters into our Anishnabe traditions. He participates in our traditional medical practices. He, himself, is the most powerful medicine. He strengthens our prayers and practices. I always ask him to enter into the healing process of persons.

"Healing is not just a physical, but also a psychological and spiritual process. Often, we have to heal the memory of the persons who come to us with their physical problem. Long before the white people, the Anishnabe have understood that healing comes from Spirit. Many of our physical troubles are caused by anxiety, stress and anger. Healing is, therefore, a spiritual process—a matter of peace and harmony.

"I believe that there is no fundamental opposition between Christianity and our Anishnabe tradition. There is not, on the one hand, an Indian God, and, on the other hand, a God of the white people. Of course, I know that many young Amerindians now reject Christianity as a religion imported from the outside. Myself, I am more and more discovering the profound correspondence between the teachings of Jesus and our own traditional teachings.

"Our traditional spirituality is based on seven simple and basic teachings : wisdom, love, respect, courage, honesty, humility and truth—the seven gifts of the Grandfathers. These gifts constitute an indivisible reality. We cannot reject a single one of these gifts. For example, we cannot replace love by hatred without jeopardizing all the other gifts and the search for wholeness and vital harmony. This is the great challenge of our traditional spirituality of which we find an echo in the gospel of Jesus."

2. Jesus: the son of Yamanhdeya

In the first part of this book we presented a brief description of the worldview of the Dene Tha in northwestern Alberta based on the research of anthropologist Jean-Guy Goulet. The religious situation of the Dene Tha can be compared to that of the Cree of Alberta Paul Hernou described. The Dene Tha have also incorporated Christian symbols into their traditional rituals.

We wanted to get a more exact picture of how Jesus is seen by the Dene Tha, in particular by their prophets and shamans. We received an unexpected answer to our question during a short visit to the Indian reservation of Assumption in June 1991, when Jean-Guy Goulet and I met with Jean-Marie Talley, a Dene prophet. The conversation was in the Dene language and concerned the naming of persons. Jean-Marie Talley met with us in the rectory of the local Catholic parish on Friday, June 27, early in the afternoon. Father Camille Piché, the local priest, first discussed the sixtieth wedding anniversary celebration of Mary and Willie Denechoan with Jean-Marie, and mentioned that according to church records the name of Willie's father was Sechuen. Jean-Marie replied that, before the arrival of the priests *(deneghadihi)*, all Dene Tha had Dene names only, and that, following the arrival of the missionaries, Dene Tha had two names, one according to the Dene Tha way *(Dene Tha k'ihhin)*, and, another, according to the way of the priest *(deneghadihi k'ihhin)*. Jean-Marie went on to offer the Dene Tha names of Willie, and of Alexis Seniantha, another important prophet whom we had visited the day before in the hospital of Peace River. Jean-Guy Goulet then asked if, today, young Dene Tha still have two names, one according to the Dene Tha, another according to the priest. Jean-Marie replied that this is not the case, that young Dene Tha only have one name, the one according to the priest. He then asked Jean-Marie if the same applied to the name of God, mentioning to him that *Ndahota* is also known to the Dene Tha as *Yamanhdeya*. Jean-Marie answered that this was correct.

Jean-Guy Goulet went on to ask him if *Yamanhdeya* is the name according to the Dene Tha, and *Ndahota* the name according to the priest. He replied that both names were according to the Dene Tha, and that *Yamanhdeya* referred to *Ndahota* when he walked around the earth before the Dene Tha existed, and that *Ndahota* was the name used to refer to *Yamanhdeya* since he had gone from this land to the other land above the stars.

Jean-Guy Goulet then asked the prophet if Jesus, who is referred to as *Ndahota chuen* (the Son of God), is also the son of *Yamanhdeya*. Jean-Marie immediately replied yes. Therefore the prophet also considers Jesus as the son of the heroic figure who, according to the Dene Tha oral tradition, "walked around the edge of the world" (which is the literal meaning of the terms *yamanhdeya* or *yamonhdeyi*), the one that tricked all the animals that lived on this land, who killed the giant animals, and who put things straight on earth.

A confirmation of this conversation can be found in the analysis by Moore and Wheelock of the mythology of the Dene in northern Alberta. These two authors also offer us an interesting interpretation of the rosary by one of the Dene elders: The larger beads of the rosary represent the places where the Son of God came on earth, while the smaller ones represent his traces.[7]

3. The gifts of the creator

The following talk by Elder Frank Cardinal offers us a glimpse of the spirituality of the Cree people in northern Alberta, and of the place of Christ in their religious experience. The talk was given by the elder on July 11, 1983, in a large meeting and prayer teepee to a group of persons (mostly Catholic priests) who were holding a traditional native fast (vision quest) in the Kootenay Plains of Alberta. The text was written from memory after the fast on July 18 by one of the participants (Jean-Guy Goulet). Fasters were not allowed to write or to read during the fasting period. The elder spoke in Cree. One of his sons translated his talk into English, sentence by sentence. The text, as presented here, can be considered a faithful reproduction of the spoken word. The meditation of Frank Cardinal:

"We are in a sacred place. Many persons come here to fast. If you look at the land around you, it will teach you many things. The trees, like the pine, you look at it from the base up to the very top and you see how it points up to the Creator. All trees point up to him for us to pray to him. The trees all point up to the Creator. They remind us of where to look for him when we come to pray.

"All the mountains you see around us, they too are part of the gifts the Creator gave us. This is how strong we want our belief to be, as strong and everlasting as these mountains. And from the mountains comes water, the springs of clear water. It flows down to all living things. This water is also given for life and we should try living a clean life, the way the Creator gives it to us. These things are here to teach us.

"With all these gifts we also received from the Creator a way of praying. We Indians have our ceremonies, our ways of thanking him and of praying to him. This is a gift he has given us on this land. We want to keep that gift and pray to our Father with it. If you look around you, you can see all kinds of trees in the forest, mostly poplar, and willows, and also pine. Pines are like the native people on this land, they belong here, they are a special kind of tree and they will remain here. And the other trees around them also grow on this land. The trees do not fight on this land. They also grow on the same land. You can look at these trees. They are all there to see. They grow in their way without fighting one another.

"If you walk on the ground around here, you can feel how soft the ground is, it is just like a carpet, it is soft and easy to walk on. The Creator put it here for us. And if you look at the rose, this is the flower of our land, the flower of Alberta. You can see its beautiful color, pink. It is sometimes used to make medicine, as all kinds of plants are also used that way. They are a gift from the Creator to us. And as we walk in the bush, we see those plants and we know how to use them, what they are good for. And so on the land the Creator has placed all kinds of animals for us to eat. We do not have to feed them or to care for them. They feed from the land and they care for themselves. They are there for us to eat and to live. This is also a gift of the Creator to us.

"When I look at the rose I wonder sometimes why it is that this rose, if a child takes it in his hands, he gets hurt. A thorn gets into the palm of his hand and his mother comes to take the thorn out of his hand. She heals him. And why is it that us adults when we walk barefoot on a thorn, right there in the middle of our foot, it hurts. It hurts so much that we swear. And why is it that sometimes we have so terrible headaches? I wonder about this, and I think this is why that we suffer where our brother, the son of the Creator, also has suffered: he had nails in his hands and feet, and he had a crown of thorns on his head, and he suffered much for us. That is also why we suffer so much in those same places.

"And when our brother died on the cross, they also pierced his side. And when our brother, the son of the Creator, died, his Father also suffered and we suffer like him when we lose someone. We suffer but we are not mad at him when someone dies, because we know we come from him and we go back to him. And us men, we should also remember that, when someone dies, it is harder for the woman than for the man. The woman suffers more than the man when the child dies, she suffers more and longer, and us men we should remember that and know that.

"I never thought or dreamed that I would see the Holy Land, or that I would travel there. I never thought of that, and a few years ago I went there. I visited the Holy Land. By the place where our brother suffered, I saw a tree with pink leaves. I forgot to ask if that tree always kept its leaves or if it lost them at a given time of the year, like the trees around here. This year, when Father Paul (Hernou; Maskwa) went there, I asked him to ask if that tree ever lost its leaves or if it always kept them. He came back with the answer, that the tree never loses its leaves, it always keeps them all the time. The leaves of that tree across the ocean on the Holy Land and the rose on our land here, must be connected. We should pray that what happens over there, people fighting and killing one another, should never happen here, on this side of the ocean, on our land. I hope that with our Indian way of praying and with the Catholic way of praying we can help one another to live in peace and we should thank the Creator for all the gifts we receive from him.

"This is all I have to say now. I never thought so many priests would want to listen to what I have to say. I thank you."

The journey to the Holy Land to which Frank Cardinal alludes in his talk took place in 1977. The trip was undertaken by a few elders after the meeting of the indigenous peoples in Geneva. Several Cree from Alberta participated in this important meeting. During the trip in Palestine, one of the elders had a vision which he shared with Paul Hernou during the annual pilgrimage of the native peoples to Lake Sainte-Anne in Alberta. On the shore of the Sea of Galilee, this elder, who was not Christian, saw the face of Christ on a rock. The meaning of this vision was not yet clear to him. But it was clear, according to him, that now the Amerindians could not eliminate Christ from their relationship with God. While sharing this vision with Paul Hernou, the elder also expressed his personal conviction that, one day, Indian prayer and Catholic prayer would meet each other.[8]

4. Jesus: a very spiritual being

In response to our survey on the Amerindian Christ, a Metis-Cree woman from Saskatchewan sent us the following letter in February 1991:

"Christ is Indian. What does it mean for me? Christ becomes man; to teach us the virtue of love and how to develop healthy spirituality. When Jesus became an adult he was spiritual and also native peoples were very spiritual at that time too.

"Healthy spirituality was handed down for many generations among native peoples: they loved and respected living things. Creation from God for us all. Jesus gave us this example too.

"God saw that man in his weakness would violate this gift (gift of life and living). Therefore, Jesus came to be born in civilized society mainly (Jewish culture) to teach this virtue of love so all humanity would benefit from it one day. I am part of that whole. And I belong to Christ. Christ is for all humanity regardless of race.

"God in his power saw that in the future native peoples would one day be very confused in their spirituality; their disconnection of their praise to God upon contact. [= They lost their traditional way of relating to God after contact with white society?]

"The upbringing of native children onward was different and society is forever changing. Humanity is fragile. These confusions are disturbing the spiritual calmness of people.

"We now have the freedom to praise God the way he intended us to praise him, but we shouldn't forget Christ our Saviour who is all loving and forgiving to us. Combination of faiths (rituals) is a must, I think. Healing is a process. Healing has to take place, and a knowledge of Jesus and his teachings for our people, so that we can get a healthy spirituality again. A healing of self—for love of self, and to others and so our love for Christ will bloom again.

"I think that priests should learn to understand different cultures and teachings while in the seminary. Because we both need a medicine man and a priest in our churches. We need to bring in native rituals without rejection of a priest because of misunderstanding.

"We need a native theology school, like the former Kisemanito Centre in Alberta, so as to understand the gospel more fully and both philosophies of God.

"I hope this is what you needed. The last part of my letter is just a suggestion. I hope I answered all the questions.

"I am living in the city of Saskatoon right now. I am a Cree (Metis) person. I move around a lot. I go where I find a job. I am still learning about Jesus and his gospels. A person has to go through a healing process to understand self and others. Jesus' gospels teach people to be whole. The challenge for me is that women were Jesus' friends and helpers too. Therefore, women should be recognized in our churches. Especially their contributions to the world. If you need more of my views or help you can write to me at this address. I am only here temporarily."

5. To be with Jesus in his suffering

The following story is told by a young Cree Indian who is living and working in one of the major cities of western Canada. It illustrates the desire and the capacity of the Amerindians to visualize themselves in the different gospel scenes and to enter into communion with the healing and reconciliatory power of Jesus' ministry:

"For several years I did not belong here (to the native parish). In fact, I was belonging nowhere. I was drinking heavily and I was totally lost. But I continued to read the Bible with the hope of finding a solution to my questions and problems. I read the Bible almost daily. One day, I came across the passage that says: 'Return to the faith of your fathers.' The faith of my fathers was the Catholic faith. My grandmother, in particular, was a very holy woman. Gradually, I found the way back to the Catholic church with the help of my sponsor in the Alcoholic Anonymous movement. At that time, I still did not know that there was a native parish in the city. But it is here that I finally ended up. I work here as a volunteer and I like to do the readings. I like to encourage others to get involved in the parish. In our church, like in the base communities, everybody should be an active member. There should be no spectators. Personally, I appreciate the use of native symbols in the Christian liturgy, like the drum, sweetgrass and other sacred herbs, and dancing. This would make our liturgies more joyful and lively.

"What does the 'Amerindian Christ' mean for me? The pope's statement means, according to me, that the hierarchy accepts and finally understands that Christ is for all peoples. This also means that Christ has become my brother and that he accepts me as his brother, just like I am. Therefore, Christ has become someone very concrete for me.

"Not too long ago I read a book on the Bible. The author invited us to meditate on the different scenes of Jesus' life and to imagine ourselves in these scenes. I then chose the passage of Jesus in the garden of Gethsemane. I saw him laying with his head against the rock. Sweat covered his face. I asked him: What

Sister Eva Solomon, C.S.J.
Ceremony with Sacred Herbs
Photo: Anglican Magazine/John Bird

can I do for you? I offered him some water. He accepted and drank it. I dried his face. I then understood that each drop of sweat represented a sin that was about to be committed. I asked him: What can I do about that? He replied: Stop sinning! I did a similar meditation on the scene of the boat on the stormy lake. I found myself among the disciples in that boat. I did this meditation at a very difficult moment of my life when I was asking myself many questions. I started disturbing Jesus in his sleep with my questions. Suddenly, he woke up and told me: Shut up! Let me sleep. I need it. I started laughing. That's all. The most important thing for me is that the church offers us a place where we can belong spiritually and freely grow as persons."

6. Jesus wants to drink from the well of our ancestors

Sister Eva Solomon, an Ojibway Indian and a member of the Sisters of Saint Joseph since 1960, understands that Jesus came into the world not only to complete the cultural and religious history of his own people, but the history of all peoples. Just as the disciples of Emmaus and the early church needed the history of the Jewish people to understand the Christ event, the Amerindians must appeal to their own traditions to discover how Christ purifies and accomplishes their history. It is the same God who created the Anishnabe and who sent them his Son and his Spirit. The Father and the Son have established their dwelling place among the Anishnabe. Sister Eva became vividly aware of this mystery during a eucharistic celebration in 1989 while reading the story of the conversation between Jesus and the Samaritan woman (Jn 4):

"Last week I had a great blessing. I was asked to be part of three or four people proclaiming the word of God from chapter four of Saint John's gospel: The story of the Samaritan woman at the well. It was very powerful for me to play the Samaritan woman because she, in that story, was asking the same question that we as native people are asking today: How can our traditional ways, and our Christian ways come together? It was Jesus himself who initiated the dialogue: 'Give me a drink.' The woman replied: 'What? You, a Jew, are asking me, a Samaritan, for a drink? You know very well that Jews and Samaritans do not associate with one another.' Jesus responded: 'If only you knew who I was, you would ask, and I would give you living water.' The Samaritan woman said: 'This well is very, very deep. Are you greater than our ancestors? Are you greater than Jacob who built this well and who came here with his sons and his cattle to drink?' Then Jesus invites her to go and get her husband. She says: 'I have no husband ...'

"This sentence reflects the honesty and the simplicity that we see in our people. It was not an issue for her that she was not with her own husband. She knew what her life was like, and so did Jesus. Jesus replied: You spoke the truth. He affirmed the truth in her. He did not condemn the way she was living. He rather said: The one you are living with now is not your husband. That's the truth. You spoke the truth. He didn't say: Look now, you have to go back to number two, or number three, or whichever one. In fact, who's to say which one was her true husband? Jesus didn't take that issue as a moral issue. He said: You spoke the truth. This affirmation opened the heart of the woman. She was now ready to hear the words of Jesus. She said: Ha, I see you are a prophet. This is what our fathers, our ancestors, have told us. They tell us that we worship on this mountain, this sacred mountain. And you, a Jew, you tell us that it is in Jerusalem that we worship...

"This question of the Samaritan woman is also *our* question, the question about our traditional ways and the institutional church—two different ways. And Jesus says: The day will come when you will neither worship on this mountain nor in Jerusalem, but you will worship in spirit and in truth. For God is spirit and God is truth. I believe that it is Jesus himself who has started the dialogue with us, the native Christian people. He, again, said: Give me to drink from this well of your ancestors. Allow me to fulfil what the Creator has given you in your past ...

"We will be a strong people when we really own our past. We will then be able to walk with dignity and hold our heads high. At the very moment when I was proclaiming the words: 'Sir, I see that you are a prophet. Our ancestors worshipped on this mountain, but you say that the place where people must worship is in Jerusalem' (Jn 4:19-20), I raised my arm up to a mountain. Suddenly, I realized that this mountain was, in fact, our sacred mountain, the *Spirit Mountain* of the Ojibwa people who live in this area of northwestern Ontario. It is there that our ancestors prayed and where those who follow the traditional way go for their vision quest and for other rituals. Suddenly, this gospel took on a totally different and new meaning for me. When I saw my arm raised to our sacred mountain, I understood that this story was truly my story, our history. Jesus came first to accomplish the history of his own people, the history of the relationship that his own people had with God before his coming into the world. If I now want to understand how Jesus also came to accomplish our history, I must know how God walked with our people in the past. I must know our own Old Testament."

IV. Christological Vignettes

During the 1990 Ontario Kateri Tekakwitha Conference at Thunder Bay (Ontario), the second gathering of Ontario's Catholic native peoples, Bishop Jean-Louis Plouffe of Sault-Ste-Marie declared: "A new face of Christ is being revealed among native people, a native face."[9] We will complete the testimonies presented in this chapter with a few christological vignettes that help us to discover this native face of Christ.

• "Jesus was a good medicine man, because he practised the same principles which our elders teach us today. Jesus has developed the skills of a medicine man to a degree that he could even perform miracles. Our elders do the same thing because of the spiritual development of the person. The difference is that the history of Jesus has been written down. The history of native spirituality has never been written ..."

Walter Linklater, Medicine man and spiritual councillor. Seventh Summer Institute of Amerindian Christian Leadership, Montreal, 1985.

• "I am a Potawatomi Indian. This is the first time I have heard "Christ is Indian." I believe Christ is for all. In my native language we call him "Zah-zho." Our name for God is "Mish-om-sen-nah." While I am Catholic, I attend the drum services of my people and have a deep respect for this type of prayer service. They are a devout people and my relatives talk of prayer often. Everything has been given us by God."

Letter from a native woman from Topeka, Kansas.

• "Who is the Indian Christ?

"I want to see him, with my hands raised, and ask him life, courage. I want to talk to him ...

"He is the power of God, the Son of God. I feel him when I ask him something, even though I do not see him. That's how I know him. Jesus, Father, my master, I ask you courage, the right road, life and justice, harmony and love ...

"It is difficult to know who Jesus is and how he lived. I think of him as an Indian. But someone who is different, like the English, will see him as English. We are different, but do we not have the same life?"

(Translated from Innu)

• "Jesus was a Jew. He was a quiet person and a good preacher. He was patient and knew how to listen to others ..."

"It is not important for me to know who Jesus was. The important thing, for me, is to know that he was born, that he suffered and he died for all of us. I know that he was a remarkable man. He loved us so much that he died for us. No one has demonstrated a similar love. It is not important [to know] who he was. He loved all the peoples ..."

"Sheshush uiashipan miam kutak auen. Tapiskut kutak auen ... Innu, Tsha-nish, Aissimeu, Akanishan, Mistukushu. Literally: Jesus has taken flesh like everybody else the same and different: Indian, Shalish, Inuit, English, French ..."

Testimonies from a few Innu from Sheshashit, Quebec - Labrador.

• "From the beginning of history, in my opinion, the Body of Christ, to use Paul's expression, is the body of humanity in the whole of creation. It is this organic whole which is the Temple of God, the Temple of Wisdom. Since its beginning, this body, indwelt by Spirit, and of the Light, has been growing, evolving from age to age. Every single human being is a member of that Body. Every religion has contributed to the building of that Temple. The church is that body, as it has been revealed, but not the institutional church in isolation. This divine mystery, the ancient wisdom, is present in the hearts of men everywhere. It is significantly present in each of the major religions. From this standpoint, couldn't one argue that Indian religion is dramatically situated? This is an awesome and magnificent context. This essential truth cannot be discovered by any process of dialectic, but is perceived only in silence through the stilling of the faculties, within the depths of soul, beyond word and thought. Indians know this, and, more important, once again, they know how to facilitate that process."

Joseph Couture, Medicine man and educator, in
"Indian Spirituality – A Personal Experience," Kerygma 16(1982), p. 89.

• "Native people see life in its totality: the physical, the mental and the spiritual. We do not have a special day set aside for worshipping God—every day is a day of worship. When the Europeans came over, whether they were Roman

Catholic or Protestant, they taught native people *their* interpretations of the Bible. Many of these interpretations were slanted. Christian fundamentalists used a particular verse to convert 'the heathen': 'For God so loved the world, that he gave his only begotten son, that whoever believeth in him, should not perish, but have everlasting life' (Jn 3:16). When *we* read 'For God so loved the world,' the native interpretation of that is that God so loved the waters, the trees, and the animals. Therefore Christ died, therefore you must respect them. That's the interpretation of the native people.

"The evangelical interpretation of that same quotation is aimed at the unconverted people. Their greater concern is not for the world, they (the missionaries) use these interpretations in a way for their own ego. This is one of the differences between native and non-native attitudes about the world: Amerindians believe that God's spirit is in everything, not just in people. The day is coming when the dominant society will turn to the native culture to help revive nature. If you applied Jn 3:16 to a greater perspective, you would not be running into all these problems today. Christians must learn to respect the native interpretations. The native interpretation of that verse could enlighten the world.

"Native peoples have been blest by the creator in a particular way. Being forced onto the reserve by European settlers has helped the native people to remain united. But many of the native people's spiritual beliefs have been lost in the process. These lost beliefs will be revealed again in due time to the people."

Excerpted and adapted from Ken Bregenser: "From a Different Perspective: A Talk with Chief John Snow," Skylines, April 1989, p. 8.

•   "During the 1990 Ontario Kateri Tekakwitha Conference, Lillian McGregor asked a group of teens to visualize Jesus in a prayer experience, to see if he came to them wearing the robes of the New Testament times or in white buckskin and an eagle-feather bonnet to the ground. The teens came back after doing the experience and said: You aren't going to like what happened. Jesus came, they said, but our Jesus was wearing a sweat shirt, jeans, and sneakers!"

Spirit. Baptism of the Lord, 3, No. 3 (1991), p. 3.

•   "This morning the question was posed, perceived perhaps to be a dilemma: For many years, the church and others as well have asked the Indian People to give up their traditions in order to embrace Christ; but now, allegedly, we seem to have reversed the situation and the Indian People are being asked to give up Christ in order to embrace their own traditions. I think that may capsulize the kind of misunderstanding that exists in this country (...) Our communities are already suffering and certainly do not need to be put through a kind of tug-of-war to see which man of prayer they should follow. They do not have to be given 'faith alternatives' or 'faith options'—because there is NO requirement ... or at least there ought not to be any requirement ... for a people to say that, on the one hand you must give up Christ whom you have come to know in order to know your own traditions; or that you must give up your traditions in order to know Christ. That sort of dilemma should not be posed for the Indian people in this country because those questions are simply not real and have no foundation in truth. They have no foundation in our knowledge of Our Father. The ways of our people CAN be brought together with the ways of other peoples. Our elders do in fact respect your church as being one of the institutions to whom our Father gave a certain knowledge and a certain truth. And they believe and accept in their own way that they too have been given a knowledge and a vision of Our Father. And they recognize that it is time ... at least that it is almost time ... to begin bringing these two traditions together so that we may be able to enrich each other; and hopefully, through that process, come to a better understanding of who we are as human beings and also to a better understanding of Our Father and what He wants of us in this world ..."

Testimony of Chief Harold Cardinal
during the General Assembly
of the Canadian Conference of Catholic Bishops in 1983.
"There is no Reason to Fear Each Other," Kerygma *18(1984), pp. 54-56.*

CHAPTER V

The Sacred Pipe
and Christ

Introduction

Many of the testimonies in the previous chapter indicate that the Amerindian religious experience constitutes the main axis for the new appropriations of the Christ figure by the Amerindians. In this chapter we will reflect on this phenomenon while concentrating on the encounter between the sacred pipe and Christ. The first part of this chapter deals with the religious symbolism of the sacred pipe and the spiritual universe it represents. We will establish parallels between the theology of the sacred pipe and the basic aspects of the Christic mystery. In the second part of the chapter we will reflect on the specific contributions of the Amerindians to the interreligious dialogue which the mainline Christian churches now consider a constitutive dimension of their mission.

I. The Sacred Pipe and the Amerindian Christ

1. The theology of the sacred pipe

In the imagination of many white people, the pipe almost spontaneously evokes the image of a proud Indian warrior preparing himself for war or concluding peace treaties. Such an association is not without historical foundation. The pipe held a central place in many alliances for peace and in making treaties. The pipe continues to have an important symbolic meaning in contemporary meetings between the representatives of the first nations and of the American or Canadian governments. This explains, to some extent, why so many non-Amerindians have a limited understanding of the theological meaning of the sacred pipe within the Amerindian spiritual universe. This indeed explains why, although its functions extend far beyond war and peace, the sacred pipe is called a "peace pipe" by most non-Indians. For the North American native peoples, the sacred pipe is more than a symbol of war and peace. It is, above all, a potent means of communication with *Wakan Tanka*, the Great Mystery. Therefore, it is appropriate to speak of *the theology of the sacred pipe*. This theology finds its origin in the legend of the coming of the sacred pipe among the Lakota people.

The mysterious origin of the sacred pipe

In the course of history, the Lakota Indians have developed a complex mythology which has triggered the interest of many anthropologists.[1] The story of the coming of the sacred pipe is a central aspect of this mythology. Even though the origin of their mythology is lost in the mists of time, the Lakota are convinced that their traditional theology is founded on the gift of the sacred pipe by the White Buffalo Woman to their people. They consider this to have been an historical event that can be compared to the coming of Jesus of Nazareth as related in the gospels.[2] The stories of the coming of the sacred pipe and of Christ are not myths but legends.

There is no doubt that the pipe was used by many native groups in North America well before the arrival of the Lakota in the western plains and before their definite settlement in the Black Hills (1775-1776).[3] The Lakota oral tradition and archeological research testify to the existence of the pipe before the coming of the While Buffalo Woman. The pipe was already in use at the time of Abraham, two thousand years before Christ. Very elaborate pipes were found among the Mound Building peoples, the paleo-Indians of the Ohio and Mississipi River valleys, who are considered to be the ancestors of the Algonquian Indians.[4] These pre-historic peoples were already living in a well-constructed spiritual universe.

At the beginning of the Christian era, the pipe was universally used by the native peoples of North America. Later on, the use of the pipe gradually declined and disappeared almost completely, especially among the southern tribes. The Lakota legend of the White Buffalo Woman, therefore, constitutes a turning point in the cultural and religious history of the Amerindian peoples. This story has consolidated the religious meaning of the sacred pipe and continues to strengthen its contemporary use.

There are a certain number of factors which permit the legend of the gift of the sacred pipe to the Lakota to be situated towards the end of the eighteenth century. The majority of the traditional Lakota calendars, the so-called winter counts, situate the event between 1785 and 1800 C.E. The few anthropologists who were allowed to see the original pipe at Green Grass on the Cheyenne Reservation (South Dakota) confirm its resemblance to several bowls of the Arikara Indians whom the Lakota visited between 1722 and 1743. The pipe which is venerated by the Lakota as the original sacred pipe in the "sanctuary" of Green Grass has been protected by fourteen successive keepers, each for an average of twenty years. Stolzman, following John L. Smith, situates the gift of the sacred pipe to the Lakota in the late 1700s. [5]

These calculations are important to the Lakota who refuse to transform their legend into a myth. Although many Lakota rituals originated in dreams and visions of individual spiritual leaders, their veneration of the sacred pipe rests on an historical event which was a community experience of a mystical nature. Therefore, it is possible to argue that the historical nature of the coming of the sacred pipe to the Lakota facilitated their encounter with Christianity which is also based on an historical event, the coming of Jesus Christ.

The legend of the White Buffalo Woman can be summarized as follows: during a period of severe famine, two young Lakota men went out to hunt buffalo. Suddenly, they saw a mysterious woman on the horizon. The woman, walking in a sacred *(wakan)* manner, was very beautiful. One of the hunters had evil thoughts. He wanted to grab her, but was reduced to a skeleton. The woman sent the other hunter back to his people to prepare her visit. Next day, she appeared in the village with a medicine bundle which contained a pipe, the Sacred Buffalo Calf Leg Pipe. She instructed the people to use this pipe when praying to God, especially in times of danger and need. When leaving the village, the woman turned into a white buffalo and galloped away.

The essential kernel of this legend has been surrounded with many details and additions which expand the religious meaning of the basic narrative. This amplification, which is characteristic of oral tradition, serves the spiritual needs of the people. The Lakota tradition has preserved many versions of the legend. The best known of all these versions is the one told by Black Elk.[6] The detailed meaning of the legend may vary from version to version, but the essential message is the same: the coming of the sacred pipe is the beginning of a new spiritual relationship between *Wakan Tanka* and the Lakota people. Something absolutely new has occurred in the religious history of the people.

The sacred pipe and the Pan-Indian movement

The historical nature of the turning point which marks the religious experience of the Lakota people was rapidly communicated to the northwestern tribes of the United States and Canada. The sacred pipe gradually became a key element in the construction of their cultural and religious identity. Practically all the spiritual leaders, shamans and elders we have met since 1982 were pipe keepers who frequently use the sacred pipe for personal prayer and group rituals. Michael Steltenkamp considers this development as an important aspect of the contemporary Amerindian renaissance and as a rediscovery of the religious meaning that the pipe once had before the arrival of the white people in North America.[7]

The sacred pipe has thus become one of the most important contemporary religious symbols and resources shared by many Amerindians. Therefore, it is practically impossible to reflect on Amerindian spirituality without considering the symbolism of the sacred pipe. Steltenkamp compares the importance of the sacred pipe ceremonies to the celebration of the eucharist among the Christians. Our own research has shown us that the use of the sacred pipe is widespread among native persons in Canada, even among those who consider themselves Christian. The sacred pipe does not monopolize the meaning of Amerindian spirituality, but it represents a central aspect of it.

The religious symbolism of the sacred pipe

Since 1982 we have been privileged to participate in a certain number of Amerindian rituals such as the vision quest, the sweat lodge, and many healing or thanksgiving ceremonies which involved the use of the sacred pipe. The use of the sacred pipe in these native rituals can be compared to the importance attached to the sign of the cross in Catholic prayers and liturgies.

But what is the basic religious symbolism of the sacred pipe? There is no dogmatic answer to this question. Amerindian spirituality has remained experiential. Therefore, the meaning of the sacred pipe can be determined only by contemplating a certain number of elements spread among the tribes which actually use the pipe in their ceremonies. These elements include the construction of this instrument of prayer, the structure of the rituals in which it is used, and the symbolic universe to which it belongs. According to the Lakota and many other native groups, these three elements are sacred or *wakan*. Since they are surrounded by mystery, they deserve our respect.

According to William Stolzman, the legend of the White Buffalo Woman has gradually lessened the emphasis on the sacred pipe as symbol of war or peace and given it a much larger religious meaning. The sacred pipe has become the universal symbol of life and death. The seven rituals mentioned by Black Elk, in relationship with the sacred pipe, aim at the restoration of cosmic harmony, and invite the Lakota to develop peaceful relationships with the other tribes. The use of the sacred pipe during the treaty-signing ceremonies in the nineteenth century can therefore be understood as a consequence of the spiritual dynamism that this prayer instrument had started to generate. The sacred pipe was becoming a source of temperance, tolerance and harmony. There is no doubt that the extended religious meaning of the sacred pipe also had a positive impact on the attitudes of the Lakota vis-à-vis the Black Robes and Catholicism. Everything was in place, right from the beginning, for the eventual encounter between the sacred pipe and the Christ mystery.[8]

The sacred pipe was given to the Lakota people by the White Buffalo Woman as a symbol of the entire universe. This universal symbolism can be found in the structure of the pipe itself. The bowl made of catlinite or another kind of stone represents Mother Earth. The Lakota seem to prefer catlinite, a red colored stone, because of its sacrificial connotation. The wooden stem represents all living beings, while the eagle feathers which are sometimes attached to the stem, represent heaven and the winged beings, the divine messengers. The centre of the bowl symbolizes the centre of the universe.[9]

Many Amerindians are convinced that the sacred pipe has the same spiritual power as the Christian sacraments. When the pipe is not used, the bowl and the stem are kept separate and are placed in a medicine bag which may also contain tobacco, other sacred herbs or objects. The spiritual power of the pipe is activated when the bowl is joined to the stem, and when the bowl is filled in a ritual manner. This ritual filling may vary from one native group to another, but the basic symbolism of the gestures is the same. These gestures once again demonstrate the universal power of the sacred pipe. The ritual filling of the pipe follows a simple but meaningful pattern. After the presider has joined the bowl and the stem, he holds the pipe in his left hand and fills the bowl with tobacco or *kinick kinick* (a mixture of tobacco and birch or willow bark) with his right. The presider holds a pinch of tobacco between the thumb and the forefinger of the right hand and places it respectfully in the bowl. This gesture is repeated seven times in honor of the four cardinal directions, heaven, Mother Earth, and the speckled eagle, a very special messenger of *Wakan Tanka*. The filling of the bowl is completed in this manner.

This filling symbolizes the coming together of all the spiritual powers which are present on earth, in heaven, and in the human person. The sacred pipe is considered to be the sacrament or the voice of these spiritual powers. This is the reason both the filling and the act of smoking are ritualized actions. We noticed that almost everywhere in Canada those who use the pipe for personal prayer or in group rituals have developed a ritual or liturgical language which expresses the same universalism: the four cardinal directions, Mother Earth, heaven, and the eagle or other divine messenger.

However, this liturgy leaves room for a great amount of personal creativity which is often inspired by the teachings, dreams or visions of the elders. Dreams or visions are often considered to be divine revelations which can modify the ritual and increase or personalize its meaning. This explains, for example, why we find Christian symbols among the different elements of the sacred pipe ceremonies in some areas of Canada. However, these Christian symbols do not substantially modify the basic meaning of the sacred pipe ceremony.[10]

Finally, we must note that the theology of the sacred pipe that developed among the Lakota Indians is also influenced by their worldview. William Powers observes that the Lakota developed the habit of visualizing the entire reality in terms of four or seven, the two sacred numbers. For the Lakota, these two sacred numbers have no absolute value. What counts, in the first place, are not the numbers, but reality itself in its totality. The numbers four and seven give a structure to their religious view of the world and allow them to see certain aspects of reality which other persons cannot see, especially those who live in a less ritualized environment.

The number four reveals the basic structure of the Lakota natural environment: the four cardinal directions of the universe, the four seasons, the four phases of human development, the four kinds of living beings, and so on. The number seven symbolizes their political and social organization. The two numbers, combined, express a sense of natural and cultural accomplishment. They represent the present and the future and determine the cyclical structure of this worldview.

Once perfection is obtained, the cycle of life is once again set in motion. Every ending means a new beginning.

This cyclical way of visualizing reality offers the Amerindians a sense of peace and security in contrast to the anxiety related to a linear vision of history, dominated by the idea of inevitable progress. The numbers four and seven permit the Amerindians to control the uncertainty and the unpredictability of human destiny and the future of the universe to some extent. The very structure of the sacred pipe ceremony and of many other native rituals reflects this fundamental vision of reality in terms of peace, security and harmony. It is important to note here that this structure does not imprison the Amerindians within a dogmatic system which forces them to see reality in a certain way. Powers correctly observes that the Lakota and other native groups are not interested in reality *as it is*, but in reality *as it should be*. The numbers four and seven offer them this insight. This is why we find these two numbers in many native rituals: in the filling of the sacred pipe, in the structure of the sweat lodge, in the sun dance ritual (see Chapter VII).

In the ritual filling of the sacred pipe, the number four represents the four cardinal directions of the universe and the four directions from which blow the four winds which are considered as personalized powers of *Wakan Tanka*. The number two represents the vertical axis of heaven and earth. The number one symbolizes a mythological birth. The number seven represents wholeness.[11]

We will now explain how this Lakota view of reality has entered into contact with Christianity which possesses its own symbolism of sacred numbers.

2. The sacred pipe and the inculturation of Christ

The use of the sacred pipe as an instrument of peace in the nineteenth century has been an important factor in the reconciliation of the different Amerindian nations. Since those days, the pipe has been adopted by many Amerindians as a potent means of communication with the Great Mystery. Many Amerindians have gradually interiorized the religious meaning of the sacred pipe so that it has now become an important factor in the reconstruction of their cultural identity. Therefore, we must reflect on what connections there might be between the sacred pipe and the Christ figure.

The data we present have been provided by a number of Amerindians and Christian pastors, whose spiritual journey has been marked by frequent prayer with the sacred pipe. At this point in our research, we will concentrate on two particular native environments: the Oglala Lakota of the Pine Ridge Reservation in South Dakota and the Cree of northern Alberta. We have had access to these two native environments through the personal experience of four missionaries: to the Lakota through Paul Steinmetz and William Stolzman, and to the Cree through Roger Vandersteene and Paul Hernou.

In the land of the Lakota

The coming of the sacred pipe among the Lakota more or less coincides with the beginning of their evangelization. The Pine Ridge Reservation, where Paul Steinmetz, S.J., worked as a missionary between 1961 and 1981, was established in 1878. According to the policy of that time, only one Christian denomination could establish itself on the reservation. The Pine Ridge Reservation was given to the Episcopalian church, notwithstanding the fact that the Oglala had often expressed their preference for Catholic priests. Due to the influence of the famous Chief Red Cloud, the first Catholic mission was established on the reservation in 1888. Today, almost all Oglala belong (at least nominally) to one of the two denominations.

They have often adopted Christianity because of the resemblance between their traditional spirituality and the Christian faith. They seemed particularly impressed by the sacrifice of Christ for his people, the fundamental equality of all peoples, and God's care for the less fortunate. They found a new source of security in the Christian churches at the very moment the American government legislated against their traditional ceremonies, especially the sun dance. A survey made towards the end of the 1960s revealed that, although the majority of the Oglala belong to the Catholic or Episcopalian church (83%), many remained faithful to their traditional religion.[12]

In his study on the religious identity of the Oglala, Steinmetz shows that the encounter between the sacred pipe and Christ has been a long and arduous road.[13] The majority of the Oglala accept the Trinity and maintain that their traditional God is identical to the God of the Christians, but the name of Christ seldom appears in their prayers (p. 39). Some Lakota easily pass from the traditional to the Christian religious system, and *vice versa* according to the spiritual needs of the moment (p. 47). Because their traditional religion offers limited information on the final destiny of souls, they welcome the resurrection of Christ as a guarantee of eternal life (p. 50). Some Lakota, followers of the Peyote religion, compare the appearances of Jesus to the disciples of Emmaus to the presence of spirits (spiritual nourishment) during their ceremonies (p. 51). When they consume the peyote, their minds turn spontaneously to the Great Spirit and to Jesus Christ (p. 100). The members of the Cross Fire section of the North American native church identify the sacrament of peyote with Christ, just as other Lakota identify him with the sacred pipe (p. 195). The sacred tree at the centre of the Sun Dance Lodge sometimes symbolizes the return of Christ and is venerated as a source of new life (p. 189). But one also encounters Lakota who have left the church and for whom the sacred pipe is a kind of Antichrist (p. 139).

Steinmetz's research reveals that certain Lakota visualize Christ as the true fulfilment of the sacred pipe (p. 177). Using Mircea Eliade's reflections on the relationship between the cross of Christ and the tree of life as his base, Steinmetz maintains that the religious symbol of the sacred pipe has come to "maturity" in Christ.[14] This conclusion is based on two important visions. Steinmetz himself had the first vision, fourteen years after his arrival among the Lakota: "On November 6, 1965, I prayed with the Sacred Pipe as a priest for the first time at the funeral of Rex Long Visitor at Slim Butte. The night before the funeral I had an inspiration that seized me emotionally, an intuition of the relationship between the pipe and Christ. A ceremony came to me that I used at that funeral and others on the Pine Ridge Reservation. I held up a pipe filled with tobacco, and taking the stem and the bowl apart, I said: 'Remember, man, that the Pipe of your life some day will be broken.' I then laid the separated Pipe on the coffin. After the ritual prayers I took up the two separated pieces and, putting them together, I said: 'Through the resurrection of Christ the life of Rex Long Visitor and all of us will be brought together into eternal happiness.' Then repeating in the four directions, I prayed: 'I am the Living and Eternal Pipe, the Resurrection and the Life; whoever believes in Me and dies shall live, and whoever lives and believes in Me shall never suffer eternal death.' After the fourth direction I touched the bowl of the Pipe to the earth in silence" (p. 36).

This new ritual, which originated in Steinmetz's personal vision, was approved by John Iron Robe, the *yuwipi* man of the commmunity (one of the main spiritual leaders), who, by the same token, legitimized this identification of the sacred pipe and Christ, and who recognized their mediating role. Steinmetz realized that he had introduced a non-authorized "innovation" into the ritual of the sacred pipe. When the bowl is filled with tobacco, it cannot be separated from the stem! It was only nine years later, while doing research on the pipe in the Library of the British Museum in London, that Steinmetz discovered that the practice of separating the filled bowl from the stem already existed among the Lakota. Before their departure for war, the keeper of the pipe filled the sacred pipe with tobacco and then separated the bowl from the stem. When the Lakota returned *victorious* from war, the stem was joined to the bowl, and the warriors smoked the sacred pipe. The discovery of this ancient ritual shows that Steinmetz's "innovation" symbolizing life and death had connected with a profound aspect of the Lakota collective psyche. One century before the funeral of Rex Long Visitor, the sacred pipe already symbolized the same fundamental truth as the resurrection of Christ.[15]

The second vision on which the identification of the sacred pipe and Christ is based took place during the life of Benjamin Black Elk, son of the famous Nicholas Black Elk, the greatest mystic of the Lakota. Like his father, Benjamin Black Elk played an important role in the development of the Catholic church among the Lakota of the Pine Ridge Reservation. But, one particular night, when talking with Steinmetz about the vision of his father and about the relationship between the Lakota religion and Catholicism, he made a startling confession to the priest. For most of his life he had believed that there was a conflict between the two religious traditions. But now he saw that the sacred pipe and Christ really were one and that they fulfilled each other. His pangs of conscience came to an end. Real spiritual peace had filled his soul. He saw that the sacred pipe had led the Lakota people to Christ as the living and eternal pipe (pp. 202-203).

The testimonies of Steinmetz and Benjamin Black Elk lead us spontaneously to the famous Nicholas Black Elk himself, whose books *Black Elk Speaks* and *The Sacred Pipe* have become classics in North American literature.[16] Steinmetz rightly considers Nicholas Black Elk as the "Saint John of the Cross" of the Lakota people. His great vision of the sacred circle and of the tree of life can easily be compared to the visions of Plato, the apostle Paul, Jan van Ruysbroeck, John of the Cross, and many other mystics. Yet, the books of Black Elk, which are based on meetings with the poet John Neihardt and John Epes Brown, more or less ignore the fact that, although he was a remarkable native mystic, he was also one of the great catechists at Pine Ridge for twenty years.

Black Elk was baptized Nicholas by the Jesuits on December 6, 1904. His entire life can be understood as a personal search for the "unknown Christ" of the Oglala Lakota. The book *Black Elk Speaks* makes no mention of this important spiritual journey of the mystic. Steinmetz uses Neihardt's fieldnotes, edited and published by Raymond DeMallie, to reconstruct the vision which Black Elk had of the Messiah (pp. 180-182). During a vision which he received while participating in the *Ghost Dance*, Black Elk saw a man with outstretched arms standing against the centre pole of the lodge which had become a tree in full bloom. During most of his life, Black Elk identified this figure with the *Ghost Dance Wanekia* (Saviour), and not with Christ, because he would have nothing to do with the white man's religion at that time. On the level of phenomenology, Steinmetz writes, Black Elk experienced a Messiah manifestation, but it was only later—after his conversion—that he would recognize the *Ghost Dance Wanekia* as Christ, the Son of the Great Spirit himself. For a long time, Black Elk wondered whether he should follow the Messiah of the *Ghost Dance* or the Christ of his Catholic faith. Only one thing, according to Steinmetz, is certain about this remarkable man: a *Lakota Christ had come to Black Elk in a Lakota vision.* Black Elk's vision has become, for many Lakota, the very foundation of their identification of the sacred pipe with Christ. Steinmetz's interpretation of Black Elk's vision is confirmed by Benjamin Black Elk who served as interpreter during his father's meetings with Neihardt and Brown.

But his identification of the sacred pipe with Christ has not necessarily been adopted by all the Lakota and the Catholic missionaries who have worked among them. Despite his personal initiation into the Lakota religion through a vision quest, William Stolzman, S.J., insists on the different functions of the sacred pipe and Christ and sees nothing more than a simple comparison or symbolic meaning between them. According to him, to say that Christ is the pipe can only be interpreted in the sense of a mystical union based on the Christian theology of divine participation in the world. It is nothing more than an affirmation of the universal presence of the Risen Christ in the world. In other words, to say that

Christ is the pipe would be no different than saying that Christ is the air, a tree or each one of us.[17]

It should be noted however that, in his book on a dialogue that took place between some Lakota medicine men and a group of Christian ministers, Stolzman offers some basic intuitions for the further understanding of the inculturation of Christ among the Lakota people. This dialogue, which was called the *Rosebud Medicine Men and Pastors Meeting*, extended over a period of six years, bringing together a group of twenty to forty persons who were interested in the relationship between the Lakota religion and Christianity nine times a year. Stolzman served as organizer and secretary of these meetings (p. 8). In his book he shows that these persons took a considerable amount of time to reflect on the comparisons between the story of the coming of the sacred pipe among the Lakota people and the infancy gospels' story of the coming of Christ (pp. 166-179). We can deduce two important intuitions which have contributed to the encounter between the Lakota religion and Christianity from this dialogue: the affirmation of the *historical* nature of the two stories, and the discovery of the *universal mediating role* of both the sacred pipe and Christ. Stolzman also reflects briefly on the symbolism of numbers in both the Lakota religion and Christianity (pp. 189-205).

The dialogue which revealed the fundamental compatibility of the meaning of the number four in the two religious traditions also focused on the connection between the number four in the Lakota cosmology and the number three in the Christian sign of the cross. Questions were raised about the relationship between the four directions or the four winds which personify the powers of *Wakan Tanka*, and the three persons of the Trinity in the Christian religion. Some dialogue participants compared the Spirit of the West with God the Father. Both mark the beginning of all things and help make them grow. The Spirit of the North, like the Son of God, shows that good comes from a life that is obedient and straight. Both show the tremendous good that flows from sacrifice for the sake of one's people. The Spirit of the East, like the Holy Spirit, is associated with wisdom, leadership, understanding, prayer, and effective communication in the spiritual order. But what about the Spirit of the South, the place where, according to the Lakota, the animal spirits live and where the human person, in ghost form, will experience earthly happiness with relatives and all the animals?

There is no fourth Person in the Christian Holy Trinity! Stolzman notes that for a time this represented a great impasse in the comparative study of the two religions. Yet, when reflecting on this, some medicine men were convinced that the Lakota tradition could help Christians deepen their understanding of God, the Great Mystery. The "communion" which exists among all the spirits in the South, according to Lakota mythology, could help Christians to highlight the corporate mystery of the "Mystical Body of Christ" more effectively. As a consequence of the incarnation of the Son of God, the mystical body of Christ is the *corporate expression* of the historical action of the Holy Trinity in the world.

We feel that we are dealing here with a profound intuition. Indeed, we will show in the following chapters that other aspects of Amerindian spirituality can help us to come to a more profound and adequate understanding of the Christian mystery of the "communion of saints" and of the universal value of the Christic mystery.

We conclude these few reflections on the encounter between the sacred pipe and Christ in the land of the Lakota with an important observation. Even though this relationship is based primarily on the testimonies of two remarkable missionaries (Steinmetz and Stolzman), these missionaries immediately admit that they are not the ones who established it. They recognize that this connection has been made by the medicine men themselves who consider the Lakota religion, centred on the sacred pipe, to be an authentic pre-Christian religion which finds its fulfilment in Christ. This is indeed an important theological statement that most Christian missionaries have only recently understood. The medicine men are greatly pleased by this development.[18] The Spirit blows where it will.

Among the Cree in Alberta

The Cree north of Lesser Slave Lake in Alberta still remember Father Roger Vandersteene, a remarkable missionary who died in 1976. The elders call him "the one who speaks our language." For Vandersteene it was not enough just to learn the difficult Cree language. He also learned to speak the cultural language of the Cree by adopting their lifestyle and opening his heart and mind to their ancestral spirituality.

Early in his missionary career, he discovered that the Cree were a "naturally religious" people. In a book he published ten years after his arrival among them, he presents a very lively picture of their customs, legends and religious rituals.[19] Unlike many missionary publications, this book does not give statistics and reports on the situation of the church in this remote area of Canada, but proposes to tell "the story of the work of grace in the soul of the Cree Indians" (p. 8). A victim of the theological language of his time, Vandersteene still uses the terms "superstition" and "paganism" when he presents the spiritual universe of the Cree. But his basic missionary intuition is to welcome the religious traditions of the Cree not as alien things but as alliances of evangelization (p. 173). He saw them as the prefigurations of the God of love who revealed himself in Jesus Christ (pp. 124-125). In this sense, Vandersteene may be considered a veritable pioneer of Christ's inculturation among the Cree.

But, I repeat that it is important to note that this significant theological intuition came from the Amerindians themselves. Vandersteene had to wait ten years before the Cree invited him to their most important religious ceremony, the *Wikkokewin*, the sacrificial meal and dance in honour of the ancestors (pp. 175-191). For all those years the missionary had tried to explain the eucharist to his parishioners. None of his explanations seemed plausible to the Cree mind. It was only after he had spent the entire night in the large tent of the *Wikkokewin* that

Vandersteene discovered that the Cree traditional ritual possessed the essential elements for a true catechesis of the eucharist: "Everything is in place! The priest, the offering, the consecration, the communion, the cross, the incense, the kiss of peace, the blessing of the church, the organs, the servants, the participation of the assembly ..." (p. 191). A true *preparatio evangelii!*

The missionary suddenly discovered that the offerings of the mass, transformed into the body and blood of Christ, always alive, could be considered as the fulfilment of the offerings which the Cree burned in the sacred fire of the *Wikkokewin* to exorcize their dead and to pacify the wrath of their ancestors (p. 178). From that moment on, the entire life of the missionary was characterized by a constant effort to facilitate the relationship between the God-Love of the Christians and the powerful *Kisemanitou* who, though often experienced with a profound feeling of resignation, was intimately present in the life of the Cree Indians (p. 115).

Contemplative and mystical by nature, Roger Vandersteene started a sort of inner dialogue with the traditional spirituality of the Cree. The sacred pipe occupied a central place in this dialogue. And not just any kind of pipe! Paul Hernou, the successor of Vandersteene, relates that, one day, Vandersteene received the visit of a Cree elder who brought him a pipe of which the bowl had been deliberately broken by a missionary, about fifty years earlier. Vandersteene managed to restore the bowl, almost perfectly, and gave it back to the elder. Shortly before his death, this elder, who felt that none of his own sons was spiritual enough to become a pipe carrier, entrusted his pipe to the missionary.

When Roger Vandersteene died in 1976, his will indicated that this sacred pipe was to be given back to the Cree people in the person of Harold Cardinal, a young chief dedicated to the political, cultural and spiritual life of his people.[20] This prophetic gesture has produced many spiritual fruits.

We personally have been able to benefit from it. Harold Cardinal and his father Frank, whose important testimony we gave in the previous chapter, played a major role in the religious initiation and inter-cultural dialogue which a group of Catholic priests and laypersons experienced in 1983.[21] Were it not for the respect that Vandersteene had shown many years before for the religion and the culture of the Cree, such an initiative would have been impossible.

Roger Vandersteene is now counted among the ancestors and the spirits who are venerated during the *Wikkokewin*, while Father Paul Hernou, introduced to the sacred pipe ritual by Harold Cardinal, continues the dialogue initiated by his predecessor. In 1987, while reflecting on his own missionary experience among the Cree, Father Hernou offered us the following testimony concerning the connection between the sacred pipe and Christ. He often starts the celebration of the eucharist with the sacred pipe ritual. In the following story, based on a conference given at Saint Paul University, Ottawa, he explains the origin and the development of this liturgical "innovation":

Cree Elder Frank Cardinal.
Thanksgiving Ceremony, Little Red River, Alberta, 1984
Photo: Achiel Peelman

"I have now been living in Trout Lake for twenty years. I never had told the people that I was a pipe holder. But the 'moccasin telegram' is an excellent means of communication! One day, a couple invited me to bless their house and told me to bring my pipe with me. We sat together on the floor of the house, smoked the pipe and blessed the house with fungus and holy water. Then we went to celebrate the eucharist. Since then, I have been doing this in many houses. In October last year, at the occasion of the twentieth anniversary of my arrival in Trout Lake, I asked the elders if it would be good to have a special pipe ceremony and the eucharist. 'It is about time you start doing this, one of the elders said. We have been waiting for such a long time now. In fact, last week we were talking about it and asking ourselves when you would finally understand what we want!'

"Some native people in the northern area are upset with the native religious ceremonies. In fact, some people in the area are upset by what I did. I am not surprised. For many years missionaries have been telling them that native religion was wrong. And now, that crazy Maskwa (that is my Indian name) is mixing the pipe with the eucharist! I also know native persons who are against the introduction of the Cree language (their own language!) in the local schools. Both the church and the Alberta school system should recognize that some of their past and present strategies are wrong. Why not be honest about that and help the native people cope with their cultural struggles?

"For me, the pipe and Christ belong together. We are not going to have two ceremonies tonight, but only one ceremony: the eucharist will be part of the pipe ceremony. This was not so in the beginning. For a while I separated the two ceremonies with a song on my drum because I felt that it was not up to me to bring the two together. But this is in fact what I have been doing, especially since October last year. I had noticed that the smoking of the pipe by elders is often followed by a period of teachings. Only at the end of the teachings is the pipe separated. This means the end of the ceremony. I have been doing the same thing.

Only at the end of the eucharist, I separated the pipe. Thus the eucharist had become an integral part of the pipe ceremony. For the elders and the native people this must have been obvious and no person told me to do otherwise! But I will have to talk about all this one day with Elder Frank Cardinal. I had been doing this in the native way. Nothing was explained in the beginning. Together we experienced something new (this is what inculturation is all about). And we will gradually come to a better understanding of the coming together of the pipe and Christ."[22]

In 1960, Roger Vandersteene wrote: "The faith of the Indians flows with difficulty in channels that are dug out in advance. It rolls its waves like a river whose capricious waters opt for a totally spontaneous freedom."[23] The previous testimony illustrates this fact very well. Just like the "unified and separated" sacred pipe of Paul Steinmetz among the Lakota, the "broken and restored" sacred pipe of Roger Vandersteene is becoming a potent symbol of Christ's death and resurrection among the Cree of Alberta. With complete freedom, they have welcomed a theological "innovation" which is deeply rooted in their traditional religious practices. In northern Alberta too, the Spirit blows where it will.

The road of the sacred pipe is difficult and arduous

Throughout this christological research we have met Amerindians who, after being separated from their cultural and religious traditions, wanted to walk once again on *the red path of the sacred pipe.* Many undertook this journey privately, while searching, whether in the United States (often among the Lakota) or in Canada, for a medicine man who was ready to teach them the theology of the sacred pipe and other aspects of Amerindian spirituality. Others organized workshops in their communities to initiate dialogue between Christianity and the traditional native religion which most community members remembered only vaguely or in a confused way. In the previous chapter we presented a few testimonies which illustrate this fact. We will complement these testimonies by briefly presenting two situations which are typical of native communities across Canada, and especially of the Cree communities which we have visited since 1982.

On the Indian reserve of Saddle Lake, in the centre of the province of Alberta, Catholicism and the traditional native religion seem to get on well. One can meet there several medicine men who are at ease in the two religious systems. On Sunday morning they may participate in the eucharistic celebration, and then, in the afternoon, enter into their sweat lodge for a healing or thanksgiving ceremony, often followed by a traditional meal in honor of the ancestors.

In November 1982, we met a young medicine man in Saddle Lake to ask him about his view of the relationship between Christianity and his native religion. Before answering our question, he invited us to smoke the sacred pipe in the company of his two very young children. "I cannot talk about my religion," he said, "without first praying and practising it." The ritual, which was held in his living room, reflected a cosmology similar to that of the Lakota Indians with its particular insistence on the four powers or directions of the universe. Following this ceremony, he drew a comparison of the two religions by referring to the symbolic way in which they use a rock or stone. The bowl of the sacred pipe is made of a stone that is carefully chosen and blessed by an elder. This stone represents the centre of the universe. Everytime the pipe is smoked, we find ourselves in the centre and the centre is in us. We enter into communion with all the spiritual powers, and are ready to live according to the teachings of the elders. "The stone of the sacred pipe," the medicine man said, "can be compared to the altar stone on which the Catholic priest places the symbols which remind us of the sacrifice of Christ."

According to him, no pipe ceremony is truly complete without the presence of at least four men and four women. The energies of the men and the energies of the women complement one another, and are activated during the ceremony. This medicine man also told us that there is a legend, well-known among the Indian tribes, that tells about a visit of Jesus to the native peoples of North America. According to this legend, Jesus had disappeared for a certain period of time. *His disciples had lost him.* This was when Jesus was visiting the Indian tribes of North America. This explains why there are so many resemblances between Christianity and the native religion, and why the teachings of the elders are so close to those of the Bible.

A few days after this meeting, three elders of Saddle Lake invited us to accompany them to the nearby village of Beaver Lake, on the occasion of the official opening of a new school, *The Amisk Community School.* The inauguration of the school started with a sacred pipe ceremony, presided over by the three elders, in the presence of all the young children. The ritual was followed by a traditional meal and a traditional dance in which the entire community, even the very young children, participated. The school was the first phase of a new educational program, under total control of the Amerindians, which focuses on the total development (academic, spiritual and social) of the children, within the Canadian context but according to the Cree traditions.

In March 1983, we found ourselves back in Saddle Lake for a community workshop on the integration of the Christian faith and native religion, organized by the *Native Pastoral Council* of the Catholic diocese of Saint Paul. We have never forgotten the two important observations made by a group of elders at this meeting, attended by young and old. First, there will never be a truly Amerindian church without the acceptance and the integration of the sacred pipe. Secondly, the church and the priest do not talk about Jesus Christ enough! There may be a mysterious relationship between the legend of Jesus' visit to the Indian tribes of North America and the two messages of these elders. If the church runs the risk of losing Jesus a second time, those who walk on the road of the sacred pipe are ready to help the church *find Jesus once again!*

While the integration of Christian faith and native religion is becoming a reality in the life of many persons in Saddle Lake, in many parts of Canada the situation is quite different. In many native communities we are only at the starting point of this process. Yet, almost everywhere, even in the native communities with a strong Catholic or Protestant faith, an increasing number of persons strongly desire to walk on the road of the sacred pipe once again.

The Catholic Mission of Saint Theresa Point is a clear illustration of this fact. This isolated community, about 350 kilometers north of Winnipeg, accessible only by air, is a strong Catholic community. Most of the persons living there have only a vague memory of the ancestral traditions. But in November 1988, a group of young laypersons took the initiative of inviting a Cree medicine man from Alberta for a workshop on the integration of native symbols in the Christian liturgy.

During his 1984 visit to Canada, Pope John Paul II seemed to have given the native people permission to undertake such a process by his own participation in a traditional native ceremony. The young people from Saint Theresa Point had not forgotten this important event. That's why they invited this medicine man, who was a Cree Indian like them and also a devout Catholic and a respected elder. With the help of this medicine man, the community seemed ready to get involved in a new enculturation process. It seemed ready to learn its own traditional Cree culture and religion.

But the message of the medicine man was sharp and clear. After he had stirred the emotions of the community in a variety of ways with his presentation of some basic teachings on the traditional Amerindian religious symbols, he told the people of Saint Theresa Point that the road of the sacred pipe was difficult and arduous. In fact, this road is nothing less than a spiritual way that must be known *and* practised. Native spirituality is based on personal discipline, sacrifice, meditation, and solitary prayer. Those who smoke the sacred pipe must be ready to live according to the values it represents. Smoking the pipe means entering into a personal convenant with the Creator.[24]

This brief journey into the land of the Lakota and the Cree has demonstrated that the theology of the sacred pipe is a very *inclusive* theology. In practising the ritual of the sacred pipe, the Amerindians place themselves at the very centre of the sacred circle of life. They enter into the presence of all the spiritual powers which the Creator makes available for their full development. This is exactly the reason why the theology of the sacred pipe is also a truly *dialogical* theology. It is the source of an inner dialogue with the spiritual powers which live in the Indians' sacred universe. It is also, often, the starting point of a new encounter between their traditional religion and Christianity.

3. Christ: the living and eternal pipe

The testimonies and reflections presented in the earlier sections of this chapter illustrate that the sacred pipe is indeed becoming a central symbol in the encounter between native spirituality and Christianity. We will now concentrate on the christological dimension of this process.

Symbolic comparisons and personal meetings

The encounter between the sacred pipe and Christ is not sheer coincidence. It has, to a large extent, been brought about by persons who have had the courage to transcend the limits of their own religious universe and to join others in a common journey toward the Great Mystery. It is not an exaggeration to suggest that this venture inaugurates a new phase in the evangelization of the North American native peoples.

From the native side, it involves the decision to "share their culture" with non-Amerindians. On the occasion of an important native gathering, the blessing of the Oldman River on the Peigan reserve in 1988, Peigan elder and spiritual leader, Joe Crowshoe, confirmed this viewpoint when he allowed non-Amerindians to watch as he performed the sacred pipe ceremony. "The world is changing. Now it is time for these things to be seen. It is important [...] You must not criticize another religion or another way. The Crees have their own way and the Blackfoot their own way. Even in other nations we all have the same thing. It is given to us, these ceremonial ways [...] I was told to pass the teaching on to you (the white) people. To love all people. I don't care who they are, we have to draw people together in unity and share the peace. And this is also important for whites."[25]

From the side of the Christian ministers and the churches, this new phase demands a willingness to develop new ways of socializing with the native peoples. It also means putting a definite end to the religious oppression that marked Christian missionary activity in the past.

We are witnessing the beginning of a new "dialogical" theology which certainly involves more people than those mentioned in the previous pages of this book. In fact, the sacred pipe represents a religious and ecumenical movement which is becoming so important that it could easily be the subject of a separate study. There is no doubt that missionaries like Steinmetz, Stolzman, Vandersteene and Hernou have played an important role in the birth and the development of this movement. But the real initiative belongs to the Amerindians themselves whose multiple and innovative theological intuitions regarding the place of Christ in their spiritual universe are forcing the Christian churches to abandon their traditional parochialism.

The history of the non-Christian peoples

The encounter of the sacred pipe and Christ offers us the opportunity to reflect on an important dimension of the Christian (christocentric) theology of salvation: the role of the history of the non-Christian peoples within this mysterious, universal economy. Because of the incarnation of God in the person and the concrete history of Jesus, Christian theology establishes a unique and indissoluble link between the church and the Old Testament, the history of the Jewish people to which Jesus belonged. Israel remains *the* people chosen by God to reveal himself to all peoples. It is therefore impossible to separate the figure of Jesus from the people of the Old Covenant. Theologically speaking, there is no justification for simply substituting the pre-Christian history of any other people for the history of Israel. But the Bible itself presents the particular history of Israel as the fundamental paradigm of universal history, i.e. the history of all the peoples. The election of Israel by YHWH is not an "exclusive" affair. The election and the covenant are the very starting point of God's special intervention in human history. This particular (biblical) revelation necessarily points to a divine Word that concerns all humankind.[26]

Therefore, it is, on the one hand, legitimate to maintain that the non-Christian peoples need the particular history of Israel, the chosen people, to interpret their own "pre-Christian history" with respect to the coming of Jesus, the Christ. On the other hand, it is equally legitimate to maintain that the Christian church, inspired by the universal message already contained in the Bible itself, must recognize that the "pre-Christian history" of the non-Christian peoples also leads to Christ.[27] The missionary church has the theological obligation to welcome this "pre-Christian history" of the peoples as a constitutive dimension of its own reflection on the universality of the Christ event, instead of rejecting it because of the special link with Israel. The church cannot forget that Jesus, an authentic Jew, did not hesitate to drink from the well of the Samaritans, despite the cultural and religious frontiers that separated him from that people.[28]

The history of the Christian missions in North America shows that the distance between Christianity and the native religions was as large as the distance between the Jews and the Samaritans at the time of Jesus. Jesus had the courage to bridge this wide gap. He went to Jacob's well and asked to drink from the water of the Samaritans, the water that symbolized their life experience, the history of their ancestors, their religious and cultural traditions. Would it be erroneous, theologically speaking, to compare the water of Jacob's well to the smoke of the sacred pipe? The gospel invites and encourages us to sit in the circle of the elders and to welcome their words and their history before we propose Christ to the Amerindians.

The "unknown Christ" of the Amerindians

The encounter between the sacred pipe and Christ invites us to consider a third theological intuition which flows spontaneously from the preceding one: the presence of the Christ in the history of the native peoples. The contemporary encounter between the sacred pipe and Christ could easily be understood to be in line with Paul's missionary intuition when he was meeting with the people of Lycaonia (Acts 14:8-18) and Athens (Acts 17:22-34). To the citizens of Lystra, Paul proclaimed that the God of Jesus Christ, the one who made the heaven and the earth and the sea and all that is in them, allowed all the nations to follow their own way, blessing them with abundant food and joy. To the citizens of Athens he proclaimed the name of the God they were already venerating. It is surely appropriate to postulate that the religious history of the Amerindian peoples contains prefigurations of Christ as significant as those found among Israel and the other biblical peoples.

The testimonies we have presented so far strongly suggest that it is impossible to develop an authentically Amerindian christology without a "Christian" reinterpretation of Amerindian history. This is an urgent and indispensable task that the Indians themselves will have to undertake, even though this implies a radical reversal of the spiritual journey imposed upon them by the church in the past. If we refuse to see how Christ was present and active among the native peoples *before* the arrival of the Christian missionaries, and *outside* the boundaries of the institutional church, the title *Amerindian Christ* will be nothing more than an empty slogan. The willingness to reorganize the connection between the sacred pipe and Christ is a decisive step in the right direction.

II. Possibilities and Limits of an Interreligious Dialogue

1. The Amerindians and interreligious dialogue

Twenty years after *Nostra Aetate*, the declaration of the Second Vatican Council on the church's relationship to other religions, the Pontifical Council for Interreligious Dialogue and the Congregation for the Evangelization of Peoples published an important document entitled *Dialogue and Proclamation* on the essential link between interreligious dialogue and the proclamation of the gospel.[29] This document unambiguously states that dialogue and proclamation, each in its own place, are component elements and authentic forms of the one evangelizing mission of the church (No. 2). This document contains three important elements which are significant for our research on the Amerindian Christ.

Three theological intuitions

The first part of the document (Nos. 14-33) presents a very *christocentric* approach to the other religious traditions and to intereligious dialogue. This theology reflects one of the oldest traditions of the church (Irenaeus) which places Christ at the centre of a universal history of salvation, and which views the cultural and religious experience of the peoples in a very positive way. The incarnation of God is seen as the centre of a universal covenant between God and all humankind. This theology is based on the universal trends of the Old Testament and on the universal mission of Jesus himself.

It should be noted that this very "traditional" theology had already provided the backbone of important Vatican II documents such as *Gaudium et Spes*, the Pastoral Constitution on the church in the Modern World (no. 22), *Nostra Aetate*, the Declaration on the Relation of the Church with Non-Christian Religions (no. 2), *Lumen Gentium*, the Dogmatic Constitution on the Church (nos. 16-17), and *Ad Gentes*, the Decree on the Mission Activity of the Church (no. 4). It can also be found in the most important writings of Pope Paul VI who in 1964 founded the Secretariat for Non-Christians (now called the Pontifical Council for Interreligious Dialogue), and in the writings of Pope John Paul II who in 1982 founded the Pontifical Council for Culture. All these documents invite us to discern how the Spirit is at work in the world before the final glorification of Christ, and how it continues to lead the peoples towards the fullness of the mystery, revealed and incarnated by Jesus of Nazareth.

The document thus proposes a positive approach of the other religions or religious traditions, based on theoretical research and the current practice of dialogue. Those involved in dialogue must remain sensitive to the spiritual and human values these religions represent and attentive to the answers they propose to the great questions of humankind. It is nevertheless important to note, in the second place, that the document presents a more extensive view of religions and religious traditions than we find in the Vatican II Declaration, *Nostra Aetate*.

While this declaration was mainly concerned with the great world religions such as Hinduism, Buddhism, Islam and the Jewish religion, the present document explicitly refers to the religious traditions of Asia, Africa and elsewhere (No. 12). This detail is very important. The Catholic Church now seems ready to recognize the authenticity and the legitimacy of the traditional, African, Asian and Amerindian religions among which she is, in fact, recruiting the majority of her new members. At the time of Vatican II, these religions were still referred to as paganism or animism.

These traditional religions were officially represented at the Day of Prayer for Peace at Assisi, on October 27, 1986. It was John Pretty on Top, of the Crow Nation from the United States, who represented the Amerindian religions. The sacred pipe ceremony was considered one of the highlights of this encounter.[30]

In the third place, the document establishes a close link between interreligious dialogue and the struggle for integral development, social justice and human liberation (no. 44). It recognizes the complex relationship between religion and culture (no. 45). These two elements are of immediate importance for this research. We have seen that religion is the real driving force of the current native cultural revival. The Amerindians remain spiritual or religious peoples. The present situation of the North American peoples is a potent illustration of what the declaration says concerning the tensions and the conflicts which often result from the coexistence of several religious cultures in the same milieu, and about the dehumanizing threat to which some traditional cultures are exposed because of modernity and the internationalization of human relations in the political and economic domaines (no. 46).

The particular situation of the Amerindians

Three factors make interreligious dialogue a particular challenge for the great majority of Amerindians: their membership in the Christian church, their socio-cultural situation, and the global context. In the first place, it is important to note that the majority of Amerindians belong at least officially to one or the other Christian church. This implies that for many of them interreligious dialogue becomes a kind of "inner dialogue," a personal effort to restore the link with their religious traditions which have never really died in their soul, but from which they have often been separated. We have quoted a certain number of testimonies which illustrate that this inner dialogue often represents a difficult struggle.

While many Amerindians want to remain faithful to the church, they now discover that she has often been an important instrument of cultural destruction. For them, there can be no inner dialogue without reconciliation. It is not surprising therefore that reconciliation was one of the major themes in the speeches of John Paul II to the native peoples of Canada in 1984. In his address to the Indian and Inuit peoples at Ste-Anne-de-Beaupré (September 10, 1984) he declared: "As disciples of Jesus Christ, we know that the gospel calls us to live as his brothers and sisters. We know that Jesus Christ makes possible reconciliation between peoples, with all its requirements of conversion, justice and social love. If we truly believe that God created us in his image, we shall be able to accept one another with our differences and despite our limitations and our sins."[31] In Midland (September 15, 1984), the Pope added: "This is truly the hour for Canadians to heal all the divisions that have developed over the centuries between the original peoples and the newcomers to this continent. This challenge touches all individuals and groups, all churches and ecclesial communities throughout Canada."[32] Finally, in his radio message delivered from Yellowknife (September 18, 1984), he repeated his message of forgiveness and reconciliation: "It is clear from the historical record that over the centuries your peoples have been repeatedly the victims of injustice by newcomers who, in their blindness, often saw all your culture as inferior. Today, happily, this situation has been largely reversed, and people are learning to appreciate that there is great richness in your culture, and to treat you with greater respect."[33]

In addition to the inner dialogue and the healing of the memory of those who have been hurt by the negative attitudes of the church towards their culture, another important dialogue is taking place at the local level in many local Christian communities about the integration of native symbols into the Christian liturgy.

The Pope's addresses also evoke the second element which must be taken into consideration: the socio-cultural situation of the native peoples within the North American context. The recent Roman declaration, *Dialogue and Proclamation*, recognizes the ambiguous role of religion with respect to cultures. Religions can be instruments of cultural alienation as well as sources of cultural reconstruction. What was the major role of the Christian churches with respect to the native peoples of Canada? We meet more and more Amerindians who openly accuse the churches of having been important agents of cultural oppression.

The famous "Oka crisis" in the summer of 1990 is but one example pointing to the urgent need for religious and cultural dialogue, in this particular case between the traditional Mohawks and the native or non-native Christians living on and around their territory. During a meeting organized by the *Centre de ressources pour la non-violence* in Montreal (September 1990), following this crisis, it was obvious that this dialogue remains very difficult because of the social, cultural and spiritual injuries the crisis caused.

Finally, there is also the global context of the ideological tensions surrounding the commemoration of the five hundredth anniversary of the "discovery" of the Americas by Christopher Columbus. This event should remind us that, though the evangelization of the Americas was the work of men and women who, generation after generation, transcended their own cultural limitations, it also caused the destruction of many native cultures because of the church's limited understanding of these cultures and because of her relationship with the colonial powers.[34] We wonder if in contemporary North America we are not on the threshold of a new evangelization which truly considers interreligious dialogue as a component of the church's mission. The question must be posed clearly because "the conflict between Indians and the rest of society [is] at its deepest level a religious confrontation."[35]

An invitation to interreligious dialogue

During the General Assembly of the Canadian Conference of Catholic Bishops in Ottawa, on September 12-16, 1983, Chief Harold Cardinal launched a vibrant appeal for interreligious dialogue. Cardinal, who was aware of the changes which had taken place in the Roman Catholic Church since Pope John XXIII concerning the church's attitudes to other religions, suggested the creation of a committee for formal dialogue between the Amerindian and the Catholic religions. He proposed a more formal approach to the challenge of interreligious dialogue and stressed its urgency in the present context of the struggle of the first nations for self-determination. It is urgent, he said, to put an end to our fears, our mutual mistrust and accusations, and to construct a better future with the help of the prayers we address to our common Father. He added that the real diversity of the prayers which he has given to the peoples in Canada must be respected.[36]

The Canadian Conference of Catholic Bishops responded to this appeal in a positive way by creating a committee which planned to meet with native elders in 1985. This meeting did not take place. Given the great variety of native cultures in Canada, a national committee may not have been the right approach. But the bishops understood that Cardinal's insistence on mutual fear and mistrust was not without foundation. Who is really ready, on the side of the Catholic church, to get involved in this type of interreligious dialogue? Who is ready on the side of the first nations?

2. The different forms of Amerindian-Christian dialogue

During an important meeting of elders from the United States, Mexico, Guatemala, Alberta and the North West Territories, which took place in Assumption, Alberta, in 1979, Peter Otcheese, one of the great spiritual leaders of the Cree, declared: "I do know, I have seen the day when the prayer of the Indians and the Catholic prayer will meet each other. When? I do not know. But those who pray according to the Indian way must ask the Creator that this day comes as soon as possible. And those who pray according to the Catholic way and according to the white way must ask the same thing."[37] Is this vision becoming a reality? What are the different forms of dialogue now developing between the native religion and Christianity? The recent Roman declaration, *Dialogue and Proclamation*, which had been preceded by another document published by the Secretariat for Non-Christians in 1984,[38] recognizes that, nearly everywhere in the world, we see four forms of interreligious dialogue, practised separately or together: (I) the dialogue of life, where people strive to live in an open and neighbourly spirit, sharing their joys and sorrows, their human problems and preoccupations; (II) the dialogue of action, in which Christians and others collaborate for the integral development and liberation of people; (III) the dialogue of theological exchange, practised by experts who seek to deepen their understanding of the different religious traditions; (IV) the dialogue of religious experience, practised by persons who share their spiritual riches with regard to prayer, contemplation, faith and ways of searching for God. Based on our own field observations since 1982, we are able to present the following tableau of the Amerindian-Christian dialogue.

The dialogue of life and action

Because of the non-institutional nature of the native religions, the Amerindian-Christian dialogue evolves primarily on the level of life and action. The majority of native communities which we have visited since 1982 are composed of traditionalists, Christians and many persons who easily move from one religious system to another. This astonishing coexistence is not easy. It creates tensions on the level of families and clans, even though religious dualism (see Part I of this book) is a well-accepted reality. The situation is made more complex by the fact that we find several Christian denominations in many native communities. The Amerindian-Christian dialogue is often handicapped by the divisions which the Christian churches have created in the native communities. In 1982, a medicine man from Saddle Lake, Alberta, told us: "What disturbs me most is that we have two cemeteries here on the reserve, a Catholic cemetery and a Protestant cemetery! How can we dialogue with people who want to remain separated, even in death?"

The Christian churches have often adopted a passive wait-and-see attitude of non-intervention with respect to Amerindians who pass with ease from one Christian denomination to another, or from the Christian religion to the native religions, and *vice versa*. They seem to lack a positive, pastoral message to assist their members in this spiritual journey. We have met many native persons who regret this lack of responsibility on the part of their church. A Dene woman from Assumption, Alberta, told us in 1982: "The Christian religion and the Amerindian religion look like a puzzle to me! How can I put the pieces of this puzzle together in my life? The only persons on whom I can count on for help are our own elders. They teach me by their example and by the stories which are transmitted from generation to generation."

The Amerindian-Christian dialogue, nevertheless, is becoming a reality in the life of many individual persons and small groups who strive for the integration of native spirituality and Christianity. One can therefore understand that the creation of a national committee (see above) had little effect, even though it reflected an urgent need for interreligious and intercultural education. More effective are the local initiatives which are emerging, for example, in Ontario, Alberta and British Columbia. The reports of the *Ontario Native Kateri Conference* (a Catholic organization) indicate that its dialogue focuses on the integration of native symbols into the Christian liturgy. In Alberta, occasional meetings between Catholic bishops and native elders deal with native spirituality in the context of the first nations' fight for their basic rights and their re-examination of the treaties.[39] In British Columbia and in the western part of the United States, the Amerindian-Christian dialogue is also associated with the quest for social and cultural justice.[40]

Since the 1970s, some of the major Christian churches in Canada have become important allies of the first nations in their struggle for basic rights through the Ecumenical Coalition, *Project North*, now called the *Aboriginal Rights Coalition*. This coalition created much ecumenical solidarity among the Christian churches themselves. Since its reorganization in 1985, the coalition has made a more consistent effort to work in partnership with the native people themselves and to pay more attention to native spirituality. On the level of life and action, the Amerindian-Christian dialogue often remains the initiative of Amerindians who have a bicultural and bireligious education, and of others who, though they have been separated from their native traditions, are now searching to reappropriate them with the help of elders and medicine persons.

The theological and pastoral dialogue

On the level of theological reflection and pastoral action, the Amerindian-Christian dialogue has not yet been able to mobilize the Christian churches of North America. The churches readily admit that they are still "moving toward dialogue."[41] They seem to find it difficult to get rid of their paternalistic attitudes vis-à-vis the Amerindians and to consider them real partners in dialogue.[42] Within this context, dialogue is often limited to discussions on the integration of native symbols into the Christian liturgy.

But there are also positive initiatives that deserve mention. We note, for example, that two major Catholic native organizations, the *Tekakwitha Conference* in the United States and the *Summer Institutes on Amerindian Christian Leadership* in Canada, pay more attention to native spirituality in their programs. Even though the main focus of these organizations remains the development of the

Amerindian Christian church, it is understood that this cannot be achieved outside the scope of dialogue with native spirituality. The same movement can be observed in centres such as the *Anishnabe Centre* in Espanola, Ontario, founded by the Jesuits, and *Kisemanito Centre* in Grouard, Alberta, founded by the Oblates. These two centres, which have been offering programs for the theological and biblical formation of Amerindians, also occasionally hold meetings with traditionalists. Only the *Centre Monchanin* in Montreal, now called the *Intercultural Institute of Montreal*, has been explicitly created to promote interreligious dialogue. It organized regular meetings with traditional Mohawks.

Among the more structured attempts at Amerindian-Christian dialogue are the *Rosebud Medicine Men and Pastors' Meetings* described by William Stolzman in his book *The Pipe and Christ*. These meetings took place between 1973 and 1979 and focused on the comparative analysis of the traditional Lakota religion and the Catholic religion. Stolzman mentions that he has always resisted referring to these meetings as "religious dialogue," even though the subtitle of his book speaks of *A Christian-Sioux Dialogue*. The objective of the meetings was to reflect on the religious synthesis already achieved by some of the medicine men. More significant, in this sense, is Paul Steinmetz's study on the religious identity of the Lakota of the Pine Ridge Reservation. He offers us probably the best examples of the "inner dialogue" that characterizes the spiritual journey of many Amerindians in North America. [43]

The dialogue of religious experience

This third form of dialogue is more in line with the experiential nature of the Amerindian religions themselves. In this perspective, the Amerindian-Christian dialogue often becomes initiation and participation in someone else's religious system.

Towards the end of the 1960s, a certain number of Indian chiefs and native Christian pastors initiated meetings on the relationship between Christianity and native spirituality. The first conference was held in Montana in 1970. Subsequent meetings took place near Morley in Alberta at the foot of the Rocky Mountains, on the traditional land of the Stoney Indians. John Snow, the well-known chief of the Stoney and an ordained minister of the United Church of Canada, was one of the great promoters of these meetings. Each year, a considerable number of Amerindians met at Morley to share their views on the Amerindian cultural and religious renaissance and on the mission of the Christian churches among the native peoples and to participate in traditional religious rituals.

This experience allowed many persons to see the basic accord between Christianity and Amerindian spirituality. John Snow confirms this viewpoint: "Our religion, the religion of this Great Island, is not contradictory to the teaching of the great rabbis of the Hebrews, nor is it in conflict with the great Christian teachers. Didn't Jesus say to the Pharisees: 'Other sheep I have which are not of this fold; them also I must bring, and they shall hear my voice; and there shall be one fold and one shepherd' (John 10:16). Didn't He say: 'In my Father's house are many mansions—I go to prepare a place for you (John 14:2).'"[44] The meetings in Morley brought together Christian pastors and traditional medicine men who were concerned with conflicts and conflict resolution between Christians and native people. This ecumenical movement gradually declined when the number of curious spectators started overtaking the number of those who really wanted to have a personal experience of the Amerindian-Christian dialogue.[45]

The meetings at Little Red River, Alberta, in which we participated between 1983 and 1987, are another example of dialogue on the level of religious experience. For five consecutive summers, these meetings brought together approximately twenty persons, mostly Catholic priests, who undertook a collective and formal training program under the direction of native elders in order to acquire a better understanding of Amerindian spirituality as it is experienced by native persons today. This initiative was a real first. Indeed, it was the first time that such a collective approach had been undertaken, at least in Canada.

The meetings involved the vision quest and other rituals such as the sweat lodge and sacred pipe ceremonies. Since most of the participants were or had been missionaries among the Amerindians in several areas of Canada, they adopted a rather "pragmatic" or practical viewpoint. They considered these meetings as a unique occasion to revise their missionary theology and to re-examine the missionary objectives of their church or religious orders. All this was done in a very experiential manner, mainly through new forms of socialization with native people and by participating in native rituals. But, very rapidly, the meetings focused on inculturation and interreligious dialogue.[46]

3. Amerindian contributions to interreligious dialogue

Religious dualism and integration

The religious situation of many Amerindians can best be described as religious dimorphism: the simultaneous or successive belonging to two religious systems. We have seen in the first part of this study that this situation does not result in the creation of independent churches, but that it is the source of a great variety of interactions on the level of personal religious experience. These interactions extend from the simple juxtaposition of the two religious systems to their almost complete integration.

In his study on the religious identity of the Lakota on the Pine Ridge Reservation, Steinmetz shows that the interaction of three elements (the Bible, the sacred pipe and Peyote) has produced five distinctive religious groups: the *American Indian Movement* (a cultural and religious movement), the *Body of Christ Independent Church* (a Native American church opposed to the traditional Lakota religion), the *Native American Church* (an independent church, composed of two subdivisions: *Cross Fire* and *Half Moon*), and two other groups, identified as *Ecumenists I* and *Ecumenists II*.[47] Those last two groups are of particular interest to this study, because they are models of the religious situation we have encountered across Canada.

The *Ecumenists I* group consists of Lakota Christians who have both Lakota and Christian identities, or a split identity. Steinmetz describes them as persons who have allowed the Lakota religion to find its maturity in Christ. He vigorously defends himself against William Powers and other anthropologists who see this movement as the result of "the religious imperialism" of the Jesuits, rather than the result of an internal evolution of the Lakota religion itself (pp. 177-180).

The *Ecumenists I* group contains the majority of the Lakota people who move back and forth between their Lakota religion (sacred pipe) and Christianity (Bible). Although their primary identity may be Lakota, their Christian identity is not superficial. Some have achieved a high degree of Lakota-Christian integration. The Lakota in the *Ecumenists I* group recognize common elements in the two religious systems, but they do not consider their Lakota religion as explicitly Christian. Those who belong to the *Ecumenists II* group, on the contrary, are persons for whom the Lakota religion has, indeed, found its maturity in Christ. They can therefore speak of a Christian Lakota religion based on the identity of the sacred pipe and Christ, or on Black Elk's identification of the Lakota *wanekia* (Saviour) as the Son of the Great Spirit himself (pp. 191-192).

Throughout this christological research we met Amerindians in all areas of Canada who could be identified, in Steinmetz's terms, as "ecumenists" who are striving towards the integration of Christianity and Amerindian spirituality. Some of these persons are involved in the development of a truly Amerindian church, beyond the present boundaries of the Christian denominations. Others would like to see the creation of an Amerindian rite within the Roman Catholic church. But most continue simply to search on the level of interreligious dialogue. Their contribution to this dialogue is twofold. In the context of the present struggle of Canada's first nations for self-determination, these individuals often represent the richness of a bicultural and bireligious life that sets an example for all those who want to develop new and positive relations with others, while maintaining their own cultural and religious heritage.

But in addition to this personal effort, there is an important social factor. It is certain that in Canada, as in many other countries, religions continue to fulfil a significant social function, despite the separation of church and state, and the impact of secularisation. Even though the churches have lost the prestige they enjoyed in the past, Christianity continues to influence politics and public life. The Amerindian religions, on the other hand, are experiencing a new awakening after a long period of oppression. The transition from religious oppression to interreligious dialogue is enormous and far from accomplished. But those who have demonstrated, primarily on the level of their personal life, that Christianity and Amerindian spirituality are not necessarily sources of division and racism can help make this transition. In fact, we do encounter an increasing number of persons for whom these two religions represent two "universes of meaning" whose interactions are significant and beneficial in a social context where, henceforth, the acculturation process is almost universal and inevitable.[48]

Amerindian ecumenism: an inner dialogue

An Amerindian prayer, inspired by the Lord's Prayer, begins: "I cannot say ... *Our*, if in my religion there is no room for the others and for their needs. I cannot say ... *Father*, if I do not accept them as brothers and sisters in my daily life."[49] This prayer reflects the fundamentally inclusive nature of Amerindian spirituality which incarnates a certain number of values of immediate importance for interreligious dialogue: freedom, tolerance, hospitality, and respect for the other. It is obvious that the Amerindians do not automatically possess these values. They acquire them in the course of their daily life, but often as the result of an inner dialogue with the global environment of creation, which constitutes the very core of their spirituality.

For many Amerindians, this inner dialogue has become difficult because of the enormous distortions of their natural environment. The forced acculturation to which they are submitted makes this inner dialogue and the dialogue with others more and more difficult. Yet, this situation has also given birth to the pan-Indian movement and to a native spirituality which is transcending the boundaries of the different tribes. Many Indian nations of North America have felt the need to meet each other on the deeper level of their spiritualities, precisely to resist the aggression of the acculturation process. William Powers describes this movement as "a system of truly ecumenical ideas" which is starting to have a universal impact. Not only in North America but even in Europe, Amerindian spirituality is beginning to capture the attention of those in search of the deeper meaning of existence.[50]

The Christian churches which often perceive the development of this pan-Indian spirituality as a threat for their own expansion have been slow in reacting to it. It is urgent to leave the idea of competition behind and welcome this new intertribal spirituality as an authentic partner in interreligious dialogue. The Amerindian effort to create a spirituality which strengthens the links between the different native tribes could serve as a model for other ethnic groups or peoples, elsewhere in the world, who are still the victims of this kind of religious war.

The future of the Amerindian-Christian dialogue

We have seen that the Amerindian-Christian dialogue operates better on a more personal and interpersonal basis than it does at the formally institutional level. This convincingly illustrates that spirituality remains the driving force of this dialogue. This is the message we received from many native elders and spiritual leaders in the course of this christological research. For them, the encounter between Christianity and their own native religion is not, in the first place, a matter of institutions and structures, but a meeting between persons with an authentic spiritual life. This does not, however, justify the restriction of this dialogue to the personal and interpersonal levels. The overall situation of North

America, which is shaped by secularization and a cultural and ecological crisis, calls for a more systematic approach to Amerindian-Christian dialogue, as Harold Cardinal suggested during the General Assembly of the Canadian Catholic Bishops in 1983.

But the Christian churches and the Amerindian peoples still face many obstacles. The time of fear may belong to the past, but the time of mutual confidence has hardly started. Right now, we find ourselves on a sort of threshold which confronts both sides with their mutual mistrust. On the one hand, the Christian churches must leave behind their traditional fear of syncretism and analyze this worldwide phenomenon more thoroughly. Marcello Zago noted that religious syncretism constituted one of the main challenges of the Day of Prayer for Peace in Assisi in 1986. They managed to avoid, he wrote, mixing Christianity with the other confessions, and the truth with error. But this important happening also illustrated the need for a Christian theology of religions which recognizes the values it shares with them and is willing to welcome their truth, while safeguarding what is specifically Christian.[51]

To participate in this movement, the churches of North America must cease to interpret the more recent developments within Amerindian spirituality (such as, for example, the Peyote cult, the American Indian Movement, the pan-Indian significance of the sacred pipe and other rituals) as *new religious movements* which fall outside of the scope of the present understanding of interreligious dialogue, at least from the Roman Catholic point of view. For the Roman Catholic church, interreligious dialogue is limited to what she recognizes as authentic and true religions.[52] This indicates, once again, that it is urgent for the Christian churches in North America to publicly affirm the validity and authenticity of the Amerindian religious experience, as it has evolved today, in order to welcome native spirituality within the family of the great world religions. Such a declaration could be modelled after the famous speech of Pope John Paul II to the aboriginal peoples of Australia in 1986.[53]

The Amerindian peoples, on their side, must cease to regard the Christian churches as unavoidable cultural aggressors who have no other objective than to destabilize their spirituality. They must welcome the 1987 pastoral message of the leaders of the major Christian denominations of Canada in which they expressed their readiness to conclude a "New Covenant" with the first nations.[54] We will refer to this message in the next chapter when dealing with the Amerindian theology of liberation.

Conclusion

The dialogue which is unfolding between the sacred pipe and Christ indicates that the Amerindian religious experience remains the main axis of our search for the Amerindian Christ. The analysis of the sun dance and the vision quest which we will present in the last chapter of this book will further confirm this viewpoint.

Yet, it is important to insist once again on the homogeneous character of the Amerindian reality. This is the reason why, in the next chapter, we will reflect on the significance of the Amerindian Christ, healer and liberator, for the present struggles of the Amerindian peoples.

CHAPTER VI

The Indian Road
to Salvation

Introduction

In this chapter we will continue our search for the Amerindian Christ by focusing on the doctrine of salvation or soteriological dimension of the Christic mystery. The Amerindians are a wounded people. Almost all the testimonies presented in this book reflect a deep need for reconciliation and for personal and collective healing. We will reflect on the place of Christ, as healer and liberator, in the Amerindian quest for identity and liberation, and in the multiple efforts to restore the social tissue of the native communities. In the first part of this chapter we will examine the relationship between Amerindian medicine and Christ. Is Christ perceived by the Amerindians as a healer or shaman? In the second part, we will present the basic characteristics of Amerindian liberation theology in relation to the struggle of the first nations of Canada for political self-determination.

I. Christ and Amerindian Medicine

1. The contemporary relevance of Amerindian medicine

In the first part of this essay we described the contemporary Amerindian renaissance while insisting, at the same time, on the precarious social situation of many native communities. The religious dimension of this movement will be further explored in this chapter in relationship with the figure of Christ as healer. For native people, religion and medicine form an indivisible reality to the point where Amerindian religion and Amerindian medicine have become interchangeable notions.

Amerindian medicine

It is important to insist that the rediscovery of Amerindian medicine is part of an international movement of protest against the contemporary evolution of technological medicine. Modern, technological medicine has become a highly specialized science at the very moment when people are discovering the importance of a holistic approach to healing. The traumas suffered by many persons as the result of technological civilization and the disturbance of their environment are more than physical evils. Their treatment requires that careful attention be paid to all the dimensions of an individual's existence: the environment, physical condition, psychological development, emotions, ethics and spiritual life.

In the treatment of any disease, the major challenge is the restoration of the integrity of the human person as individual and social being. This awareness has increased the contemporary relevance of the so-called alternative forms of medicine (natural medicine, therapeutic touch, chiropractic, acupuncture, shiatsu and so on) in reaction against modern medicine which has become too technological and impersonal.

Mention should also be made in this context of the development of many new religious movements whose orientation is often therapeutic or inspired by the philosophies of Asia. In 1973, it was estimated that there were at least 3,000 active diviners in the city of Paris alone![1] Despite the worldwide impact of secularization, the religious dimension of all these movements is obvious.

It is not surprising at all that, in the same context, many turn their eyes to the so-called primitive societies which, despite their global confrontation with the West and modernity, have maintained an holistic approach to the well-being of the human person and of society. Aylward Shorter, a well-known expert on Africa, wrote a fascinating study comparing traditional African healing techniques and the healing ministry of Jesus.[2] This study could serve as a model for a similar analysis of Amerindian medicine in relationship to Christ as healer and to the healing ministry of the Christian churches. The main objective of this chapter is to explore the basic orientations of such a study.

There is no doubt that healing was a central aspect of Jesus' ministry and mission. Jesus was using the traditional healing techniques of his time, including the exorcism of demons. We will reflect on the theological significance of his healing ministry. The therapies that were available in Jesus' own milieu can easily be compared with those still existing today in many parts of Africa and among the Amerindians. But a simple comparison of these therapies is not enough to elaborate an African or Amerindian christology or soteriology. We must insist that, while using the traditional therapies of his time, Jesus was also constantly concerned with magic, fatalism, and the link that people established between illness and sin. Jesus knew that there were different kinds of diseases and troubles, and that their treatment required an adequate perception of the global situation of the person. For him, the entire creation and the human condition as such are central parables of his mission—a mission aimed at the total well-being of the human person and of the world, here and now, and at the revelation of the kingdom of God.[3]

Shorter's book on African medicine and Christ illustrates that the western world can learn a lot from the non-western world on the relationship between humans and their natural environment, the meaning of suffering and death, and the social dimension of illness. A comprehensive study of Amerindian medicine is not yet available. Anthropologists and historians have hardly paid attention to the specifically religious or spiritual dimension of Amerindian medicine, despite the fact that Amerindian medicine has always evolved around shamans, medicine persons and traditional healers who can also be considered as the main ministers of native religion.

We have noted that the encounter between Christianity and native religion has not resulted in the creation of independent churches which, especially in South Africa, are called "Institutes of Healing."[4] This encounter, on the contrary, has resulted in a variety of syncretic actions, mostly outside the official structures of the church. The native prophets, medicine men and shamans who initiated these syncretic movements probably did not expect that the Christian churches would, one day, open their doors to dialogue with them. But, today, it is possible to meet Indian healers who are establishing positive connections between their healing ministry and the Christian understanding of salvation, inside or outside the structures of the church. Some medicine men, for example, have become ordained deacons or ministers. Others participate in Christian rituals of healing and reconciliation. Many have integrated Christian symbols into their traditional rituals. It is precisely the encounter with these "ecumenical" Amerindians which has stimulated, in part, this research on the Amerindian Christ.

The contemporary evolution of the healing ministry of these native spiritual leaders must be interpreted, in the first place, as a personal liberation from the spiritual prison in which they were kept captive by those who proclaimed the gospel to their ancestors. One wonders whether Pope John Paul II is not aware, at least implicitly, of the impasse in which the Catholic church finds itself with respect to the first nations, given the central importance of the themes of reconciliation, peace and intercultural collaboration in his 1984 speeches to Canada's native populations.

The calls for reconciliation, peace and intercultural collaboration have become crucial aspects of the church's universal mission in a world which is searching for meaning and unity.[5] This very fragmented world is the one to which the church continues to propose the gospel of Jesus as a gospel of liberation and to whom the risen Christ reveals himself as a "true medicine of life."[6] However, it has become more and more difficult to present the gospel of Christ as a road of salvation and as a source of liberation to the oppressed peoples, without encouraging them, at the same time, to drink from their own traditional wells. The example is set by Jesus himself.[7] In the following pages, we will look at the therapeutic value of Amerindian spirituality.

The sacred circle of life

In the course of history, the Amerindian peoples have developed a particular understanding of salvation, characterized by a global approach to the human person and to the universe. Reality is seen in its totality as physical, mental and spiritual. This *red road of salvation* has been transmitted from generation to generation through rituals and teachings which focus on the total well-being of the individual and the community, here and now, rather than on their ultimate destiny (eschatology). It seems that native soteriology developed this later dimension especially after contact with Christianity.

Today more and more Amerindians are asking themselves how to reconcile their Amerindian soteriology with the figure of Christ, the Saviour, who has been presented to them as the unique truth and as the unique road to fulfilment. This inner dialogue is strongly influenced by the concrete situation of the aboriginal peoples. Since the beginning of colonialism in North America, the native peoples have been exposed to radical cultural transformations. All the aspects of their life have been touched by the aggressive acculturation process dictated by western civilization.

Sometimes a people has to touch bottom before it reconnects with its vital sources. This is what happened to Canada's native peoples in the 1960s when many Indian communities were facing situations of almost total despair. Many Amerindians then reached the conclusion that the only way out was to go back to their traditional teachings and to restore the sacred circle of life by practising the ancient healing rituals once again.

Almost all the medicine men we met in the course of this research are involved in this vital process. Some have found Christ in their sacred circle of life and have given him a place in their healing rituals. Others compare their teachings with the teachings of Jesus and with the practical knowledge of their ancestors. But these comparisons are often put at a disadvantage by the official doctrine of the church concerning the absoluteness of Christ and the exclusive nature of Christian soteriology. Many medicine men struggle with the question of the relationship between Christ and the spiritual powers associated with *Wakan Tanka*, the Great Mystery. They ask themselves if the invocation of these powers during their healing rituals contradicts their Christian faith. Shorter notes that in periods of intense social transformation, certain African peoples personify the new, threatening situations in which they find themselves, and spontaneously look for extra-human and super-human explanations for the evils they are experiencing. "Bad spirits" can be seen everywhere! In periods of great social instability, the ordinary means no longer suffice to explain order and disorder, to control new diseases, and to re-establish a healthy climate.[8] This tendency can also be observed in some Amerindian communities. A certain return to magic is not excluded, at least on the level of popular perception.

But this does not eliminate the fact that the integration of traditional native medicine in the healing process of native individuals and communities is generally viewed as something positive and effective. This fact has been scientifically established by Wolfgang Jilek, a psychiatrist, and by his wife, Louise Jilek-Aall, a psychiatrist and anthropologist, who worked with certain native groups in British Columbia. Their research confirms the therapeutic value and the credibility of ancient rituals such as the spirit dance.[9] Almost everywhere in Canada the need for intercultural therapies, which take the Amerindian spiritual universe into consideration and involve medicine men, shamans and traditional healers, is recognized.[10]

Most native therapies are inspired by the traditional teachings of the medicine wheel, which is an important component of native spirituality. These teachings may vary from one native group to another, but the symbolism of the medicine wheel has become pan-Indian. The wheel or the circle represents the entire universe with all the spiritual powers or relations to which we can appeal for our harmonious development. The spiritual powers which are associated with the four cardinal directions of the universe, heaven and Mother Earth form the network of essential relations needed to enter into the circle of life. Certain native groups still personify these powers, often by associating them with animal spirits. For others, they simply constitute an ensemble of values, attitudes, skills and ways of behaving which allow them to live their life in harmony with all other living beings.[11]

The difference between these two perceptions (religious or secular) appears to be of secondary importance. Both recognize that the full realization of human life presupposes a real and universal solidarity. We will return to this important dimension of Amerindian spirituality in the next chapter dealing with the universal and the cosmic Christ.

From a theological point of view, we note that this Amerindian solidarity constitutes a challenging context for the Christian understanding of the communion of saints, an almost forgotten "article of faith" in western Christian tradition. The Amerindian spiritual universe could serve as the basis for a renewed approach to the Christian understanding of salvation because of its ecumenical and cosmic dimensions.

It would be totally wrong to identify this spiritual universe with magic. On the contrary, the Amerindians visualize the powers which are present in this universe as *free gifts* which the Creator makes available to them. These powers cannot be controlled as they are in magic but only asked for with an open mind. Finally, we have also met Amerindians for whom this universal solidarity is a sign *par excellence* of the universal salvation realized by the Creator in Christ and through the Spirit.

The ritual of the sweat lodge

The sweat lodge is without doubt the pan-Indian ritual which most effectively symbolizes the Amerindian spiritual universe. It is a ritual of reconciliation, and of personal and collective healing which is often practised in connection with other important ceremonies such as the sun dance and the vision quest.[12] We will complete these observations on native medicine with a short reflection on the symbolism of this ritual.

Like the sacred pipe, the sweat lodge has rapidly become an important component of the pan-Indian movement. For many Indian nations it is a source of spiritual nourishment and support in their political and social struggles. The sweat lodge is now part of many native healing programs.[13] It has been officially recognized by Correctional Service Canada which has been responsible for the federal prison system since 1985. Native inmates now have access to this ancient ritual as well as to the spiritual service of their own elders.[14]

The sweat lodge has even caught the attention of the ecological, feminist and New Age movements.[15] It has been adopted by some Christian Amerindians as the ritual expression of their reconciliation in Christ.[16] In fact, over the last years we had the opportunity to participate in several healing, reconciliation and thanksgiving rituals in the sweat lodge. Many of these rituals, in which the presider invited the participants to express themselves freely according to their own religious traditions, presented a rather unique blend of native and Christian symbols. Briefly, the symbolism of the sweat lodge is truly ecumenical and it is able to answer the spiritual needs of the widest possible scope of Amerindians.

The term "sweat lodge" itself is self-explanatory. The dome-shaped, hermetically closed circular little lodge is used for an intense sweat bath experience. Archeological research has revealed the circumpolar origin of this ancient ritual practised by many native tribes from Alaska to Mexico. The construction of the lodge itself is a ritual event. The lodge thus becomes a *sacred space* favoring communication and communion with the spiritual powers. The lodge is usually made of willow saplings which are forced into the earth and then interwoven at the top to form a dome encircled by four rings. Sister Eva Solomon reminds us that these four rings that shape the dome represent the four levels of knowledge beyond our world. Likewise, they bring to mind the four elements without which we could not survive: earth, water, air and fire, and the four races of humanity.

The lodge has four doors or small openings which correspond to the four directions of the universe. Only the eastern door is opened for humans to enter the lodge. The other three doors are never opened. They are the doors through which the spiritual powers enter when they come to participate in the ritual. To make the lodge air-tight and dark, it is covered with hides, blankets or canvas tarps. A little pit is dug right in the centre of the lodge to hold the stones that will be brought in. The participants sit in a circle around the hole in the middle of the lodge. The presider sits near the eastern door. He or she starts each round of prayer by pouring spring water on the rocks. He or she also invites the participants to pray or to express their intentions. A symbolic pathway leads from the door of the East to a little mound near the lodge on which are placed the sacred pipes which will be smoked at the end of the ceremony. The lodge symbolizes the universe, Mother

Earth, the maternal womb, while the little pathway between the lodge and the mound symbolizes the umbilical cord.

The ritual of the sweat lodge remains extremely sober. Like many other native rituals, it is easy to observe but difficult to explain. The ritual differs from one native group to another. The concrete procedures may also depend on the intentions of the participants (personal healing, reconciliation, purification, thanksgiving, revitalization of community or family), or on the instructions of the presider (total silence, meditation, songs, sharing of prayers). The very structure of the lodge suggests that the ritual can be seen as an experience of rebirth, which, almost spontaneously reminds Christians of the meeting between Jesus and Nicodemus (Jn 3:1-21).

The sweat lodge is a paradigmatic ritual which symbolizes a universal law of human existence and of the universe as such. There is no new life without death. The sweat lodge simultaneously evokes the finite limits of created existence, human transgressions and imperfections, and the universal capacity for pardon and reconciliation.[17]

The Amerindian path of purification is not just personal or collective, but also cosmic. The sweat lodge represents both the maternal womb and the universe (Mother Earth). In ritually experiencing their own birth, the Amerindians contribute to the renaissance of the human community and to the cosmos as such. By their own rebirth they contribute to the restoration of the universal sacred circle of life which is always threatened by the finitude and weakness of human existence. This is why this rebirth cannot occur without the help of the spiritual powers provided by the Creator. When leaving the lodge, at the conclusion of the ritual, the participants exclaim: *All my relations!* They again form a circle around the fire near the lodge and around the mound with the sacred pipes. But now they stand up. They are revitalized, renewed and regenerated. They have restored their vital link with the Great Mystery, themselves, other human beings and all other living beings of the universe.

2. Jesus of Nazareth: the wounded healer

In the course of this christological survey we noted that the figure of Jesus as healer and therapist appeals to many Amerindians because it corresponds to their cultural sensitivity and to their contemporary needs. This image appeals to those who are still struggling with their cultural identity as well as to those who are involved in the economic and political liberation of their people. Many native people seem to have no difficulty in identifying with the disciples of John the Baptist who posed the question to Jesus: "Are you the one who is to come, or are we to wait for another?" Jesus answers this question with a series of quotations from Isaiah which unequivocally illustrate his ministry as healer-therapist.

It is interesting to note that this passage can only be found in the gospel of Matthew (Mt 11:2-6) and in the gospel of Luke (Lk 7:18-23), while Mark offers us a very dramatic picture of Jesus as itinerant healer. In fact, it appears that Mark was rather unsatisfied with the image of Jesus as teacher that circulated in the Christian communities of his time.[18] We would like to support the Amerindians in their search for Christ as healer by presenting a short reflection on the healing ministry of Jesus.

The itinerant healer

The fact that Jesus was an extraordinary healer cannot go unnoticed. This fact has been confirmed by critical studies of the gospels. It is quite possible of course that Jesus himself did not read and comment on the text from Isaiah which Luke has placed like a kind of "program" at the beginning of his ministry (Lk 4:16-21). It is also possible that only two or three of Jesus' miracles which the gospels report are historical facts, and that all the others are the result of the literary genre of the times. But it cannot be denied that Jesus proclaimed the good news of the kingdom of God by healing the deaf, the dumb, the blind and the lame, by relieving the poor and the broken hearts, and by liberating the oppressed and the prisoners.

His gospel is truly a "gospel of liberation" that inaugurates a new epoque by presenting a new image of God: a God moved by compassion, a God capable of changing the human heart, a God who makes all things new. Throughout his ministry, God accomplishes his revelation by the triumph of goodness over evil in all its expressions. *Revelation* and *healing* are two inseparable aspects of Jesus' mission. Jesus offers his people a concrete experience of the humanity and the tenderness of God.[19]

From the beginning to the end, the gospels are characterized by a strong current of compassion even though the word *compassion* appears nowhere in the gospels. Jesus' power as healer-therapist resides primarily in his capacity to be with the afflicted and the oppressed, and to be shaken to the core by their suffering. The sight of the crowd without leadership fills his heart with pity (Mk 6:34). He is struck with admiration for the humility and the faith of the centurion whose slave he heals (Mt 8:5-13). He shares the sorrow of the widow of Nain (Lk 7:11-17). On the road to Galilee, he reaches out to the leper (Mk 1:41). When leaving Jericho, he opens the eyes of the blind (Mt 20:34). He is saddened by the hungry crowd which has followed him for three days without eating, and he teaches his disciples the value of sharing (Mt 15:32-39; Mk 8:1-9).

The gospels also present Jesus as a person with authentic human emotions: love, tenderness, anger, sadness and, above all, compassion. All these human emotions constitute the very basis of his total commitment to the realization of the kingdom of God. Profoundly moved and disturbed by human misery, Jesus commits himself to liberate his people from every form of anguish and suffering.

"For power came out from him," writes Luke (6:19), who, throughout his gospel, draws attention to the powerful actions of God which manifest themselves in Jesus. Jesus seems to be moved by a kind of energy which can activitate itself spontaneously, but of which he is truly aware (Lk 8:46). This energy, as we shall

The Wounded Healer
Stained-glass Window by Alex Twins
Photo: Aline Price, S.A.S.V.

see, literally explodes when Jesus, who, at least initially, saw his mission limited to his own people, meets with foreigners (the non-persons of his time).

The gospels present Jesus as an itinerant healer-therapist who looks, at least from the outside, like the other healers and shamans of his time. He adopts the same techniques as the other healers who were travelling along the roads of Galilee. He must have had the same global or multidimensional approach to illness which we still find today in many non-western cultures. But the gospels remain sober in the description of Jesus' medical practices. From the very start of his ministry, Jesus adopts a nomadic lifestyle, marked by detachment and solidarity with the poor. Nothing really spectacular: a little bit of saliva (Mk 7:33; 8:23); a slight contact with the sick person (Mk 6:56); almost no ritual formulas, incantations or invocations, only an occasional sigh (Mk 7:34). Therefore, we must not look for spectacular things when we try to compare Jesus with the Amerindian medicine men.

The power of faith

The sobriety of the gospel accounts of the miracles attributed to Jesus leaves no doubt about the basic intention of the authors of the gospels. They focus unanimously on the central aspect of Jesus' ministry: to show that, in and through the actions and the words of Jesus, God himself is at work, a God who liberates his people by the faith that he creates in them. Throughout the gospels, Jesus always follows the same pattern: faith leads to healing, not *vice versa!* Jesus does not seem to perform healings to stir up faith in his person. He calls those who are looking for signs and proofs an evil generation (Lk 11:29). He constantly revolts against the popular mentality that tries to manipulate God.

Jesus' healing activities are not the causes of faith. They are presented rather as the consequence of faith. Jesus always seems to count on the power of faith that is in his people as well as on the power of his own prayer: "Whatever you ask for in prayer with faith, you will receive" (Mt 21:22). "Your faith has made you well" is a refrain that runs through his entire ministry (Mk 5:34 par.; 10:52 par.; Mt 9:28-29; Lk 17:19; see also Mk 5:36 [Jairus]; Mt 8:13 [the centurion at Capernaum]; Mt 15:28 [the Canaanite woman].[20]

"Your faith has made you well" is for Jesus a provocative affirmation, especially when he speaks to non-Jews. But even for a Jew it was surely more appropriate to say "God has saved you," because "all things are possible for God" (Mk 10:27). But Jesus transforms this statement into "All things can be done for the one who believes" (Mk 9:23). This sublime transformation aims at two things: to let God remain God (one should not try to control this all-powerful God) and to call upon the internal dynamism of the human person, upon human confidence and responsibility. One cannot but acknowledge the therapeutic value of this approach, the most beautiful illustration of which is the story of the healing of the paralyzed man in the pool of Bethesda (Jn 5:1-18). Jesus did not laugh at the faith of the sick, blind or crippled and powerless in the Semitic or Greek healing gods who were associated with the moving waters of that pool. On the contrary, he was filled with admiration for the patience of the oldest one among them who had been disabled for thirty-eight years! Jesus simply tells him: "Do you (really) want to be made well? (Jn 5:6) ... (Then), stand up, take your mat and walk!" (Jn 5:8). The rapid disappearance of Jesus and the fact that the healed paralytic did not know the name of Jesus (Jn 5:13) are significant. It was from within himself that the old paralytic found the power to stand up ... but he could not have done it without the respect and tenderness which Jesus manifested towards him.[21]

Power-in-weakness

This comprehensive picture of Jesus as itinerant healer-therapist must be completed with a move towards the very centre of Jesus' mission. All the actions of Jesus, even his most powerful and marvellous ones, are inseparable from the mystery of the cross. The divine power which is at work in Jesus' life reveals itself paradoxically in the extreme suffering and poverty of the Son of God who dies on the cross for the salvation of the world. Jesus' entire life seems dominated by the mysterious theme of "power-in-weakness" which characterizes his approach to illness, human misery and death. We are confronted here with the paradoxical image of the wounded healer.

This is an unacceptable paradox unless we are able to see that Jesus himself understood his entire life as a *mission* and as a *gift* coming from the Father: "For I came down from heaven, not to do my own will, but the will of him who sent me" (Jn 6:38). Hans Urs von Balthasar clearly demonstrates that the entire life of Jesus must be understood as a totally receptive submission to the will of the Father, and as the faithful accomplishment of this will in virtue of a unique mission. At least, this is the general impression his disciples and their communities had of Jesus and it is the impression we find faithfully recorded in the gospels. They show us the unique configuration of Jesus' life as composed of three inseparable elements: the unique "claim" or "vindication" which radically separates Jesus from the Old Testament prophets and from John the Baptist (the famous "I sayings"); the real poverty of Jesus, expressed in his solidarity with the unfortunate ones, the sinners and the marginalized groups; and the radical "disappropriation" which forms a bridge between the first two elements, and which allows Jesus to hand over his life, unconditionally, to the Father so that the kingdom (God's glory or love) might come.[22] The entire life of Jesus can therefore be summarized in this one sentence: "While Jesus walks inevitably toward his own death, the Kingdom comes toward us, irresistibly."[23] Jesus' unique mission or project is to be totally at the service of the ultimate manifestation and realization of the kingdom through a commitment that requires the free gift of his life, and a relentless struggle against everything in this world that is an obstacle to its coming.

The Christian tradition has often felt uneasy about this paradoxical revelation. Sometimes, one finds an almost exclusive insistence on the mystery of the cross and of Jesus' death, as if dying were the only thing that Jesus had in mind! One often meets the image of a God who requires the death of his own Son—a theology focused on the notion of sacrifice in which divine vengeance seems to replace divine love. Are we really invited to believe in "a God who seemed to love suffering,"[24] a God who would find satisfaction in human misery? Jesus' Father is not the God of death but the God of life, the living God. He is not a God who loves suffering, but a God who commits himself faithfully with respect to the total well-being of the world he has created. In Jesus, this God revealed himself as someone who stands beside us in our daily efforts to combat all forms of evil and all the causes of evil. This is what Jesus himself was committed to when he freely gave his life for the salvation of the world.

In the gospels we do not find the image of a vengeful God. But the gospels do confront us with the disconcerting image of a "suffering" God. This God reveals himself throughout the entire life of Jesus, not only in the powerful and marvellous actions of Jesus, but also, paradoxically, in the scream of the one who dies on the cross, and in the silence of the one who descends into sheol—the "liturgical silence" of Holy Saturday.[25] It is therefore impossible to isolate Jesus' miracles and healing activities from the image of this suffering God. Jesus was not only an extraordinary healer, he was also a wounded healer.

3. Amerindian images of Christ as healer

"Each generation of Christians visualizes Jesus in response to its experience of faith and in relation to the sensitivities of its time. Each image of Jesus is therefore the result of a faith that searches to qualify its experience, and of desires which energize human consciousness in a positive way."[26] The figure of Jesus as itinerant healer fascinates many Amerindians. This figure is the example of an ascending christology which, inspired by the historical and spiritual experience of the man Jesus, enlightens the experience of women and men today. However, the diverse expressions and explanations given by native people to their faith in Jesus as healer (and liberator) often remain timid because many have been the victims of an evangelizing process that was characterized by a strong depreciation of their culture and religious experience.

Concrete experiences of salvation

Native languages, like the Innu language for example, are constructed around verbs. In languages of this type only concrete realities are perceived as things that happen. Affirmations such as "salvation comes" or "the kingdom of God comes," which constitute the core of the gospels, have no real meaning for the Amerindians if they are separated from the concrete figure of Jesus.[27] In fact, the Amerindians are much like the contemporary hearers of Jesus' message who experienced the coming of the kingdom through his concrete actions: the re-animation of the dead, the expulsion of devils, the healing of the sick, the support of the poor. Was this not the concrete answer that Jesus gave to the disciples of John? Amerindians love to visualize themselves in the biblical scenes and to experience personally the compassion that went out from the Jesus figure.

During the 1991 meeting of the *Native Pastoral Council* of the diocese of Thunder Bay, Ontario, dealing with inculturation and the central message of the gospel, we were able to observe that for many Amerindians salvation in Christ is experienced through the concrete transformation of their life and their community. The approximately sixty participants were invited to reflect on the questions: Who is Jesus for me? How do I experience "good news" in my life?

Group sharing on these questions revealed that the healing journey of many Amerindians is often composed of three elements. In the first place, it is a truly *personal* experience: a real meeting with Jesus in and through the brokenness and tragedies of one's personal or family life, in and through the traumatic confrontation with suicide and violent death, in the struggle against alcohol and drug abuse, but also in and through the human solidarity which is felt in these difficult situations. Secondly, it is also a *spiritual* experience. Amerindians like to pray and meditate; the Bible holds an important place in their life; the liturgies of the word and the eucharist are privileged moments of encounter with the Lord. This often leads, in the third place, to a *mystical* experience: encounters with Jesus in and through events which are apparently "insignificant," in and through dreams, visions and the splendor of nature.[28]

But, on the other hand, we also observed that answers to the question: "How do you encounter Jesus in your traditional ceremonies?" were more hesitant. Many participants had only a limited experience of these ceremonies because of their traditional, Catholic education. In fact, one of the objectives of these pastoral sessions is to promote dialogue between the Catholic faith and Amerindian spirituality, and to contribute to the restoration of the native cultural identity. But there is no doubt that the participants at the 1991 session welcomed the central message of Jesus in a very personal way and that they are becoming the agents of their own evangelization. Their faith is focusing more and more on the concrete image of God that Jesus proposed to his own contemporaries.

This is a significant evolution compared to what we observed during our 1982-1983 field research on the emergence of the Amerindian church. It was not unusual then to meet Amerindians who were unable to establish a link between God and love. During a meeting in April 1983 with a group of Amerindians in Beauval, Saskatchewan, a very Catholic environment, God was visualized, not as loving, but principally as a God of fear whose primary function was to punish human beings. The following testimony by a native mother serves as an example: "The missionaries never told us that God was good for us. The only thing I remember from my religious education is fear and hell. It was only on Easter Sunday that we heard of a God or a Christ who saves. The rest of the year, it was hell! Since I did not read the Bible during these years (it was forbidden), I did not know better. But, about two years ago, this changed. I started attending the Alcoholic Anonymous meetings and I discovered how God is really present in the others, just like he was present in the life of Abraham and other biblical figures. I started reading the Bible and the new catechism used by my children at school. I discovered the God of love!"[29]

Such a discovery corresponds to the basic objectives of Jesus' own mission. During most of his ministry, Jesus fought against the distorted images of God which were circulating in his day. He revolted against that "evil generation" that was imprisoned in its legalism and that saw nothing but sin. He revolted against the "religious terrorism" of the Jewish magisterium. He fought against the fatalism that was the opposite extreme to confidence in God. He saw that the simple people were often tormented by this attitude. This is why his entire mission as healer-therapist aimed at the triumph of faith and hope over this fatalism that had invaded the hearts of the poor, the sinners and the sick. Albert Nolan writes: "Anyone who thinks that Jesus' *motive* for performing miracles of healing was a desire to prove something, to prove that he was the Messiah or Son of God, has thoroughly misunderstood him. His one and only motive for healing people was compassion. His only desire was to liberate people from their suffering and their fatalistic resignation to suffering. He was deeply convinced that this could be done and the miraculous success of his efforts must be attributed to the power of his faith. Nor did he think that he had any monopoly over compassion, faith and miraculous cures. What he wanted to do most of all was to awaken the same compassion and the same faith in the people around him. That alone would enable the power of God to become operative and effective in their midst."[30]

Beedahbun: first light of dawn

A very beautiful illustration of Jesus' battle against fatalism can be found in the stations of the cross of Anishnabe painter Leland Bell in the church of the Immaculate Conception on the Indian reserve of West Bay, Manitoulin Island, Ontario. We will also refer to this work of art in the next chapter when we deal with the cosmic Christ. But, first, it is important to note that, for this native artist, Jesus is "the great healer who brings peace."[31] Bell had first refused to paint the stations of the cross. Faithful to the basic orientation of his own culture, he had chosen not to paint subjects filled with suffering and pain. The stations of the cross posed a particular challenge to him. They were filled with suffering and sorrow. He wondered how he could express this symbolically while remaining faithful to his own native vision. How could he reconcile the violence of the cross with the non-violence of native spirituality? He found the answer to this question in the mystery of God as love: "I found the balance in Love. With the stations it was a great time of healing, a great time of purification. That's my cultural perspective. But it was a great time of healing for people then as well as now. A time of cleansing, of people reaffirming their commitment to their Creator. It was Peter who denied Jesus three times. It wasn't just the Jews who crucified Jesus, it was the Christian people too."

Each station of the cross is shrouded in an atmosphere of profound serenity, harmony and simplicity to balance out the inevitable violence of Jesus' journey to death. Bell's paintings come from vision. Painting the stations of the cross was truly a spiritual experience for him, a sort of vision quest, an experience of communion with the Creator.

Bell decided to add a fifteenth station to the way of the cross, entitled *Jesus Abitchiba* (Jesus Risen From The Dead), the mystery that renews itself every morning when the sun rises. Bell himself comments on the fifteenth station: "Early in the morning at dawn you pray to greet the day. You announce your name, who you are and who you are praying for. Then supposedly at dusk when creation stops you announce your prayer again and your prayer is heard. You praise again and you stand still again ... All of creation is being purified. It wasn't just the cleasing of sin, but it was also the cleansing of all life. It wasn't necessary for the people at that moment to understand or to know the meaning. His resurrection shows it was for all people and all centuries. The important thing is what was provided. Life. We always celebrate his life. We can't celebrate death. What we celebrate is life!"[32]

Other native artists have made similar efforts to reconcile Christianity with native culture. In the Catholic church on the Indian reserve of Hobbema, Alberta, one can admire fourteen stained-glass windows with biblical scenes and native symbols. For the people of Hobbema, God is Indian! Jesus is shown wearing tight, neat braids when he meets with his disciples. However, in the crucifixion scene, Jesus hangs from the centre pole of the sun dance lodge; his eagle feather is broken and his hair is wild.

Native artist Alex Twins, who created this work, has often been criticized for portraying Jesus as a persecuted Indian. But Twins believes that the Bible stories speak to native people because many of them have experienced the same hatred and discrimination as Jesus and his people. Natives can identify with the sufferings of Jesus. Twins likes to portray Jesus with braids, the eagle feather and sweet grass or other sacred herbs which are often used during healing rituals. He wants to show that native spirituality and Christianity are not that far apart. His art is a form of reconciliation between the two religions.[33]

Christ: a shaman?

Jesus is considered by many native people as a great medicine man or as the most powerful of all "medicines." We have seen that this perception of Jesus is the result of both a better understanding of the Bible and of the reaffirmed role of medicine men and women in contemporary native communities. The theological and pastoral implications of this new appropriation of the Christ figure are not yet fully perceived, although they stand in sharp contrast to the traditional images of Christ proposed to the Amerindians by the missionary churches.

Yet, the history of Indian missions in North America shows that, from the very start, the native peoples were fascinated by the figure of Jesus who could easily be compared to their own cultural heroes, especially because of his capacity to communicate with the world of the spirits. But this initial perception of the Christ figure faced two major obstacles.

In the first place, there was the confrontation between Christianity as institutionalized religion and the shamanic religion of the Amerindians, the classical confrontation between the priest and the shaman.[34] The priest would gradually neutralize the shaman. Since he would from then on assume the functions performed by the shaman before his arrival, he avoided focusing on the shamanic dimensions of the Jesus figure out of fear that the Amerindians might return to their paganism. In fact, the main objective of the Christian mission was to replace the native pagan religion with the true religion of Christ.[35]

The second obstacle was the close connection between the Christian missions and colonialism. This would eventually lead to the perception of Christ as too powerful a medicine, a medicine capable of eliminating the traditional medicine of the Amerindians. It is in such a context that we normally see the birth and development of the religions of the oppressed and syncretic movements.[36]

Even today, Christ is still perceived by some Amerindians as too powerful. In 1985, for example, we met a young native man in a remote village of northern Ontario who feared that communion in the body and blood of Christ during the eucharistic celebration on Christmas day might eliminate the spiritual powers which he had received during a recent vision quest and which had helped him to reconstruct his life.

Even though, according to Shorter, Jesus *"was* a sort of witchdoctor,"[37] the appropriation of Christ as medicine man or shaman remains somewhat problematic. In Asia, Africa and Oceania, some Christian churches use Jesus' global or multidimensional approach to healing as the basis of new pastoral methods,[38] but hesitate to translate the Christ mystery into shamanic or traditional healing categories.[39] But, as far as North America is concerned, we are convinced that shamanism offers us excellent possibilities to develop new christological intuitions.

The type of shamanism that developed among the native peoples of North America is so flexible that the terms "shaman," "medicine man" and "healer" have become interchangeable. Most of the time, however, the term "shaman" refers to persons who can communicate with the spiritual powers, while the terms "medicine man" and "healer" designate those who practise traditional healing methods.[40] The widespread development of the vision quest, the traditional fast and vigil which allow communication with the spiritual powers, may also have contributed to a kind of "democratization" of North American shamanism (see the next chapter).

Native people also continue to discover that their own spiritual universe resembles the biblical universe. Consider, for example, the dreams and visions which are sources of divine revelation, or the world of spiritual powers evoked by Paul in relation to the lordship of Christ. Amerindians see that Jesus himself experienced a kind of vision quest in the desert at the beginning of his ministry. They notice his nomadic lifestyle as well as the "initiatic" structure of his entire life, his "inner light," his capacity to assume the sufferings of others in his own body, his ability to leave this intermediate world in order to descend into the underworld (sheol) or to ascend to the upperworld (heaven). All these elements confirm the shamanic quality of Jesus' life and they should encourage the Amerindians to visualize Christ as shaman, medicine man or healer more openly.[41]

A detailed analysis of Amerindian shamanism is beyond the scope of this study.[42] We are only interested in finding out how the native appropriation of Christ as shaman can contribute to a better understanding of the relationship between Christianity and native spirituality, and to the redefinition of the Christian mission among the Amerindians. Two significant points must be considered in this context. The first concerns the struggle against the fatalism and magic which are frequently instruments of oppression and which often characterize popular religion.[43] It would be naive to think that native religion totally escapes this danger. Belief in bad medicine (sorcery or magic) is still very much alive in the native communities.

In this sense, a positive evaluation of Jesus' ministry as shaman and healer may help Amerindians and others to free themselves from any form of fatalism involving natural, historical or supernatural powers which constitutes a kind of spiritual slavery. The good news of Jesus always implies a radical valorization of personal responsibility and human solidarity as roads leading to the kingdom of God. In fact, many Amerindians have told us that their faith in Christ was the best remedy against bad medicine!

The second intuition concerns the specific mission of the shamans, the priests and prophets. The Judeo-Christian tradition has often accentuated the role of Jesus as priest and prophet to the detriment of his role as shaman and healer. While the priest, as the science of religion demonstrates, is understood to be the one who manipulates religious symbols, the shaman has the capacity to experience the sufferings and the liberation of his people in his own body. This is exactly what Jesus did as he "was handed over for our trespasses and was raised for our justification" (Rm 4:25). This *pro nobis* (for us) of the Letter to the Romans and the other Pauline letters can be understood as the very core of the most primitive understanding of the Christian mystery of salvation.

There is nothing magic about all this! In carrying our sins, Jesus does not take away our freedom and responsibility. On the contrary, he radically confronts us with the very limits of human freedom and with the depth of human responsibility by accepting to die and to rise for us, in order to make our own death and resurrection possible.[44] Could the shamanic valorization of Jesus' ministry not help us to come to a better perception of this mystery of the "Christic substitution" through which the new covenant accomplishes itself? This question will be considered further in the next chapter.

II. Towards an Amerindian Theology of Liberation

1. Evangelization and liberation

Among the many challenges Canada is now facing, the issue of the basic rights of the first nations has become the most pressing because of its political, juridical and social implications. In the following pages we will concentrate on the theological significance of this native rights issue especially for those who reflect on the future of the Christian churches in native North America. We will first define the historical, geographical and cultural boundaries of this question in continuity with what we have already said about the native reality in the first part of this book. In light of this analysis, we will then reflect on the possibilities and limits of an Amerindian theology of liberation.

The basic rights of the first nations

The basic rights of the first nations, in particular their right to govern themselves, present one of the most urgent and complex questions dominating the public scene in Canada over the last twenty-five years. Until the middle of the 1960s this question hardly figured on the agenda of the Canadian people and their politicians. The two "founding peoples" of Canada, the French and the English, could quietly study their history and plan their future without the Indians who had been conquered by their ancestors and whose descendents were surviving on the periphery of the larger Canadian society in full economic expansion. This situation changed rapidly and dramatically. The native rights issue has now become a matter of increasing interest for the media, academics and political institutions.[45] It is not easy to determine exactly when this reversal occurred. Many national and international factors may have contributed to it. But, as we have seen, mention must be made, in the first place, of the extraordinary vitality of Canada's first nations themselves. The native peoples' unexpected return to central stage has demonstrated that the native cultures are truly *contemporary* cultures which want to contribute to the political and economic future of Canada on their own terms. The concepts of political assimilation and cultural integration have gradually given way to the concepts of political self-determination and collective native rights.

It is important to recall briefly that the aspiration of Canada's first nations to political autonomy is part of an international movement which aims at the protection and development of ethnic identity and the language and culture of the native peoples of the western hemisphere. In the early 1960s, the leaders of these peoples convinced the United Nations that their particular interests were not met by programs designed for Third World peoples. It was a Shuswap Indian from British Columbia, George Manuel, who therefore suggested the term "Fourth World" to designate the legitimate but dispossessed peoples who had become the "internal colonies" of nation states such as Canada and the United States of America.[46]

Since its creation in 1867, Canada has borne the marks of a kind of "original sin" whose tragic consequences can be observed even today.[47] Canada wanted to develop itself *without* and *despite* the peoples who had been living in North America for thousands of years. While it recognized the collective rights of its two "founding peoples," the new Canadian state simply forgot or put aside the aboriginal peoples. The collective and specific rights of these peoples are nevertheless enshrined and constitutionally protected by all the official laws by which Canada became an independent state.[48]

So what, then, is the problem? The major problem, up to now, is that successive Canadian governments have consistently lacked the political will to define the nature and content of these aboriginal or native rights. Canada's first nations have been systematically maintained in a situation of political, social, economic and cultural dependency (the notion of internal colonies is perfectly justified!) which is the primary cause of the cumulative human misery that can be observed in many native communities across Canada. The greatest Canadian challenge today is, therefore, to help the first nations to get out of this dependent situation by offering them the means to manage their own future, so that they can contribute, in their own way, to the establishment of a new social project that respects the cultural particularities of all the peoples who now live in Canada.

The historical and theological foundations

Before discussing the possibilities and limits of an Amerindian theology of liberation, we must briefly consider the historical and theological foundations of the aboriginal rights doctrine. There are three sources which explain the origin and the evolution of this doctrine in the legal documents of Canada.

First, it is important to note that the aboriginal rights doctrine or aboriginal title (territorial rights) is a right *sui generis* that finds its origin in the colonial policy practised by the British Crown towards the peoples and countries it had discovered, invaded or conquered. Originally, the doctrine was nothing but a collection of unwritten laws concerning the status of these peoples within the British Empire, their territorial and customary rights, and their institutions. The British Crown was willing to respect these rights to the extent that they did not enter into conflict with common law and the sovereignty of the Empire.[49]

One finds a reflection of this doctrine in the *Royal Proclamation of 1763*, the basis of the first Canadian constitution, the *British North America Act* (1867). The purpose of this doctrine was to protect the first nations against the settlers who had established themselves in North America. But, at the same time, this policy made the Amerindians totally dependent on the British government. This is to say that, for the first nations, there was no freedom unless they accepted the sovereignty of the British Crown and the Canadian state which succeeded it in 1867.

Although the new Canadian state itself wanted to get out of the colonial sphere of Great Britain, it created its first *Indian Act,* the law which applies to all those who are officially recognized as native people by the Canadian government, in 1876. This law would gradually transform the first nations into "internal colonies," totally dependent on the federal government.

Between 1871 and 1921, the Canadian government also signed eleven treaties with different native groups who were living in large territories with rich natural resources. The exact meaning and the enormous impact of these treaties is still a matter of political and juridical dispute. But while the *Indian Act* transformed Amerindians into minor citizens, the treaties suggest that they were indeed members of independent nations with real negotiating power vis-à-vis the Canadian government.

The second source of the aboriginal rights doctrine is international law as it developed after the "discovery" of the Americas by Christopher Columbus in 1492. This global event had several philosophical, theological and political implications. A new place had to be found, first of all, for the peoples of this New World in the great human family whose unity served as the foundation for the universal mission of the Catholic church and for the expansion of Christian civilization.[50] A doctrine had to be created to legitimize the colonial enterprise of the European empires and to determine their rights and those of the native peoples of the Americas. Once it was declared that these peoples were truly human beings who could be civilized and Christianized, the debate rapidly focused on whether infidels or pagans enjoyed territorial rights *(dominium)* and, if so, whether they had reached the degree of civilization required to exercise these rights.[51]

Jurists and historians recognize that figures like Bartolome de las Casas, Francisco de Vitoria and Pope Paul IV played an important role in the development of international law. But it must be noted that these key figures of the sixteenth century were largely dependent on a juridical debate which had started in the Middle Ages and which opposed Pope Innocent IV and Henri de Segusio, better known as Hostiensis.[52] Innocent IV held that, according to natural law, all rational beings, pagans as well as Christians, enjoy property rights and that they have the right to govern themselves. Hostiensis, on the contrary, maintained that the pagans did not enjoy these rights. His famous doctrine *"extra ecclesiam non est imperium"* (outside the church, no territorial rights) prevailed over Innocent IV.

The jurists and theologians of the sixteenth century had to cope with this heretical doctrine (a kind of political donatism) and also with Aristotle's philosophical doctrine of natural slavery. The application of this doctrine to the Amerindians had the effect of transforming them into inferior beings to which natural law did not apply. At the same time, it was obvious that the Catholic church was gradually losing its power and influence over the modern monarchies and their expansionist dreams. The new law of the nations gradually replaced natural law in the management of international affairs. Despite all the philosophical, theological or legal arguments used by the jurists and the theologians of the sixteenth century to defend the rights of the native peoples of the Americas, their discovery and conquest were accomplished facts. According to the prevailing ideology of the time, the Amerindians were inevitably perceived as inferior beings who were incapable of having rights, whether human or divine!

The aborignal rights doctrine, in the third place, is founded on the millennial experience of the native peoples themselves. Canada's first nations have been making two important contributions to this doctrine. Certain native groups insist on the spiritual dimension and on the divine origin of these rights. They maintain that the sovereignty of a people over a given territory comes from the Creator himself, who allows that people to live on that territory and to protect it. This vision can be compared with the Christian "divine right" doctrine of the Middle Ages, except for the fact that the native peoples do not have a pope to whom the Creator might have delegated his powers! According to other native groups, the aboriginal rights concept directly derives from the native peoples' presence, "from time immemorial," on a given territory. According to this second vision, these rights include not only fishing and hunting rights, but also the economic, political, social, cultural, and religious rights which the first nations possessed before the arrival of the Europeans. That is why we speak, in this context, of "inherent rights," rights which do not depend on any kind of foreign legislation. Many Amerindians are convinced that they have never ceded these inherent rights, despite the treaties they concluded with the European nations. According to them, these treaties were nothing more than "peace and friendship treaties," concluded between independent nations in view of their harmonious coexistence.

Evangelization after 1992

The debate on the role of the Catholic church in the Spanish and Portugese conquest of the sixteenth century and on the implications of its evangelizing mission among the Amerindians has been very polemical. The quincentenary commemoration of Columbus' "discovery" has stirred profound emotions on both sides of the Atlantic. It is certainly impossible to ignore that this discovery led to a "human—biological, cultural and spiritual—tragedy to which the whole American continent was reduced by the civilizing system of the West, made up of domination and exploitation, ethnocentrism and racism, economic colonialism and religious proselytism."[53]

But it would be wrong to think that all these things belong to the past. The International Conference of the Non-Governmental Bodies of the United Nations on Discrimination Against the Indigenous Peoples of the Americas held in Geneva in 1977 declared: "The representatives of the indigenous peoples made clear to the international community how discrimination, genocide and ethnocide were being carried out. Though the situation varies from country to country, its roots are common to all: they include brutal colonisation to open a way for the sacking of their lands and their natural resources, since commercial interests operate for the sake of maximum profit; the massacre of millions of natives over the centuries and the continued appropriation of their lands, depriving them of the possibility of developing their own resources and livelihoods; the denial of self-determination to indigenous peoples and nations, with the destruction of their systems of values and social and cultural structures. The situation clearly shows that this oppression is continuing, and its results are expressed in the destruction of the indigenous nations."[54]

A document prepared by the Mission Department of CELAM describes the human tragedy of the Amerindian peoples as one of the most important challenges that the church's evangelizing mission faces. This document establishes a close link between *inculturation* and *liberation*, two inseparable dimensions of evangelization. While the term "inculturation" confronts us with the mystery of Christ's presence among the peoples whose cultures contain the seeds of his gospel, the term "liberation" reminds us that this poor and crucified Christ is also on the side of the oppressed peoples who struggle for their basic rights. "The poor and crucified Christ wants to come into the light, grow and rise; he wants to join the despised and oppressed communities with him in his resurrection."[55]

This poor and crucified Christ can also be met among the Indian populations of Canada. Even though their situation can be described as less tragic than that of the native peoples of Latin America, Canada's first nations remain dispossessed, oppressed and marginalized peoples. This is why a link must be established between the aboriginal rights doctrine and this search for the Indian Christ. The aborginal rights doctrine is at the very centre of the historical relationship between the first nations and the rest of the Canadian population. The recognition or the rejection of these rights is crucial for the future of the native peoples.

How does Christian theology react to this situation? We will try to answer this question by adopting the perspective of liberation theology. We will ask ourselves what happens to liberation theology, which originated in Latin America, when it is applied to the North American native peoples' struggle for their basic rights.

2. Native people and liberation theology

According to Vine Deloria, Jr. (Dakota Nation), one of the best-known North American native writers, liberation theology seems no more than the latest "gimmick" to keep minority groups circling the wagons with the vain hope that they can eliminate the oppression that surrounds them. Liberation theology, he maintains, does not seek to destroy the roots of oppression, but mainly to change the manner in which oppression manifests itself. The root of the problem is the submission of the Amerindians to a western worldview from which they are, in practice, unable to separate themselves. Liberation theology too easily assumes that the common experience of oppression is sufficient to mobilize and unify minority groups in their sruggle against the dominant society. By placing all these minority groups under the same theological heading, liberation theology risks overlooking their specific claims, and obstructing their profound transformation and real liberation.[56]

This judgment may seem exaggerated, but it certainly is in line with the critical analysis of liberation theology by some Latin American theologians themselves.[57] Deloria, who received a solid juridical and theological education while being raised by a family of Episcopalian ministers, clearly points to the fact that once liberation theology has left Latin American territory, it can easily become one theological system among others, instead of remaining a theological movement that originates in, and develops from, the grassroot communities.

When he appeals to the old Indian saying, "The White man has ideas ... the Indians have vision," he seems to suggest that the particular contribution of the Amerindians to liberation theology must be situated on the level of critique of the ideologies which command the present evolution of the world and the universal mission of the church. We would like to show that these contributions do in fact connect with the basic orientations of liberation theology itself. The evolution of liberation theology within Latin America clearly indicates that the main challenge is not to construct a new theological system *for* the poor and the oppressed, but the practice and understanding of Christian faith *within* a world of oppression and *in communion with* the struggle of the oppressed for liberation.[58]

God of liberation and God of conquest

The first contribution of the Amerindians to liberation theology deals with its biblical foundations: the exodus and the covenant stories with their image of a liberating God who chooses the side of the oppressed and the poor, the non-persons, and transforms them into his chosen people and leads them to the promised land. The appropriation of these biblical symbols by the Amerindians constitutes an enormous problem. They rapidly discover that their situation very much resembles the situation of the aboriginal Canaanite peoples who were conquered by Israel with the help of a God who ordered them to abstain from any social relations with these peoples and commanded them to destroy the aboriginal religions.

The biblical story, adopted by liberation theology, does have two sides. It is a story of liberation and a story of conquest.[59] The Amerindians, who received the Bible from the Europeans in exchange for their land (an ironic statement often heard in native North America), soon discovered that the biblical God of liberation is also a God of conquest. They cannot set their own liberation in motion without telling the whole biblical story and without knowing that, when they became Christian, they were asked to adore the God of the peoples who invaded their land. Amerindians learn to read the Bible with the eyes of the Canaanites!

It is important to draw a line between what happened historically and the biblical accounts of the historical events. What matters here is not the comparison between the historical events of the conquest of Canaan and the conquest of the Americas, but the religious symbols which legitimize these conquests and the religious symbols which mobilize the oppressed in their struggle for liberation. The results of the historical-critical research on the real relationships between Israel and Canaan do not erase the narratives as recorded in the Bible.[60] These stories can be read today by the peasants of Solentiname, the members of Brazil's base communities or the Indians of North America. In fact, one of the basic characteristics of liberation theology is to read the word of God in connection with the concrete situation of the people, the poor and the oppressed. But the situation of these groups is far from identical. In its contextualized reading of the Bible, each group must find the mechanisms which allow it to distinguish the symbols of oppression and the symbols of liberation within the biblical narratives.

This is precisely what Robert Allan Warrior of the Osage Nation, United States, has done. In applying the biblical narratives of the exodus and the covenant to the particular situation of the North American native peoples, he invites us to place the Canaanites at the very centre of the interpretation of these narratives. Amerindians who believe in the Judeo-Christian God and who would like to adopt these narratives as the foundation of their liberation, must seriously consider all the violence which these narratives contain. According to Warrior, we must learn to listen to the ignored voice of the Canaanites, if we want to apply liberation theology to the North American native peoples. He even suggests that it might be better for native people to look elsewhere for their vision of liberation, justice and peace. Maybe, for once, he writes, we will just have to listen to ourselves, leaving the gods of this continent's real strangers to do battle among themselves.[61]

In making his assessment of liberation theology, Warrior may have underestimated its historical evolution. Since the CELAM Conference of Medellin (1968), the political landscape of Latin America has changed dramatically. Liberation theology now focuses more on the symbol of captivity than on the symbol of the exodus and the entrance into the promised land.[62] It also concentrates on the true powers of liberation which are present in the peoples and the human groups who remain oppressed or exploited. Because of this important evolution one should not be quick to ignore liberation theology's ability to offer an analysis of the situation of global dependency in which the North American native peoples find themselves.

Another native theologian, William Baldridge (Central Baptist Theological Seminar), agrees with Warrior that the native Americans are the Canaanites of the biblical narrative. But he also reminds us that there is another narrative in which this forgotten people play a central role: the story of the meeting of Jesus with the Canaanite woman who comes to him and begs him to heal her child (Mt 5:21-28; Mk 7:24-30). This story is no less symbolic than the exodus and covenant narratives. At the beginning of this story, Jesus identifies himself totally with the destiny of his own people, Israel, out of faithfulness to the mission he has received from his Father: "I was sent only to the lost sheep of the house of Israel" (Mt 15:24). He even refuses the status and dignity of a human being to the Canaanite woman: "It is not fair to take the children's food and throw it to the dogs" (Mt 5:26). But the woman continues to challenge Jesus and to request his service as healer until the very moment when Jesus liberates himself from his exclusive link with Israel and from the commandment of his Father. What happens next, Baldridge writes, is a miracle! The real miracle which produces itself in this narrative is perhaps not, in the first place, the healing of the child of this pagan "non-person," but the transformation of Jesus' mind and heart.[63]

This transformation can be compared to the one proposed by Jesus himself to Nicodemus (Jn 3:1-21). For Jesus it is like a second birth and a second baptism. While his first baptism in the river Jordan confronted him with his own people's misery and desire for salvation, his encounter with the Canaanite woman and the other non-Jewish figures in the gospels urges him to assume personally the message he addresses to Nicodemus. God, his Father, does not love only Israel, but the entire world (Jn 3:16-17).

As far as the Canaanite woman is concerned, the story does not tell us if she became a disciple of Jesus or if she continued to venerate her own gods. We will come back to some of the theological and pastoral implications of this story which, quite obviously, invites the Christian churches to examine whether the God they continue to propose to native people is truly a liberating God—a God who, like Jesus facing the Canaanite woman, is liberated from any form of racism, sexism and imperialism; a God who allows himself to be transformed by the peoples who encounter him and who still want to count on him for their liberation and their integral development.

Artisans of their own liberation

Liberation theology is constituted by theological reflections and social practices which allow non-persons to become once again the artisans of their own history. Segundo, however, has observed that liberation theology oscillates between two tendencies. The first tendency considers the poor as the *object* of a theology which analyses their oppression and proposes channels of liberation. The second tendency sees people as the *subject* of their own liberation and theological reflections.[64] Gutierrez affirms that: "Even the poor have the right to think. The right to think is a corollary of the human right to be, and to assert the right to think is only to assert the right to exist (...) The right to engage in theological reflection is part of the right of an exploited Christian people to think."[65]

Since the 1930s we have been accustomed to interpret this movement as a "sign of the times" or as a manifestation of the salvific presence of God among his people.[66] This theological interpretation of history, with its profound biblical and patristic foundations, had an enormous impact on the Second Vatican council. We must ask ourselves if such an interpretation of history can be found among those who are involved in the Amerindian revitalization movement which we have analyzed in the first part of this book.

This revitalization movement is clearly transforming the native people into artisans of their own history. But despite this fact, their situation can still be described as one of global captivity and dependency. This is the meaning of a powerful dream shared by a young native woman of Norway House, Manitoba, during the first Native Convocation of the Anglican Church of Canada in Fort Qu'Appelle, Saskatchewan, in 1988. In her dream, Rose Evans saw a beautiful eagle feather, symbol of Amerindian leadership, coming from the sky. She did not want it to touch the ground. She was going to catch it. But, all of a sudden it was pulled up. She heard voices laughing, and looked up. It was the white people. They were controlling this feather. She could see the strings. And her people were trying to get the feather. They were crying. But they were controlled by white society. And whatever the white people wanted, it happened. Because they had this feather.[67]

This dream captures the central aspect of the first nations' struggle for liberation better than any historical or political analysis. The eagle is the symbol of power and clear vision. The dream shows without any doubt that the only power now possessed by the first nations is the one ceded to them by the dominant society. It is the dominant society which continues to control the vision which native peoples have of themselves and their place within Canada. This is the real tragedy of Canada's Indians, the dark side of their history.[68] The churches have told them that their religion was evil. The governments have despised their social, juridical and political institutions. Their subsistence economy has collapsed under the pressure of the excessive economic demands and technological developments of the dominant society. They receive the crumbs that fall from our table.

White Canadian society is scandalized when it sees the annual budget of the federal government's Department of Indian Affairs and Northern Development, and when it witnesses the ongoing failure of its assimilation policy. This failure is acknowledged, but almost nothing is done to entrust the first nations with the responsibility for their own destiny. For those who observe this situation with the eyes of a theologian, the symbols of captivity and exile are certainly more appropriate than the symbols of exodus and covenant.

While the figure of Christ as healer appeals to many Amerindians across Canada, especially medicine men, we were able to observe that few Indians perceive Christ as liberator. This figure, which has been put forward by theologians like Leonardo Boff, Jon Sobrino and Claus Bussmann in the context of Latin America, is almost totally absent from the North American native scene.[69] There seems to be a certain divorce between the Christian faith of many Amerindians and their socio-political commitments. We have seen that their experience of Christ is above all personal, spiritual and mystical. The focus is on interior liberation (the liberation, for example, of the victims of alcohol and drugs) and on social liberation (the victims, for example, of family violence), rather than on political and economic liberation. The native peoples are aware of the fact that their dependency is caused by national and international, oppressive structures. But only a small minority establish an explicit link between their faith in Christ and this situation.

Integral liberation

Vine Deloria writes that true liberation requires a paradigmatic shift on the level of the worldview that has dominated our life for almost two millennia: "Liberation, in its most fundamental sense, requires a rejection of everything we have been taught and its replacement by only those things we have experienced as having values."[70] This succinct statement reminds us once again of the fact that the present confrontation between Canada's first nations and the dominant society is not just a political and economic issue, but a truly spiritual debate. It is a confrontation between two worldviews. On the one side, we have native spirituality, a metaphysics of nature that must adapt itself, and is willing to do so, to the modern and contemporary historical conditions. On the other side, we have a fragmented western civilization whose Judeo-Christian messianism has been largely replaced by secularized, political and economic soteriologies, dictated by the law of the most powerful. On the one side, a world to discover and respect. On the other, a world to conquer and exploit. We observed in the second chapter of this book that the greatest distances separating the native peoples and the other populations in Canada are not the immense geographical spaces of the North, but the cultural perceptions of their development.

An Amerindian approach to liberation theology may help us to understand that the Amerindians are becoming the "Good Samaritans" whom western civilization desperately needs to heal its self-inflicted wounds caused by its obsessive desire for progress and its disproportionate taste for material comfort. Let us be aware that with the disappearance of each native culture in our contemporary world we are losing an important dimension of our own human experience. Every time the fundamental rights of native peoples are violated, we do violence to our own existence.[71] Indeed, one of the great strengths of the Indian peoples and other aboriginal peoples lies in their interior communion with the archetypal world of the collective consciousness. This is manifest in their capacity to explore the intuitive, affective and mystical dimensions of the human mind and in their use of the symbolic power of dreams and visions. The Indians have managed to maintain and to develop this capacity of communication which the western world has largely lost because of its exclusive emphasis on the rational process and the phenomenological ego. But the western world is now discovering that it is exactly because of their capacity to communicate with the deepest levels of existence that the Indians have been able to do a better job than we do of absorbing the inevitable shock of cultures.[72]

Vine Deloria is right when he maintains that the western world has constantly produced new ideas but that it has never questioned its basic worldview. The new ideas have simply replaced the old ones within a framework of interpretation that has virtually remained unchanged for almost two millennia. We have seen, for example, that natural law was replaced by the new law of nations after the "discovery" of the Americas. But the West has hardly been able to free itself from its Eurocentric perception of the world. Christianity has become a world religion. But it has not really been able to free itself from its Middle Eastern and Mediterranean cultural ties. In such a geopolitical and georeligious context, it is rather easy to understand why Christianity continues to be seen by many Amerindians as the religion of the oppressor and why this perception constitutes an enormous challenge to the Christian churches when they try to develop new relations with the aboriginal peoples of North America.

3. A new covenant

In February 1987, on the eve of the last constitutional conference on aboriginal rights, the leaders of the main Christian churches published a declaration, entitled *A New Covenant*. This pastoral message focused on the constitutional recognition and protection of the basic rights of Canada's first nations: the right to be considered as distinct peoples, the right to have an adequate landbase, and self-government. Those who signed this document considered this constitutional conference as an historical and critical moment for concluding a new covenant with Canada's first nations and for doing something concrete in view of their full participation in the future of Canada.[73] This declaration was the follow-up of another small document, entitled *"You can contribute to write the next chapter in*

Canadian history," published by the Aboriginal Rights Coalition (Project North) in 1984.

We will conclude this chapter by asking ourselves what such a contribution implies for the Christian churches in Canada.

Inculturation and liberation

The native appropriation of Christ as healer or liberator demands, in the first place, that we define the concept of *liberation* with respect to the concept of *inculturation* which we have adopted as the key notion for this study of the Amerindian Christ. Contemporary missiology often leaves the impression that the strategy of liberation better suits the Latin American church, while the concept of inculturation or indigenization corresponds more to the cultural sensitivities of the African, Asian and Amerindian peoples. Therefore, it would appear that "liberation theology" belongs to Latin America, while the other parts of the Third and the Fourth World should develop a "theology of culture." The difficulties involved in applying liberation theology to the Indians of North America, as we pointed out earlier, seem to confirm this classification, at least on the level of the missionary strategies of the Christian churches.

But this opposition between liberation and inculturation loses its significance when we place ourselves on the level of a truly ecumenical theology which visualizes Christ both as a liberator and as the one who accomplishes the culture of those who welcome his gospel. The term inculturation focuses more on the mystery of Christ as the accomplishment of human destiny, while the term liberation points to the cultural transformations which may result from the encounter with the gospel. Therefore, it is legitimate to consider liberation theology and the theology of culture as the two complementary sides of a contextualized theology that affirms the universal meaning of the Christic mystery.[74]

The application of liberation theology to the North American native scene remains an enormous challenge. We must not forget that Amerindian cultures have remained so-called "primitive" cultures in which the religious factor determines all aspects of life. The Amerindian peoples have remained spiritual or religious peoples. For liberation theology, this situation poses a real dilemma. This is clearly illustrated by the attitudes of the Latin American liberation theologians vis-à-vis popular religion with its syncretic blend of Christian, African, Amerindian and aboriginal beliefs. There is no doubt that this popular religion is often a source of oppression, fatalism and alienating images of God. At the same time, popular religion remains the religion of millions of people who are members of a type of Christian church (Christendom) which remains closely associated with the political and economic powers of Latin America.

Certain liberation theologians are, therefore, convinced that they must first promote the secularization of these so-called primitive cultures and popular religion in order to create a basis for their authentic evangelization and liberation. But they realize that their secularization attempts may eventually lead to the radical transformation or the destruction of these cultures. "Secularization, mercantilism and the despoilment of land lead practically to a direct destruction of the (Amerindian) community and of the presence and action of God in that community."[75]

The church claims the right to evangelize all peoples and all cultures. She proposes the gospel as a gospel of liberation. But does she have the right to participate directly or indirectly in the radical transformation of cultures? The church recognizes that evangelization must respect the cultural identity and evolution of a people. She cannot, of course, ignore the religious dimension of the native cultures. The evangelization of these cultures requires that the church commit herself to fight against all the oppressive powers which maintain the Amerindians in a situation of global dependency (the axis of liberation theology), and that she respect the traditional religious experience of the Amerindians (the axis of inculturation).

We are well aware that this new approach to evangelization presupposes a critical look at the theology which legitimized the church's mission in the past. Liberation theology presupposes the liberation of theology itself, while inculturation requires that those who are involved in this new approach to evangelization be willing to undertake a journey which is marked by spiritual detachment and be ready to leave their own cultural perceptions behind in order to discover how Christ is present in the life that people lead.[76]

The requirements of partnership

It is also important to insist on the development of a true partnership with the Amerindians within the Christian churches themselves. More than any other kind of church members, native people have been considered as "objects" of the pastoral and missionary action of the church. Finding themselves most of the time at the receiving end, they have had almost no possibility of putting their cultural values and spiritual gifts at the service of their own Christian communities. The Christian churches must stop thinking of the first nations as their "missionary territory" and welcome them as peoples who have achieved a high degree of spiritual maturity. A group of native persons in Winnipeg observed: "After more than a century of bringing Christianity to native people, however, most pastoral agents are still non-native. Sometimes we still refer to our churches in native communities as 'missions.' The local mission compound is usually set apart from the native community's life. This 'apart' is where the non-native pastoral agents live, and frequently they are self-sufficient. The non-native Church does not seem to need the native church. The non-native church seems to be there because it is bringing something to the native people, not the other way around. The non-native church continues the white dominance and the white interpretation of the native experience."[77]

Since we started this christological research, we have witnessed an increasing interest in the development of a specific native pastoral approach and in the creation of a truly Amerindian church. But so far the efforts hardly go beyond the pre-Vatican II strategy of adaptation. Despite everything that has been said about inculturation over the last few years, most churches seem afraid to submit themselves radically to the law of incarnation and to participate in the transformation of a world where millions of people are struggling for survival. The true evangelization of this world—the proclamation of the gospel as a message of liberation and accomplishment—is impossible without decoding human history in order to denounce what makes no sense in this history. One of the things that makes no sense in Canada is the long socio-political history of assimilation to which the Amerindians have been subjected by all the Canadian institutions, including the churches. The churches cannot participate in the native peoples' struggle for liberation and in the development of an Amerindian theology of liberation unless they let go of their attitudes and their strategies of assimilation. They must adopt a truly intercultural approach which publicly affirms the validity and the authenticity of the Amerindian cultural and religious traditions.[78]

Partnership postulates a certain number of concrete social attitudes and practices which appear to be more and more urgently needed in the Canadian context: the struggle against the latent forms of racism which manifest themselves every time the first nations claim their rights[79;] the struggle against the negative stereotypes of the Indians which the dominant society has interiorized, sometimes unconsciously, since the beginning of conquest;[80] adequate information and education of the Canadian population concerning native rights and the real situation of the first nations.[81] However, it would be unjust not to recognize the work already accomplished by the churches in this field since the mid-1970s.

Memory, penance and commitment

Dom Fragoso insisted before the Fourth CELAM Conference, which was held in San Domingo in 1992, that we must leave room for those who have the courage to reflect on the evangelization of the Americas according to the schema "memory, penance, commitment": "... we must have a correct memory of what has happened, without triumphalism, and recognize what was good and what was bad. We must recognize that the crushing of the civilizations that were here is a crime called genocide ... and we must do penance. The entire church must do penance, because she has been guilty. And then, we must commit ourselves to work again with all those who were trampled, but whose cultures have resisted and survived..."[82]

What about the application of this schema to the North American scene? During the World Assembly of the First Nations, held in Regina, Saskatchewan, in 1982, Bishop Remi de Roo of Victoria, B.C., acknowledged that the Christian churches have much to be forgiven for because of their past attitudes and actions vis-à-vis the first nations: "It is my hope and prayer that by forgiveness and mutual reconciliation we can develop attitudes of trust which will enable us to learn together from our experiences and to build bridges for more beneficial collaboration as we fashion the world of tomorrow."[83] The churches should avoid developing a guilt complex that simply deplores their missionary past. They must, however, have the courage to ask the aboriginal peoples for forgiveness if they want to conclude a new convenant with them.[84]

It is indeed impossible to isolate completely the historical relationship which has developed between the churches and the first nations in Canada from the attitudes and the strategies which, elsewhere in the world, caused the political, cultural and religious oppression of the aboriginal peoples. Are we ready to recognize that what happened elsewhere may also have happened here?[85]

The Canadian churches cannot conclude a new convenant with the native peoples unless they recognize that, as institutions, they have consciously participated in the destruction of the aboriginal cultures, despite the authentically evangelical commitments of many of their members, ministers and missionaries. The participation of the churches in the liberation movement of the first nations presupposes their own liberation and purification from their "original" and historical sin.

Conclusion

In this chapter we focused on the figure of Christ as healer and liberator. The appropriation of this Christ figure by the Amerindians is an important dimension of the dialogue which is developing between Christianity and native cultures. These cultures continue to be profoundly religious cultures which are concerned with the integral development of their members. The fact that the application of liberation theology to the situation of the native peoples of North America raises some questions, especially on the level of the biblical foundations of this theology, does not mean that it is impossible to propose the gospel of Jesus as a gospel of liberation to the Amerindians. But we must acknowledge the shadow that falls on the figure of the Amerindian Christ because of the past negative attitudes of the churches with respect to the Amerindian cultures and religious experience. We will show in the next chapter that the Amerindians are capable of transforming this negative history into a positive experience by offering Christ a place in their most important religious rituals.

Tree of Life
Painting by Blake Debassige
Photo: Anishnabe Spiritual Centre

CHAPTER VII

The Universal Christ

Introduction

During this christological research we found that the Amerindian visions of Christ often focus on the historical person of Jesus. This general impression can be deduced from many testimonies. Jesus is visualized by many Amerindians as a true companion who supports them in their daily struggles. They speak about him in a simple and direct way. They love to situate themselves in the gospel narratives which are read in a contextual manner. But we want to conclude this study by showing that this Amerindian christology is not limited to the discovery of the historical person of Jesus. It also contains powerful intuitions of the universal meaning of the Christic mystery.

In the first part of this last chapter we will show that the Amerindian eco-theology is part of the contemporary effort to construct a planetary theology which maintains an intrinsic link between the mystery of creation and the mystery of redemption. The figure of the cosmic Christ will serve here as the main reference. In the second part, we will continue the reflection we started on the relationship between the sacred pipe and Christ. We will present two other important native rituals, the sun dance and the vision quest. For some Amerindians these pan-Indian rituals have become unique forms of meditation on the place of Christ within their spiritual universe.

I. The Challenge of a Planetary Theology

1. Christ and creation

More than a decade after Vatican II, Karl Rahner observed: "Theologically speaking, there are three epochs in Church history, of which the third has only just begun and made itself observable officially at Vatican II. First, the short period of Jewish Christianity. Second, the period of the Church in a distinct cultural region, namely, that of Hellenism and of European culture and civilization. Third, the period in which the sphere of the Church's life is in fact the entire world."[1]

This new and almost unexpected situation represents a unique challenge for theology, in particular for christology. Even though Christianity, more than most other religions, has managed to implant itself in almost all parts of the world, we must admit that its theological reflection on the salvific meaning of the Christ event remains strongly dependent on western thought. But the further we are in time and space from the historical event of Jesus, which is the foundation of the Christian faith, the more we must reflect on its universal meaning in terms of the particular cultural situations of those who welcome the gospel today. We must also reflect on the international movements of our planet. We need a theology which is both contextualized and planetary, observes Tissa Balasuriya (Sri Lanka), to account in depth for all the dimensions and the implications of the Christic mystery.[2] In the context of this study on the Amerindian visions of Christ we would like to insist briefly on the fact that this type of theology invites us to reconsider the link between creation and redemption in Christ.

The limits of western theology

The new cross-cultural situation in which Christianity finds itself today allows us to assess more accurately the limits of its western incarnations. With the exception of orthodoxy, classical western theology is characterized by a separation between redemption and creation. This separation is not a fortuitous thing. It is the result of a long historical evolution in which three outstanding thinkers have played a major role: Augustine, Thomas Aquinas and René Descartes. Their works are representative of the general pattern of western theology when it reflects on the role of Christ with respect to redemption and creation.

The theology of Saint Augustine (354-430) seems largely dominated by the biblical narrative of the fall and by the doctrine of original sin. Augustine looks at creation primarily as a fallen reality or as a state of corruption, separated from Christ. Christ enters into history in view of another and totally new creation, the city of God, of which the church is the sign. In this Augustinian perspective, theology focuses almost exclusively on soteriology, the doctrine of redemption, and ecclesiology, doctrine of the church as sacrament of salvation. There is practically no room for a theology of creation or a positive reflection on the original beauty and goodness of creation, and on Christ as the accomplishment of this divine mystery. Augustine was strongly influenced by the philosophy of Plato for whom the abstract world of ideas prevailed over the concrete, material world.

One of the great achievements of Saint Thomas Aquinas (1225-1274) was that he "baptized" the philosophy of Aristotle and put it at the service of theology. This philosophy offers a solid basis for a more positive reflection on creation. But Thomism remains characterized by a sharp distinction between two orders of reality: the order of nature, God's creative work, and the order of grace, God's redemptive work. Contrary to Augustine, Thomism was able to develop a theology of creation in which nature is not visualized as something corrupted by sin, but as a reality which is finite, precisely because it is created by God. But in this Thomistic perspective, the doctrine of creation developed as an autonomous theological treatise which did not account for the role of Christ in the creative work of God.

René Descartes (1596-1650) completed this historical evolution that is characterized by Augustine's unilateral insistence on redemption and by Thomas Aquinas' distinction between the order of nature and the order of grace. Everything that comes under nature (material objects) from now on becomes the field of the modern sciences, while philosophy focuses on human beings as thinking subjects, and theology on their eternal salvation. The implications of this compartmentalization are multiple. It allows each specific science to develop autonomously and to determine its own field of research. It also inaugurates the end of the unified or synthetic type of thinking that was a hallmark of the West.[3]

This large picture of the evolution of western theology explains to some extent the opposition which has developed between the scientific vision of the world and the Christian interpretation of history and the separation between the cosmos and God. Western theology has become increasingly "a-cosmic" while western cosmology has become increasingly "a-theological." Gérard Siewalt rightly observes that this evolution of western thinking results in a theology without cosmology and in a scientific cosmology without theology: on the one side, a God without cosmos and, on the other, a cosmos without God.[4] There has been a divorce between nature and history. Nature has become the exclusive domain of scientific thinking, while history is interpreted as a "history of salvation," the locus of the interventions of God in favour of humankind.

Western systematic theology, especially in its Protestant expressions, has strongly accentuated the theology of history to the detriment of the theology of creation. According to Claus Westermann, this is largely due to the fact that, since Luther, the Greek term *soteria* has been translated by the Latin term *salus* and the German term *Heil*. These translations have produced a radical change in the biblical understanding of God's salvific action. In the Old Testament, this action is not limited to the special interventions of God in the salvation history of his chosen people, but also includes his presence and interventions in its pre-history (universal history) and in nature.

In the Old Testament, God's salvific action or blessings means both a condition or situation of integrity and accomplishment, and a deliverance. In western theology, however, the term salvation has been gradually reduced to the special liberative and redemptive interventions of God in the particular salvation history of which the church is the sign and sacrament. God's salvific action has been reduced to one of its dimensions.[5] At the same time, we also observe a certain spiritualization and individualization of salvation in which God is seen as the saviour of souls. This stands in sharp contrast to the Pauline and Johannine meditations on the cosmic and universally historical dimensions of the Mystery (Eph 1:9) of which Christ is the centre.

The implications of this reduction of the biblical understanding of God's salvific action are enormous. We observe, for example, that Christian theology has been rather silent about the ecological crisis. It seems unable to produce a truly theological and christocentric assessment of this planetary phenomenon. We do not seem to have a truly Christian ethics for the cosmos that would help us determine the responsibilities we have for its well-being.

It is also important to note that the radical separation between God and the cosmos in western thinking is also at the origin of a series of other dualisms or separations which have profoundly influenced Roman Catholic and Protestant theology: cosmos-history, nature-grace, body-spirit, profane-sacred, world-church, individual-society, man-woman. This evolution has been analysed and assessed by theologians like Paul Tillich and Karl Rahner.[6]

This Platonic-Cartesian dualism and its political or ideological use by churches which continue the western incarnations (or captivity) of their theology has been rightly criticized by feminist and Third World theologians. Tissa Balasuriya vigorously denounces the ethnocentric orientation of this traditional theology which is culture-bound, church-centred, male-dominated, age-dominated, procapitalist, anticommunist, non-revolutionary, overly theoretical and bereft of social analysis.[7]

The biblical foundations

The separation established by western theology between creation and redemption stands in sharp contrast with the biblical understanding of the salvific work of God in Christ and through the Spirit. A careful reading of the Old Testament reveals that, even though the canonical text of the Bible starts with two creation narratives, the mystery of creation is not the beginning or the centre of Israel's faith. Israel discovers the mystery of God as creator in and through the experience of the proximity of God in its history. The experience of God as liberator and saviour leads the chosen people to the revelation that its God is also the creator, the God of heaven who governs the world and who is also the God of the other peoples. In the Old Testament there is a close connection between the mystery of creation and the covenant.[8]

We are confronted here with a very dynamic image of creation. The world created by God is not a lifeless world, something thrown into existence, but an immense project in which God himself is involved. As Israel discovers the dimensions of this mystery, it becomes increasingly aware of its own responsibilities as the chosen people vis-à-vis itself, the other peoples and the entire world. Israel becomes the miror of humankind as a whole.

In the Old Testament, the mystery of creation is embedded in a truly universal history of salvation in which the dramatic relationship between God and his chosen people always figures in the foreground.[9] The New Testament adopts the same perspective, but places the figure of Christ at the centre of this universal history as its accomplishment. Every time the New Testament deals with the mystery of creation, it assumes the Old Testament tradition while interpreting it in the light of the total Christ event. This is well illustrated by the great Pauline and Johannine meditations on the mystery of creation. Special attention must be given here to the cosmic texts of Paul and to the prologue of the fourth gospel.

Paul's meditation on creation rests entirely upon his own experience of the risen Christ. This experience leads Paul to three basic convictions: (I) Christ is the unifying centre of the world created by the Father (1 Cor 8:6); (II) He is the recapitulation or summary and the head or summit of everything that the creative love of the Father has produced in the world; in him appeared the fulness of time (Eph 1:9-10); (III) Jesus Christ is the living synthesis of the creative and redemptive power of God, being the first-born in the order of creation and the order of redemption (Col 1:15-20). Paul's meditation on creation is both a prayer of praise and a prayer of supplication. It reflects the early Christians' desire to be personally and definitely integrated into this Mystery (Eph 1:9) which has Christ at its centre. They sensed that all of creation was waiting for its conclusion and fulfilment (Rom 8:18-22).[10]

While Paul's meditation is based on his experience of the resurrection, John's meditation derives from his intimate contact with Jesus during his earthly life. It focuses directly on the mystery of the Trinitarian God. The drama of creation and redemption is truly at home in the eternal love of God as Father, Son and Spirit. This summit of divine revelation, of which John is the privileged witness, sheds a threefold light on the mystery of creation: (I) God *is* (exists), while the world becomes or begins (Jn 1); the world receives its existence from the creative relationship which exists "before the foundation of the world" (Jn 17:24) between God and his Word, between the Father and the Son. (II) The insurmountable distance between God and the world is once and for all mediated by Jesus himself in the symbolism of the vine (Jn 15:1-11)—there is an intimate connection between Jn 1:3, everything is through him, and Jn 15:4-5, without me you can do nothing, between God's creative and God's redemptive Word. (III) The love which exists from all eternity between the Father and the Son constitutes a third person whom the New Testament designates as Spirit.

This "third person" lacks a proper name, precisely because she is the Spirit of the Father and the Spirit of the Son, their mutual and perfect gift of self (their existence-for-the-other in fullness) and their ultimate divine gift to the world— the Spirit who hovers over the surface of the waters (Gn 1:2), God's breath who gives life to the human being (Gn 6:3) and all other beings (Ps 104:30).[11] She is the Spirit who universalizes and interiorizes the redemptive work of the Son so that the grace of the new creation might penetrate into the depth of each being and extend itself to the outermost bounds of the universe.[12]

Rethinking the mystery of creation and redemption

The preceding biblical data may help us to perceive more adequately the challenge that rethinking the mystery of creation and redemption from a christo-centric and universal perspective poses. Although the meditations of Paul and John adopt a universal perspective, they remind us that we cannot separate the mystery of creation from the mystery of the one who died on the cross for the salvation of the world. They also invite us to welcome everything in this world which is *capax gloriae Dei*, capable of manifesting the glory or love of God.

In fact, the dogma of creation is the only dogma which is not exclusive to Christianity! That the world is created by a supreme being or that it emerges out of the sphere of the divine is not a specifically Christian belief. It has been part of the universal religious patrimony of humankind from its beginnings. Therefore, the dogma of creation could be perceived as a unique place of encounter for all those involved in the future of the world and humankind. Their common commit-ment to this future may eventually produce a truly ecumenical theology which respects and integrates peoples' profoundest convictions, their quest for meaning, their dreams of transformation and accomplishment, and their experience of the Great Mystery. The Christian churches can participate in the development of such a planetary theology by redefining their specific mission in the context of interre-ligious dialogue, by examining their own quality of life, and by remaining faithful witnesses of the unique word and the unique light that God freely offers to the world in the person of Jesus, the Christ.

2. Amerindian eco-theology

It is obvious that the development of such a universal theology concerning human responsiblity vis-à-vis the universe calls for the best elements in every culture and worldview. It also calls for new encounters between the more techno-logical and scientific culture of the West and the more organic or traditional cultures which are still very much alive in many parts of the world. The Amerin-dian peoples have often expressed the desire to participate in such a global adventure. They have become increasingly aware of the extraordinary persistence of their traditional values and want to put them at the service of other peoples.[13]

The limits of this essay do not allow us to explore all the aspects of this enterprise. But we will concentrate, once again, on the particular images of Christ which emerge within the context of this Amerindian eco-theology. We will do so without idealizing the native cultures and by remaining attentive to the tragic situation in which many native communities find themselves.

Traditional values – new challenges

It might be useful to turn again to the different speeches made by Pope John Paul II during his 1984 and 1987 visits to the native peoples of Canada. While celebrating their faith in Christ with the native people, John Paul II also welcomed the fact that Canada's first nations have been able to maintain and to develop their traditional cultural values. In his speech to the native people in Sainte-Anne-de-Beaupré, on September 10, 1984, he mentioned their acute sense of the presence of God, love of the family, respect for the aged, solidarity, sharing, hospitality, respect for nature, and the importance given to silence, prayer, and faith in providence (no. 3). He shared their fear about how the impact of economic, social and cultural changes will affect their traditional ways of life (no. 4).

In his speech in Midland, on September 15, 1984, he recalled how the worthy traditions of the Indian tribes were strengthened and enriched by the gospel message and that the church herself has been constantly enriched by these traditions. These traditions include a unique awareness of the presence of God, the ability to discover him in creation, a sense of gratitude for the land and responsible stewardship of the earth, a reverence for all his great works (no. 5).

In his radio message from Yellowknife, September 18, 1984, he called upon the native peoples to use their talents to build an even more authentic civilization of justice and love for the common good of Canada. He again mentioned their responsible stewardship of nature, especially at a time when pollution and environmental damage threaten the earth (no. 9).

During his later visit to Fort Simpson on September 20, 1987, Pope John Paul II delivered substantially the same message while supporting the first nations in their claim for political and economic self-determination. Again he insisted on the importance of preserving and developing their traditional cultural values: sharing, family-based community life, positive relations between the young and the elders, creation-centred spirituality, care for the environment (no. 5).

What is striking about these papal speeches to native people is the close connection between, on one hand, culture, political self-determination, economic development and freedom, and, on the other, traditional values, spirituality and the particular relationship with the land. Pope John Paul II seems very much aware of the fact that all these elements constitute a harmonious and indivisible reality. All the values mentioned by him have a profound religious dimension. This may explain why in his speech at the Shrine of the Canadian Martyrs in Midland he established a direct relationship between the Indian Christ and Amerindian culture, while declaring that Christ must be placed in the centre of each culture. Let us once again quote this important text: "Thus the one faith is expressed in different ways. There can be no question of adulterating the word of God or emptying the Cross of its power, but rather of Christ animating the very centre of all cultures. Thus, not only is Christianity relevant to the Indian peoples, but Christ, in the members of his body, is himself Indian."[14]

It is regrettable however that, although these papal addresses to the native peoples of Canada very strongly affirm their cultural values, they do not explicitly recognize the authenticity and validity of their traditional religious experience and of their aboriginal religions. This omission is partially made up for by the Amerindian purification ritual to which the Pope submitted himself in Midland (1984) and by the native ceremony he presided over at Fort Simpson (1987). This last ritual, composed by a Dene spiritual leader, was explicitly Amerindian and only implicitly Christian. Many native persons have told us during this research that these two rituals were more important than any papal speech on the Amerindian religions possibly could be. We must recognize in any case that the speeches of Pope John Paul II, in continuity with a long tradition of the Christian churches in Canada, seem to affirm that Christ is indeed the centre of the Amerindian cultures, but that they do not extend his incarnation beyond the threshold of the religious dimension and expression of these cultures. The official discourse of the Christian churches of Canada concerning native people seems therefore to be characterized by a basic ambiguity. They place the native peoples before a dramatic choice: to become more fully Indian (affirmation and recognition of native cultures), but to abandon their traditional religions which are, or should be replaced, by Christianity. For most native people, such a choice is practically impossible and basically ambiguous. One must affirm here, once again, that in the Amerindian communities culture and religion constitute an indivisible reality. Amerindian cultures remain spiritual cultures and the fact of the matter is that many native people have opted for Christianity without abandoning their traditional religious experience.

It comes, therefore, as no surprise that the official discourse of the Catholic Church on the relationship between Christ and Amerindian cultures constitutes a source of profound uneasiness for many native people. We have observed this throughout this research, especially when we asked them the question: Is there room for Christ in your traditional ceremonies and in your Amerindian worldview? Many answered this question by saying that they perceived no basic opposition between their Amerindian religion and Christianity "because we all address ourselves to the same God and that there is only one God." Many consider the two religions to be two roads leading to the same Mystery. But such an answer is basically *theistic* rather than Christian or christological. Few native people mentioned Christ when answering this question or seemed able to make the passage between the historical Jesus and the universal Christ. Many native people are impressed by the historical personality of Jesus and find many elements in the Bible which resemble their traditional religious experience. But they do not seem to place Christ in the centre of their culture. But a more personal and intimate relationship with some of them, especially in the context of the traditional ceremonies in which we were allowed to participate, indicated that their initial response to our question contained hidden and profound christological intuitions gravitating around the mystery of the cosmic Christ, even though this term was never explicitly mentioned during our research.

The Amerindian "milieu divin"

Whatever the official attitude of the church in respect to the contemporary renaissance of the first nations, we cannot ignore the fact that the native worldview has remained a religious worldview. We cannot ignore that it is exactly this religious worldview that determines the Amerindian participation in the development of a truly ecumenical and interreligious eco-theology as well as their acceptance of Christ. Therefore, to grasp all the aspects of the Amerindian visualizations of Christ it might be appropriate to recall the basic aspects of native spirituality.

In the second chapter of this book we presented this spirituality as a metaphysics of nature. This term, borrowed from Joseph Epes Brown,[15] is of course a western notion. It expresses, for better or worse, that nature or the cosmos remains for native people the primary meeting place with the Great Mystery. The Amerindian religious experience is profoundly mystical and sacramental. The term "meta-physics" does not really do justice to this religious experience. The Great Mystery is not situated "above" nature or the cosmos, but is an intimate dimension of it. The total reality of nature or the cosmos can therefore be conceived as an immense iconography which contains concrete signs of the Great Mystery.

All the rituals which allow native people to enter into contact with this Great Mystery reproduce this global sacramentality of the cosmos. The symbolism of the four directions in the sacred pipe ceremony as well as the structure of the sweat lodge illustrate this cosmic dimension of native spirituality. This will be further confirmed by our description of the sun dance and the vision quest.

Before presenting these two rituals and their christological reinterpretation, we must insist, once again, on the intimate link within this metaphysics of nature between symbol and reality, between the ritual forms and the meaning they produce. This symbolic efficacy has been clearly observed by Claude Lévy-Strauss in his analysis of certain Amerindian healing ceremonies.[16] It is a type of efficacy that can be compared to the *opere ex operato* (the signs produce grace) of the classical Christian understanding of the sacraments. But one should not be too quick to compare the native rituals with the Christian sacraments. The grace of Christ produced by the Christian sacraments always presupposes a concrete link with, and an explicit reference to, the historical person of Jesus who is the unique source of this grace and, therefore, the sacrament par excellence. Amerindian sacramentality, on the contrary, is immediate and intuitive. This is why Amerindian spirituality is both sacramental and mystical. The cosmos (world, nature, creation) in which the Amerindians encounter the Great Mystery is, as such, a mystical reality: a "milieu divin" (Teilhard de Chardin), a holy land (Frank Cardinal) or a *Wakan* environment (the Lakota).[17]

It is important to insist that this mystical dimension of the Amerindian religious experience did not disappear after the native religions had contact with Christianity and possibly interacted with it. During this research we were also able to observe that the Amerindian approach of Christ is often very mystical. We met native people who were profoundly aware of the fact that the person of Jesus presented to them by the Christian churches was already present, as Christ, in their own "milieu divin." In fact, they often perceive the cosmos and the Bible as the two basic sources of revelation. Traditional native people often declare that the

Bible was given by God to the white people, because they needed Jesus to be saved, while the native peoples had already found everything in nature!

In the last stage of this research we are therefore interested in seeing how these two sources of revelation eventually connect with each other. What is the relationship, for traditional Indians, between the historical figure of Jesus and the one designated by the Christian tradition as the cosmic Christ?

The Son of the Creator, our older brother

The designation of Jesus as "the Son of the Creator, our older brother" is one of the most beautiful images of Christ we encountered during this research. Varieties of this title can be heard almost everywhere in Canada, but especially among the Anishnabe in Ontario and the Cree in Alberta. It is often used in their sacred pipe ceremonies and sweat lodge rituals. We were able to perceive the originality of this title while participating in these rituals.

There is no doubt in our mind that this title represents a unique aspect of the development of Amerindian christology, something that may be compared to the "two natures" doctrine of the Council of Chalcedon. This is the Amerindian way of affirming that Christ belongs both to the human and to the divine world. The subtle substitution of "Son of the Creator" for the title "Son of God" indicates that there is, indeed, room for the historical figure of Jesus in the religious cosmology of the Amerindians.

For many native people, however, the question concerning the place and the role of Christ among the spiritual powers associated with *Wakan Tanka* remains very delicate.[18] The native people have accepted Christ, but without necessarily abandoning their traditional belief in, or knowledge of, these spiritual powers. One could compare this situation with the attitude of the apostle Paul vis-à-vis the powers and the principalities that were part of his worldview. For many native people, the term "Son" affirms the link between Jesus and the Great Mystery, while the term "brother" designates him as a member of their native community and of the human family as such. Therefore, this full title can be understood as a confession of faith in the uniqueness of Jesus as Christ. But when answering the question about the relationship between Christ and the powers, most native people limit themselves to stating that Christ is the most powerful of all medicines and that he offers them protection against bad medicine and the obscure elements which threaten their existence.[19]

It is also important to note that the title "Son of the Creator, our older brother," and all the other titles mentioned in this book are, from the native point of view, more soteriological than ontological. The Amerindians are not particularily concerned with defining the ontological status or the exact nature of the spiritual powers and Christ. While situating Christ among the powers, they recognize that he, like these powers, is personally involved in the drama of human existence. The Son of the Creator thus becomes for some of them the very symbol of the solidarity of the spiritual powers in their struggle against the forces of evil.

We find a very beautiful illustration of this confession of faith in Anishnabe painter Leland Bell's *Stations of the Cross*, to which we referred in the previous chapter. According to the Anishnabe tradition, the sun is seen as the Grandfather or the Creator. The sun dominates each of the stations painted by Leland Bell. The Creator is involved in the drama of his Son while he is walking towards his death. In the painting of the first station (*Jesus Bibakona Tchi Nibod*; Jesus Is Condemned To Death), a dark sun (black, brown, yellow-green) hovers over the human trial of Jesus. The Creator, who is the only being who can pass judgment, looks with sadness on the condemnation of Jesus. In the second station (*Jesus Od Odapinan O Tchibaiatigoman*; Jesus Picks Up His Cross), the blue circle around the white sun is broken, but the colour that comes out of it in the four cardinal directions is to show that Jesus is not alone, even though he carries the burden of the cross alone. In the fourth station (*Jesus O Nagishkawan Ogin Keshkendamin-idjin*; Jesus Meets One Who Is Very Sorrowful), a suffering sun is painted in the same colors as the robe and the cross of Jesus. The Creator shares the sufferings of his Son. In the fifth station (*Simon Cireneing Ga-Ondjid O Widokawan Jesusas*; Simon of Cyrene Goes To Help Jesus), the three circles are the Trinity watching over Jesus who walks the path, the way of the cross. The circles and the path are painted in the same blue-white colors. In the sixth station (*Kitchitwa Veronik O Gassingwewan Jesussan*; Holy Veronica Wipes the Face of Jesus) there is no circle to represent the Creator, but there is the woman who, according to Bell himself, symbolizes not just comfort but compassion. It's the woman giving compassion, or Jesus consoling the woman.

On the seventh station (*Jesus Minawa Pangishin Tchibaiatigo-Makanang*; Jesus Again Falls On The Road Of The Cross), Bell comments: "Here I try to show the fall, not so much that Jesus collapses under a great burden, but more in the sense that he tries to gather strength in the form of prayer. The Trinity watches over him. He is going to a high place to receive a vision; he is going to the mountain to pray. Simon remains beside Jesus; he is the support ..."

Each of the stations of this remarkable way of the cross is like a Byzantine icon. With its vivid colors and elongated figures, each station leaves us with the impression of a unique movement. We see the figures walk in a sacred *(Wakan)* or solemn manner as actors in a cosmic ritual of which the Creator himself is the choreographer and the main actor. Leland Bell, whose Indian name is *Bebamino-jmat* (talking straight or honestly), has managed to speak his own cultural language to express the universal and cosmic meaning of Jesus' death and resurrection.[20]

Other native people have found other symbols within their own spiritual universe to express the same mystery. For Frank Cardinal, a highly respected Cree elder from northern Alberta, who often uses the title "Son of the Creator and our elder brother," the thorns of the wild rose of Alberta are the symbol of the passion of Jesus. The wild rose, the trees and the living water that flows from the Rocky Mountains are the gifts of the Creator to his people in view of the coming of his

Jesus Minawa Pangishin Tchibaiatigo-Makanang
Jesus Again Falls On The Road To The Cross
Leland Bell (1953-) acrylic on canvas, 50 cm x 45 cm
Photo: Tomiko Publications

Son. All these gifts express a mystical link between the land of Jesus and the land of the Indians.[21] The entire creation remains for him and for many other native people the principal sacrament of their communion with the Christic mystery.

3. The cosmic Christ

Contemporary efforts to develop a planetary theology often imply a revaluation of the cosmic Christ image in order to stress the universal meaning of the Christic mystery. This image, which finds its origin in the above-mentioned meditations of Paul and John, indicates that we cannot limit ourselves to a purely anthropological or historical interpretation of the salvific work accomplished by the Father in Christ and through the Spirit. "When we think about Christ's universal kingship today we become aware of some rather difficult questions. How can the event of Christ reach beyond our human world and affect the whole universe? As human being Christ is indeed one with God and the eternal Word, but how can he, as human being, mean something for the whole universe and even occupy a dominant position in this universe?"[22]

The thinking of western theology on this question has been handicapped for a long time by the classical dispute on the motive of the incarnation. The negative answer of the Thomists to the hypothetical question "Would God have become man if Adam had not sinned?" has dominated theology to the detriment of the positive answer offered by the Scotists. Therefore, we have been accustomed to see Christ as someone who enters into history "afterwards," once human sin has endangered the integrity of divine creation, rather than seeing him as the one who was included in divine creation as its source and fulfilment "before the foundations of the world."

The contemporary evolution of the world and humankind invites us to visualize Christ as the one who comes from the most intimate heart of the world and the one from whom we learn about the most intimate heart of the world.[23] It should be noted here that this rediscovery of the central place of Christ in the creative work of God is one of the most remarkable results of the confrontation of Christianity with the non-western cultures.

The cosmic meaning of Christ

Even though the question of the relationship between Christ and the cosmos has drawn the attention of many theologians since the beginning of Christianity, the term "cosmic Christ" appeared only in the nineteenth century, first in Germany and then in the English-speaking world.[24] It generated an extensive literature during the first half of the twentieth century, including many commentaries on the Letters to the Ephesians and Colossians. It did not, however, impose itself as the starting point for a renewed christology and ecumenical theology. Under the influence of Rudolf Bultmann's school, biblical scholars often limited themselves to the demythologization of the cosmic powers or "gnostic elements" mentioned by Paul. In systematic theology, the debate soon focused on the works of Pierre Teilhard de Chardin (1881-1955) whose christological intuitions clearly went beyond the official teachings of the church.

In fact, it is only since 1961 that cosmic christology started having some negative or positive impact on the collective imagination of the Christian churches. On the occasion of the third Assembly of the World Council of Churches in New Delhi (1961) dealing with the theme "Jesus Christ, the Light of the World," Professor Joseph A. Sittler from the University of Chicago, an ordained minister of the United Lutheran Church of America, delivered a remarkable conference on the unity of the church and the cosmic design of God.[25] This conference was based on Colossians 1:15-20 and explored the possibilities of a cosmic christology. Sittler insisted on placing the doctrine of redemption within the wider doctrine of creation, and developing a christology based on Irenaeus's notions of recapitulation and fulfilment of creation in Christ to limit the influence of Augustine and his nature-grace dualism: "A doctrine of redemption is meaningful only when it swings within the larger orbit of a doctrine of creation. For God's creature of earth cannot be redeemed in any intelligible sense of the word apart from a doctrine of the cosmos which is his home, his definite place, the theater of his selfhood under God, in corporation with his neighbour, and in caring-relationship with nature, his sister."[26]

The debate stirred by this conference illustrates to what extent western theology has focused almost exclusively on the mystery of redemption.[27] Theological reflections on the relationship between Christ and the cosmos are, therefore, rapidly perceived as a danger for classical theology and as a return to gnosis and to the mystical currents of Eckhart, Ruysbroeck, and Böhme which have no value for "real theology."

Among the positive reactions to Sittler's conference, one must note an article by the Protestant missiologist Horst Bürkle.[28] He considers the first chapter of the Letter to the Colossians as a truly missionary discourse and he welcomes the mystery of the cosmic Christ as the foundation for the encounter between the ecumenical and the missionary movements. The mission of the church must promote the unity of the church, while the unity of the churches must find expression in their common mission to the world. Bürkle maintains that the term "cosmic Christ" has become a key concept for a more comprehensive or extended christology which reflects our contemporary human experience.

At the Assembly of New Delhi it was obvious that this was particularly true for the representatives of the young churches of Africa and Asia. Paul David Devanandan (1901-1961), founder of the Christian Institute for the Study of Religion and Society, Bangalore, followed in the footsteps of Sittler by launching a vibrant appeal to redefine the nature of Christian witness as a testimony to the mystery of the New Creation in Christ. He proposes that the risen Christ be recognized and proclaimed as the ultimate factor which gives world history significance and direction.[29] For M. M. Thomas, Devanandan's successor in Bangalore and the president of the Central Committee of the World Council of Churches (1968-1975), the pauline vision of the cosmic Christ is the starting point for a new interpretation of history, based on three convictions: (I) the gospel of Christ transcends all cultural and political orders and all social, ideological and ethical systems; the church must be involved in a positive but critical way in all the movements for the renewal of the world but without absolutizing them. (II) The redemption and the judgment of Christ do not concern merely the individual, but have a social and cosmic dimension. Consequently, they affect science and technology, culture and society, theologies and religions. (III) Christ is at work in today's world where he enters into constant dialogue with persons and peoples by the power of his love. He acts through the great revolutions of our times and we cannot limit his actions in the world to the actions of the church.[30]

For the great majority of the non-western theologians, the figure of Jesus remains the centre and the norm of their cosmic christology. It must be noted that most of these theologians did not participate in the western debate on the relationship between the historical Jesus and the kerygmatic Christ. But they insist with vigour on the need to make the leap from the particular history in which the incarnation of God presents itself to the history of the peoples who welcome the gospel today.[31] This "theological leap" challenges the western appropriations of the Christic mystery. The non-western contributions to the development of a cosmic christology indicate that it will be difficult for western Christianity to get beyond its "mystique of redemption" without the new visions of Christ which are emerging in the context of creation-centred spiritualities.[32] We find a unique expression of this spirituality in the sun dance and the vision quest rituals, as well as in the symbol of the tree of life which constitutes the centre of native spirituality.

The tree of life

The tree of life belongs to a very ancient and complex system of symbols which Mircea Eliade designated as *the symbolism of the centre*.[33] According to this famous historian of religions, the powerful symbol of the tree and the related symbols of the *axis mundi*, the totem and the sacred mountain have represented a great variety of functions throughout the centuries: image of the cosmos, place of theophanies, symbol of life, centre of the world, mystic union with animals, symbol of resurrection and rebirth, and so on. All these symbols and images reveal a central truth: the unlimited power of life of which the tree, as centre of the cosmos, becomes the symbol par excellence. We are dealing here with a cultural and spiritual tradition which should not too rapidly be assigned to a past mythological age, because it continues, even in its contemporary expressions, to connect us with the fundamental questions of life and death, with the cycle of seasons, the struggle between good and evil, the ultimate destiny of the human being, the origin and the order of the universe.[34] This has been confirmed by the research of Carl Jung for whom the "philosophical tree" is the archetype of human consciousness, which has the ability to express the fundamental aspects of the human mind, while adapting itself to a multitude of ideologies.[35]

The symbolism of the tree can be found everywhere in the contemporary cosmology and spirituality of the Amerindians who can be defined as the "People of the Centre."[36] It can be found among the ancient rock drawings in Peterborough, Ontario.[37] But we will focus instead on the contemporary expressions of this symbolism.

In 1931, the great Oglala prophet, Black Elk, declared: "The nation's hoop was broken, and there was no centre any longer for the flowering tree." [38] Black Elk was contemplating the sufferings of this people and its religious-cultural destruction following the massacre of Wounded Knee in 1890. However, he also had an important vision that can be compared to that of the author of the Book of Revelation (Apoc 22:1-3). Black Elk not only saw the restored circle of his own people, but many other circles which, together, formed but one reality, the circle of the universe. At the centre of this circle where all the peoples were called to live in harmony as the descendants of a single mother and father was the sacred tree.[39]

The contemporary native renaissance can be interpreted as the fulfilment of this vision. It promotes the cultural reconstruction of the native communities as well as the rebuilding of their relations with other peoples. The tree of life remains an important symbol of this renaissance.[40] We refer here, above all, to the symbol of the central pole *(axis mundi)* of the sun dance lodge. The structure of the sweat lodge and many other native rituals, as we have seen, also symbolize the cosmos and its centre. The elaborate totem poles of the native tribes in British Columbia were originally simple trees surmounted by a bird.[41] The Anishnabe Midewiwin society also developed the same symbolism.[42] Because of the flexible nature of Amerindian religions, some of these developments have also integrated Christian elements. We will see later that some native people associate the central sun dance pole with the Christ figure. We must consider whether we are dealing here with a simple accumulation of religious symbols (cumulative acculturation) or with true forms of religious integration.

Can we consider the christological meditations which developed around the sun dance ritual as authentic Amerindian contributions to the long theological tradition of the tree of life and Christ association? Indeed, we should recall, briefly, that the early Christians did not hesitate to affirm the cosmic significance of Jesus' death. John affirms that it is for the love of the world (cosmos) that God has sacrificed his only Son (Jn 3:16). This text has a unique significance for the Amerindians. Adam Cuthand, a native Anglican priest, explains: "Western man does not access or analyze the real truth of the statement—the key word being 'world' which in the original Greek was 'Kosmos,' when properly translated, means the Universe and everything in it—the earth, mountains, rocks, stones, trees, birds, animals, plants, insects and all other living things."[43]

Because of its four directions the cross of Christ is often interpreted as the centre of the universe. The cross finds itself, so to speak, midway between the tree of paradise (Gn 3:24) and the tree of the apocalypse (Rev 22:1-2). For Hippolytus, Bishop of Rome in the third century, the cross means "the home of all things, their resting place; the foundation of planet earth, the centre of the cosmos."[44] Several centuries later, Joachim of Flore (1135-1202) would be captivated by the same symbolism and would construct a theology of history which would have a great impact on the evolution of western thinking.[45] The cross of Christ, with its four directions and its central cosmic symbolism, has a special meaning for native people who have integrated Christ into their sacred pipe rituals.[46]

History and cosmos

The particular contributions of the Amerindians to the development of a universal, christocentric theology can best be appreciated by comparing two different paintings which explore the tree of life symbol. The first painting, entitled *"Christ on the Tree of Life,"* is the work of the Italian artist Pacino De Bonaguido (beginning of fourteenth century). The second, entitled *"The Tree of Life,"* is a work by Anishnabe artist Blake Debassige, produced in 1983 for the Jesuit Anishnabe Center in Anderson Lake, Ontario.

The painting by Placino De Bonaguido is inspired by Bonaventure's *Lignum Vitae*, a work of 12 chapters dealing with the origin, passion and glorification of Christ.[47] The painting represents a tree with twelve branches. The four inferior branches show the origin of Christ in medallions, while the four middle branches deal with his passion, and the four upper branches with his glorification. On the top of the tree or the cross, a pelican symbolizes Christ's sacrifice. At the bottom of the painting, we find the stories of Genesis. The entire painting is dominated by the glorified Christ, the Virgin Mary, the angels and saints.[48]

Blake Debassige's painting (see page 194), on the contrary, is influenced by the Anishnabe Midewiwin religion. The tree itself is a cedar, known and respected by the people for its medical purposes. The naked Christ is totally incorporated into the tree. He is male and female—symbol of the fullness of life. The entire painting is a celebration of life. But the owl, which is set atop the tree, reminds us that people are mortal. Death is part of our living. There are two representations of the Holy Trinity: three birds sitting on the treetop and three circles above them. Birds are considered the medium by which the soul travels. Each bird represents people who have died, but whose presence is still felt around us. The various faces within the tree represent the people living today, at various ages. When one counts all the faces, they add up to twelve. At the bottom of the painting, two serpents appear as if through cracks and crevices in the earth with only the head and tails visible. They represent temptation and the spirit of evil. Each one is grasping at small white butterflies but is unable to grasp them securely. This symbolizes the dark side of life. The dying Christ holds wild roses in his hands. This recalls the practice of giving flowers when a person dies and expresses the triumph of life over death.[49]

By their common tree of life symbol, these two paintings represent two specific appropriations of the Christ mystery. Pacino De Bonaguido offers a specifically western, historical interpretation of the Christic mystery, while Blake Debassige situates Christ at the centre of the Amerindian metaphysics of nature. The two paintings focus on the universal meaning of the Christ event. They celebrate the universal Christ. But Blake Debassige's painting reminds our western society, dominated by its mystique of redemption and its obsession with progress, about the urgent need for a cosmology that views the universe as a living organism and as the meeting place with the Great Mystery. His painting enriches

Placido De Bonaguido's "history of salvation" with a "theology of creation" that integrates both the historical (crucifixion) and the cosmic meaning of Christ.

II. Amerindian Celebrations and Meditations

1. The sun dance

The sun dance can be considered one of the rituals which incarnate practically all the major aspects of Amerindian spirituality. For the Amerindians it represents what Holy Week means for the Christians: the very centre of their "liturgical year," their sacred space and time. The ritual appeared in the eighteenth century among the Plains Indians at the apogee of their civilization. Despite the fact that the ritual was prohibited by the American and Canadian governments from the end of the nineteenth to the middle of the twentieth century, it managed to survive in a variety of forms and even gained new vitality during the 1960s. In fact, the sun dance contains all the cultural and religious elements which the pan-Indian movement wants to promote. We will present a brief overview of the origin, the historical evolution and the theological significance of this ritual while also illustrating the possibilities it offers to Christian native people for the celebration of their faith in Christ.

The sun dance ritual

The prehistorical and mythological origin of the sun dance is situated among the nomadic peoples of North America whose survival depended entirely on the buffalo. It appears that these peoples developed a ritual to acquire the medicine or the spiritual power of the buffalo—a ritual that could be compared to the rite of the sacred bull in Egypt and in the classical semitic cultures of Antiquity, as well as to the Roman ritual of the Sun God.[50] This buffalo ritual developed east of the Rocky Mountains from northern Texas to Manitoba. Under the influence of the Arapao, the Cheyennes and the Oglala Lakota, it became a more and more elaborate ceremony whose significance expanded considerably from the nineteenth century on.

Like all native rituals, the sun dance expresses and celebrates the vital link of the human being with the Great Mystery and the spiritual powers. In fact, the sun dance can be understood as an elaborate form of the vision quest. It activates a considerable number of native symbols, such as the circle, the medicine wheel, the tree of life, the sacred pipe, and the four directions, which constitute the "milieu divin" of the Amerindians.[51] This may explain why the ritual has been adopted by a large number of Indian tribes and is not limited to one particular native culture or linguistic group. In the twentieth century the sun dance will become a truly pan-Indian celebration.

Because of this historical evolution, it is not easy to grasp the profound meaning of the sun dance. Ake Hultkrantz remarks that the majority of anthropological studies on the sun dance tend to focus on its political and economic context. Few studies deal directly with its religious meaning.[52] Some interpret the sun dance as a nativistic movement involving a radical return to ancestral traditions, others as a syncretic revitalization movement which blends traditional and Christian elements.[53] A complete study of the ritual should therefore take into consideration the particular situation and the historical evolution of each tribe that has adopted the sun dance.

The general description of the ritual which we shall offer is based on the conviction that the sun dance can be interpreted as a sacrifical rite for the revitalization of the individual and the community. Joseph Epes Brown writes: "The annual sun dance ceremonies of the Plains Indians of North America give to these peoples—as indeed to all peoples, today as in the past—a message through example affirming the power of suffering sacrifice, revealing in rich detail the mystery of the sacred in its operations, in all life, and through all creation. Where there is no longer affirmation or means of sacrifice, for 'making sacred,' where the individual loses the sense of the centre, the very energy of the world, it is believed, will run out."[54]

It should be noted, however, that the English or French names of the ritual, sun dance or *danse du soleil,* do not entirely do justice to its sacrificial meaning. The sun occupies a central place in the ritual and mythology of certain tribes, such as the Sioux, where the dancers constantly stare at the sun. The Lakota call the sun dance *wiwanyank wapici,* they dance while staring at the sun.[55] Other tribes, such as the Arapao, speak of the "Dance of the offering(s) lodge" or the "Dance for world and life renewal."[56] Today, the sun dance ritual varies among the different native groups. We will limit ourselves here to a generalized account of the ritual.

The sun dance is celebrated annually, in the middle of summer. It is a truly community celebration, inspired by the commitment of some individual members of the community to dance and to sacrifice themselves for the community. Among the Plains Indians, the sun dance is often undertaken in fulfilment of a vow made by an individual, woman or man, who is seeking spiritual power. The basic motivation for undertaking the sun dance can be one or more of the following:

1. To fulfil a personal vow.
2. To obtain spiritual power for oneself.
3. To obtain spiritual power for others.
4. To become a holy *(wakan)* person through sacrifice and prayer.

The entire sun dance is divided into four stages spread over several months:

1. The announcement of the sun dance by those who pledge to dance.
2. The instructions by the elders and medicine men for the dancers.
3. The organization of the sun dance camp.
4. The sun dance proper.

The organization of the four-day camp, the sun dance ritual and the other rituals associated with it are supervised by holy *(wakan)* persons among whom the spiritual leader of the dance is chosen. The sun dance proper lasts four days. Only blue or sunny clear days are ceremonially active and must be awaited. During these four days all the activities are highly ritualized:

1.   The rites of the first day concern the choice of the site for the sun dance: a perfect circle in the exact middle of which a hole is made to plant the sacred tree. A man is chosen to scout in the nearby forest for this tree, which is to be felled to become the sun dance pole. Others meanwhile start the construction of the sun dance lodge.

2.   The rites of the second day concern the capture and bringing in of the Sacred Tree. The tree is struck like an enemy. After it is felled, it is stripped of its branches and bark up to the fork which is left at the top. Sometimes, a panache of foliage above the fork represents an eagle's nest. The tree is carried to the camp in a solemn manner. It may be decorated with sacred objects, like the four colours, which symbolize the universe. Many tribes choose a cottonwood which is considered the most sacred of all trees. Its inner grain takes the form of a five-pointed star, a representation of the Great Spirit, while its leaves rustle constantly, thus sending continual prayers to the Great Mystery. Generally speaking, native people do not explain why the tree is carried to the camp like a captive enemy.

3.   The rites of the third day concern the erection of the sun dance pole in the centre of the lodge where the dance will be held. All the other ritual elements, drums, sacred pipes, and so on, are prepared. The day closes with a feast for the entire community, with the exception of those who will be tomorrow's dancers and who, therefore, start their fast. These men and/or women have been isolated from the community since the official beginning of the ceremony. They prepare for the dance by fasting and by sacred pipe and sweat lodge rituals according to the instructions of the elders who supervise the dance. In the past, in some tribes this preparation included physical mutilations. Sometimes, cuts were made in the shoulder blades or on the back of the dancers through which leather thongs were thrust to attach the dancers to the central pole. This practice may have contributed to the prohibition of the sun dance. It accentuated the more spectacular aspect of the sun dance, especially for the non-native observers, to the point of obscuring its profoundly theological meaning.

4.   The fourth day is very sacred. The day starts with a solemn evocation of the sun power and the immediate preparation of the dancers. The dance itself and the mortifications which are freely assumed by the dancers vary from tribe to tribe. Generally speaking, the dancers move all day long around the central pole until they are totally exhausted. They are supported by the prayers and songs of the community.

In some tribes, the dance is composed of four military elements: the capture, torture, captivity and release of the dancers. The exact meaning of these elements remains obscure. Hartley Alexander suggests that warfare is used here simply as a metaphor for the drama which is embodied in human life.[57] Other commentators, like Black Elk, speak of suffering as an intrinsic element of human life and of the sacrificial meaning of suffering.[58] The sun dance ends with a solemn banquet.

The theology of the sun dance

All the symbols implied in the sun dance suggest a dramatization of the cyclical rebirth of the world in a ritual of thanksgiving. The fast and the other mortifications of the dancers can be understood as a form of purification, a ritual of healing and a quest for spiritual power. The sun dance is thus a kind of synthesis of the main elements of Amerindian spirituality.

According to Alexander, the ritual "is essentially an interpretation of life, of the meaning of nature for man, and of man's sense of his own significance in the midst of nature—in short, of that which we call a philosophy of life."[59] According to this American *Urphilosophie*, the human being participates in the ongoing process of creation, but is not to be considered the summit or centre of this creative process. Humans remain pitiful beings who can do nothing without the spiritual powers emerging from the Great Mystery.[60] According to this original native philosophy, all living beings are related to one another in and through the Great Mystery.

The sun dance is the annual celebration and ritual dramatization of this universal solidarity. The suffering, freely assumed by the dancers, symbolizes the efforts of each individual to enter into this communion. The sun dance also symbolizes the struggle against the chaos which constantly threatens this harmony. It is both a celebration of thanksgiving and a ritual of personal or collective purification. It is a ritual effort to restore the universal order of things by means of the sacrifice which the dancers accept for themselves and for others so that their community may again become whole and holy.

The sun dance can be considered as the centre of the Amerindian eco-theology. The Amerindians know that everything comes from the Great Mystery, the Creator, and that everything must return to the Great Mystery. The sun dance dramatically re-creates the sacramentality of the entire universe. The circular lodge is a microcosmos, a likeness of the universe. Each of the poles around the lodge represents some particular object of creation, so that the whole circle is the entire creation. The tree at the centre, upon which all the poles rest, is *Wakan Tanka*, which is the centre of everything. The central pole indicates the road to the Creator. The suffering caused by gazing at the sun, while dancing to exhaustion, and the other forms of mortification, dramatically symbolize the participation of the human being in the renewal or rebirth of the universe. The cosmic renewal runs through the personal renewal of each individual human being. The Amerindians encounter the universal expression of this "paschal mystery" everywhere in nature in, for example, the annual cycle of the seasons.

Joseph Epes Brown correctly states that the sun dance is not centred on the human person as such: "The sun dance is not a celebration by humans for humans; it is an honoring of all life and the source of all life that life may continue, that the circle be a circle, that all the world and humankind may continue on the path of the cycle of giving, receiving, bearing, being born in suffering, growing, becoming, returning to the earth that which has been given, and finally being born again. Only in sacrifice is sacredness accomplished; only in sacrifice is identity found. It is only through suffering in sacrifice that freedom is finally known and laughter in joy returns to the world."[61]

Christological meditations

Within the limits of this research it is impossible to do complete justice to the ritual and the theology of the sun dance which J.R. Walker once described as the most developed metaphysical system that can be found among the American native peoples living north of Mexico.[62] But our brief description of the sun dance has already given us an inkling of its possible christological interpretations. The sun dance contributes to the revelation of the hidden face of the Amerindian Christ.

It is important to note, in the first place, that many contemporary versions of the sun dance present a blend of Amerindian and Christian symbols. In fact, since the middle of the nineteenth century, certain Christian reinterpretations of the sun dance have been recorded. The question is whether we are dealing with a form of "cumulative acculturation" or with a real transformation of the meaning of the ritual.[63] Jorgensen mentions that for some native people the central pole of the sun dance lodge represents life, personal sacrifice for the life of others, the human being, Jesus Christ, the cross of Christ, the Spirit of God, spiritual power and so on.[64] Hultkrantz has met native people for whom the lodge symbolized the tomb of Jesus from which one rises, at the end of the dance, as a renewed being. Other native people compare the central pole to the cross of Jesus or to Jesus himself, our brother (the fork at the top of the pole can be compared to the sign Y which signifies brother in the native sign language).[65]

It is quite possible that in the nineteenth century some native spiritual leaders fabricated this christological reinterpretation of the sun dance to make it acceptable in the eyes of the representatives of the government and the churches. If we go back to the starting point, we may be dealing with a so-called accidental increase of meaning rather than with a true effort to integrate.[66]

But, today, the situation has radically changed. In the United States and in Canada native people can now celebrate the sun dance in total freedom and they are doing it more and more, all over the North American continent. This is why we have met traditional native people who are totally opposed to any Christian interpretation of the sun dance and others for whom the same ritual has become an important expression of their faith in Christ. It is easy to observe that for many native people the sun dance has become a ritual of initiation to their Indianness through a return to the ancestral traditions and a counterculture. But one can also observe that at least a limited number of native people have made the passage from "cumulative acculturation" to religious Amerindian-Christian integration as far as the basic meaning of the sun dance is concerned. The testimonies which we were able to collect represent three major orientations.

The first orientation concerns the christological interpretation of the central pole of the sun dance lodge. Since 1982, we have met a few native people, mostly medicine men, for whom this sacred tree represents the cross or the person of Jesus. An explicit link is established between the tree of life symbol and Jesus Christ.

Paul Steinmetz, S.J., and Sylvain Lavoie, O.M.I., two Catholic priests who have had the opportunity to participate in sun dance celebrations which are not easily accessible to non-native people, report meeting persons who think of Christ while dancing (Steinmetz) or for whom the poles of the lodge represent Christ and his apostles (Lavoie).[67] Since the early 1960s, Steinmetz has even been invited to celebrate the eucharist during sun dance rituals and to offer communion to the dancers.

This christological reinterpretation of the sun dance is confirmed by the research of Hultkrantz who writes that the central pole was traditionally understood to be a channel of communication between the world and God. The pole was perceived as a mediator, invested with divine power, between the cosmos, symbolized by the circular lodge, and God, symbolized by the sun. The dancers did not address their prayer directly to the pole or to the sun, but to God or to the Great Mystery. Today, some dancers address their prayers to Christ, mediator, when facing the central pole, and identify the sacred tree with Christ.[68] Christ is perceived by them as the true centre of the Amerindian spiritual universe and as the unique road leading to God.

The second orientation concerns the sacrificial aspect of the sun dance. One of the traditional motivations of the dancers was to assume personal sacrifices for the healing of others, to obtain spiritual power for others or to dance for the well-being of the entire community. Since 1982, we have met persons who explicitly assume this dimension of the sun dance in communion with Christ who carried his cross for the salvation of the world. In 1982, at Frog Lake, Alberta, we met a medicine man who represented this second orientation. He shared with us his hesitation about making the sun dance pledge that year because of the immense responsibilities and the suffering it represented. He was wondering if he was still able to carry the sufferings of others.

We are dealing here with a profound appropriation of the mystery of "substitution" which constitutes the centre of Paul's christology (Rm 4:25) and the Christian creed. In fact, it should be noted that the Amerindians have always been fascinated by the ascetic aspects of Christianity. It comes therefore as no surprise that some establish a concrete link between the sacrifice of Christ for the salvation of the world and the sacrifices of the sun dancers for the holiness (becoming *wakan*) of their community.

The third orientation concerns the symbolism of the light. This symbol has been analyzed by William Stolzman in his meetings with the Lakota Medicine men. This dialogue established a significant connection between the sun dance ritual and the paschal vigil. The sun dance is, within the religious system of the Plains Indians, what the *triduum paschale* represents for Christianity.

The two religious systems explore the symbolism of light. The early Christians, for example, associated the resurrection of Christ with the sunrise. They chose December 25, the octave of the Roman celebration of the winter solstice, as the date of Jesus' birth. The sun rise symbolizes the transforming power of Christ. It came therefore as no surprise that the Lakato medicine men and their pastors established parallels between the ritual of the Easter Vigil and the sun dance (Christ = the paschal candle = the central sun dance pole = the sun), and that they compared the sun dance pledge to the renewal of baptismal vows. Both type of vows were important reminders of their Amerindian and Christian responsibilities.[69]

2. The vision quest

The vision quest is one of the most important rites practised by many native peoples in North America. The Lakota call it *hanbleciya*, literally, "crying for a dream." Most of the time, the ritual takes place in an isolated area. It consists of a total fast lasting for an average of four nights and three days. The faster meditates and keeps vigil from sunset to sunrise, and rests during the day without leaving the ritually prepared location. The vision quest leads us to the very heart of the Amerindian religious experience. We offer here a basic description of the general structure and the theological meaning of this experience, while again asking how the ritual can contribute to the discovery of the Indian Christ.

The ritual of the vision quest

The vision quest can be found among almost all the Indian peoples of North America with the exception of those who live in the extreme eastern part of Canada, the Algonquians and Cree of the Atlantic coast and the Naskapi, who consider spiritual power as a sort of super-ego *(mistapeo)* that is innate in the human person and manifests itself in dreams.[70] In the other native cultures, this power is quested for and eventually obtained by way of an ascetic (fasting) and meditative (vigil) ritual, under the guidance of a medicine man or elder whose own spirituality has been put to the test.

The vision quest can be considered a kind of democratized form of shamanism.[71] Together with the sacred pipe ceremonies, the sun dance and the sweat lodge rituals, it has become a pan-Indian experience which is practised by an increasing number of adults. In a short study on the historical evolution of the ritual, Hultkrantz notes that, at the beginning, the vision quest was, at least in a certain number of tribes, a rite of initiation imposed on their young members (compulsory for boys, not always for girls) at the age of puberty. The successful accomplishment of the ritual, often through the reception of a spiritual power associated with an animal spirit, allowed the young person to enter fully into the human community and into the Amerindian spiritual universe. Today the vision quest has become a common but not exclusive means by which native adults establish their relationship with the Great Mystery by searching for the vision that gives a lasting meaning to their life.[72]

Because of the highly individualized nature of the vision quest, it is difficult to offer a precise description of the ritual itself. We have to rely, basically, on the testimony of persons who have accomplished the ritual successfully. But even then, it is difficult to have access to the subjective vision experienced by these successful vision seekers. The following description of the ritual corresponds to the tradition of the Plains Indians and to our own personal experience of the vision quest.[73] The ritual form of the vision quest varies considerably from tribe to tribe, but, typically, includes the following eight stages.

1. *The decision to do the vision quest*

In traditional native societies there was great pressure on young men to go on a vision quest. Today, such an experience depends totally on the free initiative of the individual person who starts the process by contacting a spiritual person, elder or medicine man. The decision must be made without internal or external pressures. Because of the demanding nature of the experience a careful preparation is necessary.

2. *Sweat lodge purification ritual*

The vision quest proper begins with a sweat lodge purification ritual. This ritual symbolizes the many spiritual relations in which the seeker of the vision is already involved. The purpose of the purification ritual is to establish the proper relationship with these powers and to summon them to be present during the quest.

3. *The solitary vigil*

The vision quest centres on the moment when the seeker goes out to the ritually prepared place to meet the spiritual powers during a solitary vigil of total fasting. In traditional native societies the vigil was often related to bravery and courage, the main virtues of warriors and hunters. Contemporary native people stress the element of personal sacrifice.

4. *Gift of vision*

The reception of a vision constitutes the centre of the experience. But there is no unanimity among the Amerindians (or non-Amerindians commentators) on the exact nature of the vision phenomenon. But the medicine men know the difference between hallucinations and authentic visions. The vision is interpreted as something real or as a response of the spiritual powers to the seeker. This subjective reality can be compared to the visionary and auditory experiences of Christian and other mystics.

5. Relationship with a guardian spirit

For many native people, the main purpose of the ritual is to meet their guardian spirit, a supernatural being (often an animal spirit) that becomes their personal mediator with the spiritual powers or with the Great Mystery. Again, there is no unanimity on the exact role of this animal spirit and on its link with the Great Mystery.

6. Gift of power

A successful vision quest often implies that the individual has received special powers. Two types of power are available: power to increase one's personal abilities in ordinary activities, and power to perform extraordinary things. The first type is more common. The second type is often interpreted as a special gift to be put at the service of the community.

7. Reception of a material token

A successful vision quest is often confirmed by the reception of a material token. The range of possibilities is considerable. It can be an amulet, a new prayer or song, or even instructions for a new ritual. These various objects remind the seekers of the importance of their vision and help them to maintain their relationship with the Great Mystery.

8. Interpretation of the vision

In some native tribes, the quester is expected to share his or her vision with the medicine men or with the entire community. But in most native societies the vision is kept secret. In fact, most native people are reluctant to talk about their experience and to share their vision with others, out of fear that they might lose the spiritual powers which they have received.

The theology of the vision quest

The theology of the vision quest is structured around the basic conviction that a human being needs supernatural assistance to fulfil his or her life journey. Amerindians seek and obtain this assistance through the vision quest, the sacred pipe ceremony, the sweat lodge and other rituals. These rituals allow them to establish a significant relationship with powers greater than themselves.

However, it is important to note that the vision quest has nothing to do with magic. The purpose of the ritual is not to gain control over the spiritual powers, but, on the contrary, to enter into the right network of spiritual relationships (the Amerindian "communion of saints") needed for the full development of the individual's existence in harmony with others.

The vision quest reveals an important dimension of Amerindian anthropology, especially in native cultures, like the Anishnabe culture, where the ritual was perceived as a compulsory rite of initiation.[74] Anishnabe writer Basil Johnson states: "No man begins to be until he has received his vision."[75] According to the

Anishnabe and other native groups, the human person is a composite being, made of spiritual and material elements. Just as the entire universe is the result of Kitche Manitou's dream or vision, human beings are called into existence to realize the vision that the same Great Spirit has reserved for them. This vision permits the person to become a truly ethical being.

The vision is, at the same time, a gift and a call (vocation). It is the gift of the spiritual power that a person needs to fulfil his or her life, and a call to walk on the road indicated by the vision. The basic purpose of the vision quest is to provide this orientation. It offers the human person a veritable life program that produces, sometimes, a real conversion or turning point in his or her existence.

This also explains why, in traditional native societies such as the Anishnabe, the vision quest was followed by a name-giving ceremony during which the young person received a new name which symbolized the direction of his life. Despite the fact that the vision quest has ceased to be a compulsory rite of initiation in these societies, the name-giving ceremony is still practised.

It should be noted that among the Anishnabe the vision quest was not compulsory for girls. Women were considered complete beings. As women and mothers, they had already fulfilled the basic purpose of existence as givers of life and as participants in the creative act of Kitche Manitou.

The quest for vision or spiritual power remains one of the main characteristics of contemporary Amerindian religions. Adults who freely decide to seek vision prepare themselves carefully for this experience. The vision quest, as noted above, is not a magic ritual but a spiritual journey or a profoundly religious and ascetic experience. In fact, the purpose of its ascetic dimension (fasting) is to eliminate all the obstacles in and around the human person in order to allow that person to connect with the spiritual energy which is the very source of existence, and to live in harmony with all creation. All the ritual elements of the vision quest, like those of the sun dance, symbolize a universal communion (all my relations): communion with the members of one's family, clan or tribe, communion with all other living beings, with the spiritual powers (ancestors, guardian-spirits) and, finally, with the Great Mystery which is the centre and the source of all these relations.

The vision quest, finally, symbolizes that the individual human person is an incomplete being. Human life receives meaning only through the relations that the individual maintains with all the other living beings in the universe. The vision quest allows individuals to find their proper place in that universe.

Even though it is practised today only by a limited number of adults, the vision quest reveals one of the most profound challenges of human existence. As long as we do not know who we are, that is as long as we lack vision, and we do not know our spiritual energies or relations, we cannot live in harmony with others and develop as truly ethical beings. The vision quest suggests that spirituality is the quintessence of ethics and moral existence.[76]

Christological meditations

There is no doubt that, within the contemporary Amerindian revitalization process, the vision quest is helping many native people to affirm or to reconstruct their cultural identity. This has been the case for most of the Amerindians we have met since 1982. But among them we have also met several for whom the same ritual has also become a powerful means to affirm and strengthen their Christian identity. For them, the vision quest has become a kind of "Indian retreat" which has allowed them to establish a more profound relationship with the person of Christ. The vision quest is also practised by non-native people, including Christian ministers, who want to strengthen their own spiritual life in relation to the Amerindians, and who choose this initiatic approach to redefine their mission among the Amerindian peoples.[77]

Native people as well as non-native people affirm that they are inspired by the example of Jesus himself who at the beginning of his ministry went out into the desert to seek his own vision (Lk 4:1-13). The testimonies which we have received from these persons indicate that the vision quest leads to a profound interiorization of the Christic mystery and to the affirmation of its cosmic dimension. We were able to observe three major forms of interiorization.

A first level of interiorization of the Christic mystery can be found among those who compare the vision quest to certain Christian rituals like the sacrament of confirmation or the ordination to the priesthood.[78] The focus here is on the special grace received by candidates when these sacraments are given. The spiritual power received by the Amerindians who have accomplished the vision quest successfully is compared to this grace. In both cases, this grace or spiritual power is a personal gift to be put at the service of the community.

As a rite of initiation in adolescence or as search for spiritual power in adulthood, the vision quest symbolizes the spirit of service and solidarity which are the hallmarks of the Amerindian communities. We have met native people who do not hesitate to compare their understanding of community life with the diaconal and charismatic structure of the early Christian communities. The vision quest has helped them to visualize Christ in a more profound way as the foundation and source of their human and Christian solidarity.

A second level of the interiorization of the Christic mystery was observed among the persons with whom we experienced the vision quest between 1982 and 1987. This interiorization sometimes focused on the image of Christ as light or energy. Here we are dealing with an explicit transition from the historical person of Jesus, who was proposed to the Amerindians by the missionary church, to the universal Christic mystery.

The explicit reference to this Christic mystery is similar to the major intuitions which can be found in the works of Pierre Teilhard de Chardin. The scientific and theological accomplishments of this remarkable man are radically christocentric. Christ is the keystone of his world vision, just as he was the centre of Paul's theology of history. Teilhard is one of the few thinkers who has been able to visualize and express the universal Christ mystery in terms which reflect a modern, dynamic and evolutionary worldview. However, it is important to note that his christology was not simply the consequence of his scientific research. He had three ecstatic visions or mystical experiences which left a profound impact on his life.[79]

Teilhard speaks of the Christ mystery in three different but complementary ways. At the starting point of his christology we always find the figure of the historical Jesus, the Word incarnate, by whom God enters the universe, historically and phenomenologically. But this God-who-became-man is also the cosmic Christ, the principle of universal vitality and the Omega point to which the entire universe is converging. And, finally, Teilhard also speaks of the universal or mystical Christ, the mystical body constituted by all the human beings who accede to supernatural or Christic life.[80]

The vision quest is a unique contemplative experience that allows the seekers to become more profoundly aware of the spiritual network which shapes their life. There is no doubt that this ritual, when experienced within the perspective of Christian faith, almost spontaneously leads its participants to the pan-christic theology of Teilhard de Chardin. The vision quest helps them to bridge the cultural distance between the historical figure of Jesus and the universal presence of Christ today. Christ, Jesus of Nazareth, can be visualized both as the permanent historical foundation of the Christian faith and as the universal power which forms the most intimate core of each living being and the entire universe.

Finally, a third form of interiorization of the Christic mystery is related to the death-resurrection theme that dominates the vision quest ritual as we have experienced it ourselves. Even though, according to Hultkrantz, this theme does not seem to be a traditional aspect of the vision quest,[81] it is almost spontaneously mentioned by those who fast today in solitary vigil. The ritual beginning and coming out of the fast symbolize the temporary interruption of ordinary, daily life. It symbolizes a kind of return to the origins of existence in order to connect with the energies which generate a new beginning and a new existence. Just as the sweat lodge ritual almost spontaneously evokes the encounter between Jesus and Nicodemus (is it really possible to be born again?), the vision quest ritual evokes, in a more radical fashion, the mystery of Jesus' own death and resurrection. The experience of total fasting in an isolated area can become a form of almost physical communion with this central mystery of the Christian faith: the paschal mystery of Christ. This third form of interiorization indicates that the vision quest, notwithstanding its cosmic connotations, does not necessarily separate the Christian believer from the historical figure of Jesus. The vision quest leads to specifically Amerindian appropriations of Christ which—to use the words of Pope John Paul II—"do not empty the cross of its power." The vision quest can lead us to the very centre of the Christian faith.

Conclusion

The main purpose of this book was to evoke the cultural climate of the contemporary native American appropriations of the Christ figure following the statement by Pope John Paul II that Christ is Indian. We wanted to show, in the first place, that the answers of Amerindians to the question "And you, who do you say I am?" are very contextualized answers. These answers deserve their place in the sun along with the many theologies which are developing among the people of God, especially in non-western cultures. The fact that these answers have not yet developed into a systematic christological discourse does not in any way diminish their theological meaning and value.

Throughout this christological research we have met many Amerindians for whom Christ is real and concrete. We have been able to admire their simple but living faith. More than any other contextualized christology, the native visions of Christ develop from below. They are emerging out of the fierce struggle of the first nations for their basic rights in the North American context. They are often associated with radical, cultural transformations and with the quest for cultural identity.

The situation of this emerging native christology is unique. It is not yet supported by truly native Christian communities and liturgies such as we find them in many African countries. It is far from having the impact and the scope of the liberation christologies of Latin America and the christologies which are developing in the Asian context of interreligious dialogue. In fact, the Amerindian christologies still find themselves in a sort of theological "no man's land." They have not yet found a place for themselves. From an ecclesial point of view, the Amerindians are still searching for their own culturally-based communities within the churches of North America. From the social, political and economic point of view, they remain dispossessed peoples. The "Amerindian Christ" inevitably reflects this double marginalization. At present, there is no home for him except in the heart of the native women and men who have welcomed his gospel and who count on his presence.

The christology which can be deduced from the many testimonies presented in this book remains experiential. Its dramatic and esthetic approach to the Christ figure cannot be ignored. It bears the marks of the experiential mode of learning which is so typical of the native cultures. In these cultures, to know is to have experienced. Amerindians cannot and will not speak of an Amerindian Christ unless they have met, heard or personally experienced him in their lives. It will always be difficult to evaluate this type of christology in dogmatic terms or from the point of view of its content. What counts here, in the first place, is not the content, but the process: the journey of the Indian mind to the Christ figure and the concrete native appropriations of the gospel message.

Finally, we must recognize that the declaration of Pope John Paul II has been welcomed by many Amerindians as a confirmation of their culture. They believe that the Pope has given them not only the mission, but the *permission* to express their Christian faith in their own cultural language. In this book we wanted to highlight one of the most beautiful aspects of the Amerindian cultures, their mystical capacity. The cultural language of the Amerindians is the language of the human heart and of the intuitive mind. Therefore, it is also a universal language. To the extent that the native peoples of North America are invited to speak this language freely within the Christian churches, the entire Christian community will be better prepared to visualize all the dimensions of the universal Christ mystery.

Notes

Notes to Introduction

1   Pope John Paul II, "Celebration of the Word. Martyr's Shrine, Huronia. September 15, 1984," *Canadian Catholic Review* 2(1984), No. 9, 368.

2   See Jacques Dupuis, *Jesus Christ at the Encounter of World Religions*. Maryknoll: Orbis Books, 1991.

3   Walbert Bühlmann, *The Coming of the Third Church. An Analysis of the Present and Future of the Church*. Maryknoll: Orbis Books, 1978.

4   See "Different Theologies, Common Responsibility: Babel or Pentecost?" *Concilium* 171(1/1984).

5   See Robert Schreiter, *Constructing Local Theologies*. Maryknoll: Orbis Books, 1985.

6   See Thomas Berry, "The Indian Future," *Cross Currents* 26(1976): 133–142.

7   See Harold Turner, "Old and New Religions Among the North American Indians: Missiological Impressions and Reflections," *Missiology: an International Review* 1(1973): 47–66; John Webster Grant: *Moon of Wintertime. Missionaries and the Indians of Canada in Encounter Since 1534*. Toronto: University of Toronto Press, 1984.

8   See "Missions of the Canadian North. Statement by the Bishops of the Eight Dioceses of the Canadian North at the Plenary Assembly of the Canadian Conference of Catholic Bishops in 1985," *Kerygma* 21(1987): 127–131.

9   See Achiel Peelman, *L'inculturation. L'Église et les cultures*. Paris: Desclée; Ottawa: Novalis, 1988.

10 See Schreiter, *Constructing Local Theologies*.

11 In this book, the first inhabitants of the Americas are referred to collectively by the terms aboriginal peoples, native peoples, Amerindians, Indians, native North Americans, first nations.

Notes to Chapter 1

1   Pierre Duchaussois, *Mid Snow and Ice: The Apostles of the North-West.* London: Burns & Oates and Washbournen, 1923, p. 13.

2   See Douglas Cole, *Captured Heritage.* Washington: The University of Washington Press, 1985. Quoted by Jon W. Magnuson: "Echoes of a Shaman's Song: Artifacts and Ethics in the Northwest," *The Christian Century* 104/14(1987): 406-408.

3   See Michael Asch, *Home and Native Land. Aboriginal Rights and the Canadian Constitution.* Toronto: Methuen, 1984, pp. 62-63.

4   See Ton Lemaire and Frans Wojciechowski, eds., *Terugkeer van een verdwijnend volk. Indiaans en Inuit activisme nu.* Nijmegen: Instituut voor culturele en sociale anthropologie, Katholieke Universiteit, 1985.

5   Quoted by Bill Kenkelen, "American Indians: Higher Spirits," *National Catholic Reporter,* September 9, 1983, p. 3.

6   Emma Laroque, *Defeathering the Indian.* Agincourt: The Book Society of Canada, 1975, p. 27.

7   In this book, the term "Indian (Amerindian) Medicine" has the same meaning as Amerindian spirituality or religion. See, in particular, Chapter 6.

8   See Vincent Cosmao, *Changing the World. An Agenda for the Churches* (Maryknoll: Orbis Books, 1984), pp. 46-49.

9   See Bernard Cleary, *L'enfant de 7000 ans. Le long portage vers la délivrance.* Sillery: Les Éditions du Pélican/Septentrion, 1989.

10 United Nations Economic and Social Council, Sub-Commission on the Prevention of Discrimination and the Protection of Minorities: "Study of the Problem of Discrimination against Indigenous Populations," U.N. Doc. E/CN./4/Sub.2/1983/21/Add.8, par. 379. Quoted by Richard Mulgan: "Should Indigenous Peoples Have Special Rights?" *Orbis* 33(1989): 379.

11 See Kenkelen, "American Indians: Higher Spirits," pp. 11-12.

12 See Rudolph Ryser, "Fourth World Wars: Indigenous Nationalism and the Emerging new International Political Order," in Menno Boldt and J. Anthony Lang, eds., *The Quest for Justice. Aboriginal Peoples and Aboriginal Rights* (Toronto: University of Toronto Press, 1985), pp. 304-315.

13 See Harold Cardinal, *The Unjust Society. The Tragedy of Canada's Indians.* Edmonton: M.G. Hurtig Ltd., 1969; *The Rebirth of Canada's Indians.* Edmonton: Hurtig Publishers, 1977.

14 See Vine Deloria Jr, *Behind the trail of Broken Treaties. An Indian Declaration of Independence.* New York: Dell Publishing Co., 1974.

15 See Lee Sweptson, "Indigenous and Tribal Populations: A Return to Central Stage," *International Labour Review* 126(1987, No. 4): 447-455; "Geneva, 1977: A Report on the Hemispheric Movement of Indigenous Peoples," *Basic Call to Consciousness.* Edited by the Periodical *Akwesasne Notes,* Mohawk Nation, Rooseveltown, N.Y., 1982.

16 See *Report of the Fourth Russell Tribunal on the Rights of the Indians of the Americas.* Volume I: Conclusions. Amsterdam, 1980.

17 See Boyce Richardson, ed., *Drumbeat. Anger and Renewal in Indian Country.* Toronto: Summerhill Press - Assembly of First Nations, 1989.

18 See Julien Harvey, "Réveil mondial des autochtones," *Relations,* No. 566 (December, 1990): 303.

19   See Bernard Cleary, "L'urgence d'un nouveau contrat social," *Relations*, No. 566 (December, 1990): 299-302.

20   See *Tradition, Change and Survival. Proceedings, World Conference: Indigenous Peoples' Education*. June 8-13, 1987. Vancouver: International Indigenous Peoples' Association, 1987, 13.

21   Joseph Epes Brown, *The Spiritual Legacy of the American Indian*. New York: Crossroad, 1982.

22   Thomas Berry, "The Indian Future," *Cross Currents* 26(1976): 133-142.

23   See Jean Barman, Yvonne Hebert, Don McCaskill, eds., *Indian Education in Canada*. Volume I: *The Legacy*. Vancouver: University of British Columbia Press, 1986; Volume II: *The Challenge*. Vancouver: University of British Columbia Press, 1987.

24   See Janet Somerville, "Cariboo Council Probes School Wounds," *Catholic New Times* 15(1991), No. 15, pp. 1, 12-13. Also Celia Haig-Brown: *Resistance and Renewal. Surviving the Indian Residential School*. Vancouver: Tillacum Library, 1988.

25   See Daryold Winkler, "Native Language Revitalization in Canada," *Kerygma* 21(1987): 225-231.

26   See Achiel Peelman, "Dynamisme spirituel, sagesse et communauté. Quelques observations et réflexions sur la figure et le rôle des anciens chez les Amérindiens," *Église et Théologie* 16(1985): 39-77.

27   House of Commons (Canada): Minutes of Proceedings of the Special Committee on *Indian Self-Government*. First Session of the Thirty-second Parliament, 1980-81-82-83. Issue No. 40: 34-35.

28   See Achiel Peelman, "Traditional Native Spiritual Practice in Canada's Federal Prisons," *Kerygma* 20(1986): 101-119.

29   See Maggie Hodgson, "The Eagle Has Landed," *Kerygma* 20(1986): 195-203.

30   See Wolfgan Jilek, *Indian Healing. Shamanic Ceremonialism in the Pacific Northwest Today*. Surrey/Washington: Hancock House, 1982.

31   David Young, Grant Ingram, Lise Swartz, eds., *Cry of the Eagle. Encounters with a Cree Healer*. Toronto: University of Toronto Press, 1989.

32   In the radio message delivered to the Native peoples at Fort Simpson (because of a heavy fog, the Pope was unable to land in Fort Simpson and delivered the message from Yellowknife), Pope John Paul II said: "Today I want to proclaim that freedom which is required for a just and equitable measure of self-determination in your own lives as native peoples. In union with the whole Church I proclaim all your rights—and their corresponding duties. And I also condemn physical, cultural and religious oppression, and all that would in any way deprive you or any group of what rightly belongs to you." John Paul II: "To the Native Peoples. Fort Simpson. September 18, 1984," *The Canadian Catholic Review* 2(1984), No. 9: 380.

33   See Maggie Hodgson, "The Eagle Has Landed," *Kerygma* 23(1989): 195-203.

34   See Michael Foster, "Canada's First Languages," *Languages* 1982, pp. 7-15; Daryold Winkler: "Native Language Revitalization in Canada," *Kerygma* 21(1987): 225-231.

35   According to the 1981 Census, only 29% of the aboriginal population reported having a native language as mother tongue (the language first learned as a child and still understood). The 1966 census reports that only 11% of aboriginal persons living off-reserve use an aboriginal language as mother tongue, compared to 45% for the aboriginal population living on-reserve. Only 7% of all persons of aboriginal origin living off-reserve still speak an aboriginal language at home compared to 35% of persons of aboriginal ancestry living on-reserve. When compared with the corresponding figures for mother tongue—11% and 45% respectively—it appears that retention

of aboriginal languages is limited among persons of aboriginal origin living both off- and on-reserve.

36   In 1982, while visiting the native (Nootka) village of Ahousat on Vancouver Island we met a native person who was a professional fisherman with a radar-equipped boat, but whose daily life was profoundly marked by his ancestral spirituality. In February 1984, we were invited to attend a sweat lodge ritual in northern Alberta, presided by a Cree chief who, one month later, would participate at the Constitutional Conference of the First Ministers on Aboriginal Rights, where his political analysis did not go unnoticed.

37   See Bernard Cleary, *L'Enfant de 7000 ans*, pp. 7-10.

38   See Thomas Berger, "Native History, Native Claims and Self-Determination," *B.C. Studies* 57(1983): 14.

39   See Michael Asch, *Home and Native Land. Aboriginal Rights and the Canadian Constitution*, p. 5.

40   While the category of status or registered Indian is based on an objective fact, i.e. being on the official list of the Canadian government, the categories of non-status Indians and Métis have a subjective foundation or perception. The category of non-status Indians regroups those aboriginal persons who, for one reason or another, are excluded from the official register, but who consider themselves as having aboriginal ancestry, while the Métis category is composed of persons who consider themselves descendants of the Métis of the nineteenth century, a specific socio-cultural group.

41   Before the Canadian federation (1867), the administration of the Indian Affairs was the direct responsibility of the British Crown or Imperial Government, which dictated from London all the laws concerning the relationship between the colonists and the Amerindians. From 1867 on, this responsibility was taken over by the Canadian Federal Government which in 1880 created a Ministry of Indian Affairs. From 1936 on, the aboriginal populations of Canada came under the jurisdiction of the Ministry of Mines (given the increasing importance of the industrial development of northern territories), while in 1950 they moved to the Ministry of Citizenship and Immigration. Did native peoples become aliens in their own country? Since 1960, we have had the Department of Indian and Northern Affairs.

42   See Sametz, *Economic Geography of Canada*. Toronto: Macmillan, 1964, pp. 33-54.

43   See Louis-Edmond Hamelin, *Canadian Nordicity: It's Your North Too*. Montreal: Harvest House, 1979; Andrew Siggner, "The Socio-Demographic Conditions of Registered Indians," Rick Ponting ed., *Arduous Journey. Canadian Indians and Decolonization*. Toronto: McClelland and Stewart, 1968, pp. 57-83; William Wonders, "Changing Role and Significance of Native Peoples in Canada's Northwest Territories," *Polar Record* 23(1987): 661-671; Lyne Paquet and Jeannine Perreault: "Un demi-million d'Indiens inscrits au Canada en l'an 2001?," *Cahiers québécois de démographie* 13(1984): 101-115; Louise Normandeau and Victor Piché, eds., *Les Populations amérindiennes et inuit du Canada: Aperçu démographique*. Montreal: Presses Universitaires de Montréal, 1984; Norbert Robitaille and Robert Choinière, "L'accroissement démographique des groupes autochtones du Canada au XXe siècle," *Cahiers québécois de démographie* 16(1987): 3-35.

44   Sources: The Assembly of First Nations. Ottawa: 1990.

45   See Kathleen Jamieson, *Indian Women and the Law in Canada: Citizens Minus*. Ottawa: Ministry of Supply and Services Canada - Advisory Council on the Status of Women. Indian Rights for Indian Women, 1978.

46   See Virna Kirkness, "Emerging Native Women," *Canadian Journal of Women and the Law* 2(1987-1988): 408-425. See also the witness of a group of native women from the Indian reserve of Tobique (New Brunswick): *Enough is Enough: Aboriginal Women Speak Out*. Toronto: The Women's Press, 1987.

47 See Patrick Johnston, *Native Children and the Child Welfare System*. Toronto: Canadian Council on Social Development in Collaboration with James Lorimer & Company, 1983.

48 See Geoffrey York, *The Dispossessed. Life and Death in Native Canada*. Toronto: Lester & Orpen Dennys, 1989, pp. 201-227.

49 See Larry Krotz, *Indian Country. Inside Another Canada*. Toronto: McLelland & Stewart, 1990.

50 See Johnston, *Native Children and the Child Welfare System*, pp. 78-79, who bases his remarks on Peter Hudson and Brad McKenzie: "Child Welfare and Native People: The Extension of Colonialism," *Social Worker* 49(1981), No. 2.

51 See Wolfgang Jilek, *Indian Healing*.

52 See Rick Ponting and Roger Gibbings, *Out of Irrelevance. A Socio-Political Introduction to Indian Affairs in Canada*. Scarborough: Butterworths, 1980.

53 See Bruce Richardson, ed., *Drumbeat. Anger and Renewal in Indian Country*. Toronto: Summerhill Press - The Assembly of First Nations, 1989.

54 See, for example, Richard Ponting, "Conflict and Change in Indian/non-Indian Relations in Canada: Comparison of 1976 and 1979 National Attitude Surveys," *Canadian Journal of Sociology* 9(1984): 137-158.

55 See Mark Nagler, *Indians in the City*. Ottawa: Canadian Research Centre for Anthropology, Saint Paul University, 1973; William Stanbury, *Success and Failure. Indians in Urban Society*. Vancouver: University of British Columbia Press, 1975; Andrew Siggner, *An Overview of Demographic, Social and Economic Conditions Among Canada's Registered Indian Population*. Ottawa: Indian and Northern Affairs Canada, 1979; Larry Krotz, *Urban Indians. The Strangers in Canada's Cities*. Edmonton: Hurtig, 1980.

56 See Achiel Peelman and Jean-Guy Goulet, "La réalité autochtone et la dimension socio-politique de la mission," *Kerygma* 17(1983): 127-157; Edward Weick: "Northern Native People and the Larger Canadian Society: Emerging Economic Relations," *American Review of Canadian Studies* 18(1988): 317-329; Kenneth Coates and Judith Powell: *The Modern North. People, Politics and the Rejection of Colonialism*. Toronto: James Lorimer & Company, 1989.

Notes to Chapter 2

1 For an overview of studies on the Amerindian religions, see Ake Hultkrantz: "North American Indian Religion in the History of Research: A General Survey," *History of Religions* 6(1966), pp. 91-107; 6(1967), pp. 183-207; 7(1967), pp. 13-14; pp. 112-148; Ake Hultkrantz and Christopher Vecsey, eds., *The Study of American Indian Religions*. New York: Crossroad, 1983.

2 See Ake Hultkrantz, *Native Religions in North America. The Power of Visions and Fertility*. San Francisco: Harper & Row, 1987, pp. 9-19.

3 See Carl Waldman: *Atlas of the North American Indian*. Maps and Illustrations by Molly Braun. New York: Facts On File Publications, 1985, pp. 1-22. Note, by way of comparison, that in the Middle East (prehistory of the Judeo-Christian civilization), the first habitations are built around 9,000 B.C.E.; ceramics started around 4,500 B.C.E. The ancient Egyptian empire and hieroglyphic literature began in 3,100 B.C.E.; the construction of the pyramids started in 2,600 B.C.E.

4 See Josef Haekel, *Kosmischer Baum und Phahl in Mythus und Kult der Stamme Nordwestamerikas*, Wiener Volkerkundliche Mitteilungen. Vienna: 1958, Vol. 4, pp. 33-81; Chester Chard: "Maritime Culture in the North Pacific: Age and Origin," *Proceedings of the*

International Congress of Americanists 34(1960): 279-283; Gudmunt Hatt, "North American and Eurasian Cultural Connections," *Proceedings of the Fifth Pacific Science Congress, Canada 1933.* Toronto: University of Toronto, 1943, Volume 4.

5   See Hultkrantz, *Native Religions of North America*, pp. 14-15.

6   See Joseph Epes Brown, *The Spiritual Legacy of the American Indian*. New York: Crossroad, 1982, pp. 1-27.

7   See Peggy Beck and Anna Walters, *The Sacred. Ways of Knowledge. Sources of Life*. Tsaile (Navajo Nation), The Navajo Community College Press, 1977, pp. 8-30.

8   See William Stolzman, *The Pipe and Christ. A Christian-Sioux Dialogue*. Chamberlain, S.D.: Tipi Press, 1986.

9   See Brown, *The Spiritual Legacy of the American Indian*, pp. 47-55; Jamake Highwater, *The Primal Mind. Vision and reality in Indian America*. New York: Harper & Row, 1981, pp. 55-167; Sam Gill: *Native American Traditions. Sources and Interpretations*. Belmont: Wadsworth Publishing Company, 1983, pp. 19-85.

10   See Brown, *The Spiritual Legacy of the American Indian*, pp. 64, 71, 110; Catherine Albanese, *Nature Religion in America. From the Algonkian Indians to the New Age*. Chicago: The University of Chicago Press, 1990, pp. 16-46.

11   In the second part of this book we will present a certain number of these ceremonies and rituals in their relation to the Christ mystery.

12   See Sam Gill, *Native American Religious Action. A Performance Approach to Religion*. Columbia: University of South Dakota Press, 1987, pp. 129-146.

13   See Carl Starkloff, "Religious Renewal in Native North America: A Contemporary Call to Mission," *Missiology. An International Review* 13(1985): 81-101.

14   See Jean-Guy Goulet, "Representation of Self and Reincarnation Among Dene-Tha," *Culture* 8(1988): 3-18; David Young and Jean-Guy Goulet, eds., *Being Changed by Cross-Cultural Encounters. The Anthropology of Extraordinary Experience*. Peterborough: Broadview Press, 1994.

15   See Achiel Peelman, "Christianisme et cultures amérindiennes. Présentation et analyse d'une démarche théologique interculturelle," *Église et Théologie* 22(1991), pp. 131-156.

16   See Hartley Burr Alexander, *The World's Rim. Great Mysteries of the North American Indians*. Lincoln: University of Nebraska Press, 1953, p. 163.

17   See Joseph Jorgensen, *The Sun Dance Religion. Power of the Powerless*. Chicago: The University of Chicago Press, 1972.

18   See Vine Deloria, Jr, *God is Red. A Native View of Religion*. Second Edition. Golden: North American Press, 1992, pp. 78-97.

19   See Achiel Peelman: "Dynamisme spirituel, sagesse et communauté. Quelques observations et réflexions sur la figure et le rôle des anciens chez les Amérindiens," *Église et Théologie* 16(1985): 39-77.

20   See Edward Evans-Pritchard, *Theories of Primitive Religion*. London: Oxford University Press, 1956.

21   See Vine Deloria, Jr, "Religion and the Modern American Indian," *Current History* 67(1974): 250-253.

22   Edward Tylor, *Primitive Culture*. 1871.

23   See Brown, *The Spiritual Legacy of the American Indian*, p. 70.

24   See Carl N. Gorman, "Navajo Vision of Earth and Man," *The Indian Historian*, Winter 1973. Quoted by Brown, p. 70.

25   See Deloria, *God is Red*, pp. 79-80.

26   See "Native American Thanksgiving. As told by Princess Red Wing," *Modern Liturgy* 10(1983): 4.

27   See Joseph Epes Brown, *The Sacred Pipe. Black Elk's Acccount of the Seven Rites of the Oglala Sioux*. Baltimore: Penguin books, 1971, p. xx.

28   Stolzman, *The Pipe and Christ*, p. 181.

29   William Powers, *Oglala Religion*. Lincoln: University of Nebraska Press, 1975, pp. 45-46.

30   See Paul Steinmetz, *Pipe, Bible and Peyote Among the Oglala Lakota. A Study in Religious Identity*. Knoxville: The University of Tennessee Press, 1990, pp. 39-40.

31   Jacques Dupuis, *Christ at the Encounter of World Religions*. Maryknoll: Orbis Books, 1991, p. 239.

32   See Eva Solomon, "Gitchi-Manitou as We Know Him," *Kerygma* 21(1987): 117-120.

33   See Hultkrantz, *Native Religions in North America*, p. 26.

34   See Brown, *The Spiritual Legacy of the American Indian*, p. 110.

35   See Ton Lemaire, "De Indiaanse houding tegenover de natuur. Indiaanse ecologie als uitweg uit onze milieucrisis?," Wouter Achterberg and Wim Zweers, eds., *Milieucrisis en filosofie*. Amsterdam: Ekologische Uitgeverij, 1984, pp. 171-188.

36   See Calvin Martin, *Keepers of the Game. Indian-Animal Relationships and the Fur Trade*. Berkeley: University of San Francisco Press, 1978.

37   See Achiel Peelman, "Scheppingsgeloof en Ecologie," *Objectief* 13(1979): 1-45.

38   See Robert Bunge, "Awareness of the Unseen - The Indian's Contact with Life," *Listening* 19(1984): 181-191.

39   Basil Johnston, *Ojibway Heritage. The Ceremonies, Rituals, Songs, Dances, Prayers and Legends of the Ojibway*. Toronto: McLelland & Stewart, 1982(1976), p. 119.

40   See the Russian linguist, Lev Semenovich Vygotsky (quoted by Bunge), *Thought and Language*. Cambridge: Massachussetts Institute of Technology Press, 1962, p. 71.

41   Scott Momaday, "Native American Attitudes to the Environment," Walter Holden Capps, ed., *Seeing With a Native Eye*. New York: Harper Forum, 1976, p. 80; Scott Momaday: *Commencement Address*. Geneva (NY): Hobart and William Colleges, 1980.

42   Christopher Vecsey, *Imagine Ourselves Richly. Mythic Narratives of North American Indians*. New York: Crossroad, 1988.

43   See Antonia Mills, "The Meaningful Universe: Intersecting Forces in Beaver Indian Cosmology," *Culture* 6(1986): 81-91.

44   See Hugh Brody, *Maps and Dreams*. Vancouver: Douglas & McIntyre, 1981.

45   See Antonia Mills, "Preliminary Investigation of Cases of the reincarnation Type Among the Beaver and Gitksan Indian." Paper delivered at the Canadian Ethnology Society Meetings, May 1985. See also Jean-Guy Goulet, "Representation of Self and Reincarnation Among the Dene-Tha," *Culture* 7(1988): 3-17.

46   See Kenneth Coates and Judith Powell, *The Modern North. People, Politics and the Rejection of Colonialism*. Toronto: James Lorimer & Company, 1989.

47   See the Preface of Martin E. Marty to the book by Albanese, *Nature Religion in America*, pp. xi-xiv.

48   See Richard Nelson, *Make Prayers to the Raven. A Koyukon View of the Northern Forest*. Chicago: The University of Chicago Press, 1983.

49   See the documentary movie *Attiuk*. Crawley Films - National Film Board of Canada, 1979.

50 See Adrian Tanner, *Bringing Home Animals. Religious Ideology and Mode of Production of the Mistassini Cree Hunters*. New York: St. Martin's Press; London: C. Hurst, 1979.

51 See Arthur Amiotte, "Eagles Fly Over," *Parabola. Myth and the Quest for Meaning* 1, No. 3 (1976): 28-42. Also published in Sam Gill: *Native American Traditions. Sources and Interpretations*. Belmont: Wadsworth Publishing Company, 1983. pp. 90-104.

52 See Walter Holden Capps, ed., *Seeing With a Native Eye. Essays on Native American Religion*. New York: Harper & Row, 1976.

53 See Basil Johnston, *Ojibway Ceremonies*. Toronto: McClelland & Stewart, 1982.

54 See Nomaday, "Native American Attitudes to the Environment," pp. 79-85.

55 See Hans Urs Von Balthasar, *Love Alone*. New York: Herder & Herder, 1969, pp. 11-42.

56 See Jennifer Brown, "Northern Algonquians from Lake Superior and Hudson Bay to Manitoba in the Historic Period," Bruce Morrison and Roderick Wilson, eds., *Native Peoples. The Canadian Experience*. Toronto: McClelland & Stewart, 1968, p. 222.

57 See, for example, the journal of George Nelson, a fur trader at the beginning of the nineteenth century. Jennifer Brown and Robert Brightman, eds., *The Order of the Dreamed: George Nelson on Cree and Northern Ojibwa Religion and Myth, 1923*. Manitoba: The University of Manitoba Press, 1988.

58 See Frank Speck, *Naskapi. The Savage Hunters of the Labrador Peninsula*. Norman: University of Oklahoma Press, 1935.

59 See Tanner, *Bringing Home Animals*.

60 See Bunge, "Awareness of the Unseen," pp. 187-188.

61 See Graham Watson and Jean-Guy Goulet, "Gold In; Gold Out: The Objectivation of Dene Tha Accounts of Dreams and Visions," *Journal of Anthropological Research* 48(1992): 215-230.

62 For an overview of anthropological studies on this question in the subarctic area of Canada, see Robin Ridington, "Knowledge, Power, and the Individual in Subarctic Hunting Societies," *American Anthropologist* 90(1988): 98-110.

63 See Hazel Hertzberg, *The Search for an American Indian Identity. Modern Pan-Indian Movements*. Syracuse: University of Syracuse Press, 1971.

64 See, for example, John F. Bryde, *Modern Indian Psychology*. Vermillion (South Dakota): The University of South Dakota, Institute of Indian Studies, 1971, pp. 2-87; George J. Jennings, "The American Indian Ethos. A Key for Christian Missions?," *Missiology. An International Review* 5(1977): 487-498.

65 *In A Sacred Manner We Live. Photographs of the North American Indian by Edward S. Curtis*. Introduction and Commentary by Dom D. Fowler. New York: Weathervane Books, 1972.

66 Brown, *The Spiritual Legacy of the American Indian*, p. 124.

67 See Beck and Walters, *The Sacred. Ways of Knowledge. Sources of Life*, pp. 8-33.

68 See Deloria, *God is Red*, p. 81.

69 See Douglas Schwartz, *Plains Indian Theology. As Expressed in Myth and Ritual and in the Ethics of the Culture*. Ann Arbor: University Microfilm International, 1984, p. 205.

70 See Powers, *Oglala Religion*, p. 51.

71 These reflections are based on Thomas Berry, "The Indian Future," *Cross Currents* 26(1976): 133-142.

72 See Harold Turner, "Old and New Religions Among North American Indians: Missiological Impressions and Reflections," *Missiology. An International Review* 1(1973): 47-66.

73   See Mary E. (Beth) Southcott, *The Sound of the Drum. The Sacred Art of the Anishnabe*. Erin: The Boston Mills Press, 1984.

74   Première Performance, Ottawa, November 16-17, 1988.

75   See Carl Jung, *Alchemical Studies* (Collected Works, Vol. 13). London: Routledge and Kenan Paul, 1967, pp. 251-349; Carl Jung, *Mandala Symbolism*. Princeton: Princeton University Press, 1973.

76   See Berry, "The Indian Future," pp. 136-137.

77   See Conrad Arensberg and Arthur Niehoff, *Introducing Social Change. A Manual for Community Development*. Chicago: Aldine Publishing Company, 1971, pp. 207-231.

78   See Thomas Berger, *Northern Frontier, Northern Homeland. The Report of the MacKenzie Valley Pipeline Inquiry*, 1977. Also, Thomas Berger, *Village Journey. The Report of the Alaska Native Review Commission*. New York: Hill and Wang - The Inuit Circumpolar Conference, 1985.

79   See Gibson Winter, *Liberating Creation. Foundations of Religious Social Ethics*. New York: Crossroad, 1981, pp. 94-105.

Notes to Chapter 3

1   John Webster Grant, *Moon of Wintertime. Missionaries and the Indians of Canada in Encounter Since 1543*. Toronto: University of Toronto Press, 1984, p. 239.

2   See Achiel Peelman and Jean-Guy Goulet, *The Amerindian Reality and the Catholic Church in Canada*. Brussels: Pro Mundi Vita Bulletin 93, 1983/2.

3   See James Ronda and James Axwell, *Indian Missions. A Critical Biography*. Bloomington: Indiana University Press, 1978.

4   See Henry Warner Bowden, *American Indians and Christian Missions. Studies in Cultural Conflict*. Chicago: University of Chicago Press, 1981; James Axtell, *The European and the Indian. Essays in the Ethnohistory of Colonial North America*. Oxford: Oxford University Press, 1981; James Axtell, *The Invasion Within. The Context of Cultures in Colonial North America*. Oxford: Oxford University Press, 1985; Bruce Trigger, *Natives and Newcomers. Canada's "Heroic Age" Reconsidered*. Manchester: Manchester University Press; Kingston-Montreal: McGill-Queen's University Press, 1985.

5   Robert Berkhofer: *The White Man's Indian. Images of the American Indian from Colombus to the Present*. New York: Vintage Books, 1979, p. 10.

6   Oliva Dickason, "The Concept of L'*Homme sauvage*," Marjorie Halpin and Michael Ames, eds., *Manlike Monsters on trial. Early Records and Modern Evidence*. Vancouver: University of British Columbia Press, 1980, p. 66.

7   See Anthony Pagden, *The Fall of Natural Man. The American Indian and the Origins of Comparative Ethnology*. Cambridge: Cambridge University Press, 1982.

8   See Robert Berkhofer, *Salvation and the Savage. An Analysis of Protestant Missions and American Indian Response, 1787-1862*. Lexington: University of Kentucky Press, 1965.

9   See Henri Maurier, "Missiologie et Sciences. Évangélisation et Civilisation," *Cultures et Développement* 1-2(1981): 6.

10   See William Hutchison, *Errand to the World. American Protestant Thought and Foreign Missions*. Chicago: University of Chicago Press, 1987.

11 See Claude Champagne, *Les débuts de la mission dans le Nord-Ouest canadien. Mission et Église chez Mgr Vital Grandin, o.m.i. (1829-1902)*. Ottawa: Éditions de l'Université d'Ottawa - Éditions de l'Université Saint-Paul, 1983.

12 Quoted by Jean-Guy Goulet, "Liberation Theology and Missions in Canada," *Église et Théologie* 15(1984): 300-301, Note 16.

13 See Jan Grootaers, "La fonction théologique du laïc dans l'Église," *Théologie. Le service théologique dans l'Église*. Mélanges offerts à Yves Congar. Paris: Les Éditions du Cerf, 1974, pp. 83-112.

14 Champagne, *Les débuts de la mission dans le Nord-Ouest canadien*, p. 230.

15 On the origin and development of ethnohistory, see Trigger, *Natives and Newcomers*, pp. 164-172; Axtell: *The European and the Indian*, pp. 3-15.

16 See Kenneth Morrison, "Discourse and the Accommodation of Values: Toward a Revision of Mission History," *Journal of the American Academy of Religion* 53(1985): 365-382.

17 See Elisabeth Jones, *Gentlemen and Jesuits. Quests for Glory and Adventure in the Early Days of New France*. Toronto: University of Toronto Press, 1986; James Ronda, "The European Indian: Jesuit Civilization Planning in New France," *Church History* 4(1972): 385-395; Michael Pomedli, "Mythical and Logical Thinking: Friends and Foes?" *Laval théologique et philosophique* 42(1986): 377-387; Michael Pomedli "Beyond Unbelief: Early Jesuit Interpretations of Native Religions," *Studies in Religion* 16(1987): 275-287.

18 See Harold Turner, "Old and New Religions Among the North American Indians: Missiological Impressions and Reflections," *Missiology. An International Review* 1(1973): 47-66.

19 See Cornelius Jaenen, "Amerindian Responses to French Missionary Intrusion, 1611-1760: A Categorization," William Westfall et al, eds., *Religion/Culture. Comparative Canadian Studies. Études canadiennes comparées*. Association for Canadian Studies. Association des études canadiennes, Volume VII, 1985, pp. 182-197. Also Cornelius Jaenen, *Friend and Foe. Aspects of French-American Cultural Contact in the Sixteenth and Seventeenth Centuries*. New York: Columbia University Press, 1976.

20 See Grant, *Moon of Wintertime*, pp. 239-263.

21 Grant, *Moon of Wintertime*, p. 244.

22 Grant, *Moon of Wintertime*, p. 262.

23 See Kenneth Morrison, "The Mythological Sources of Abenaki Catholicism. A Case Study of the Social History of Power," *Religion* 11(1982): 235-263.

24 See the sources cited by Morrison, in particular, Jeanne Guillemin, *Urban Renegades. The Cultural Strategy of American Indians*. New York: 1975, pp. 102-110; Edward Jack: "Maleseet Legends," *Journal of American Folklore* 9(1985): 194; Silas Rand, *Legends of the Micmacs*. New York: 1894; Frank Speck, "Penebost Tales and Religious Beliefs," *Journal of American Folklore* 48(1935): 1-107.

25 A similar syncretic process can be found among the Amerindian tribes that were evangelized by the Russian Orthodox Church. For the Tlingit Indians of Teslin (Yukon), see Margaret Denis, "The Reserve Revisited. A People Rediscovered," *Kerygma* 6(1972): 78-89; Sergei Kan, "Russian Orthodox Brotherhoods Among the Tlingit: Missionary Goals and Native Response," *Ethnohistory* 32(1985): 196-223. For the Kodiak Aleut People (Alaska), see Michael Oleksa, "Orthodoxy in Alaska: The Spiritual History of the Kodiak Aleut People," *St Vladimir's Theological Quarterly* 25(1981): 3-19; Lydia Black, "Ivan Pan'kov - An Architect of Aleut Literacy," *Arctic Anthropology* 14(1977): 94-107. See also Wendell Oswalt, *Mission of Change in Alaska*. San Marino: The Huntington Library, 1963; Jay Miller, "Tsimshian Religion in Historical Perspective: Shamans, Prophets, and Christ," Jay Miller and Carol Eastman, eds., *The Tsimshian and Their Neighbors*. Seattle: University of Washington Press, 1984.

26 See Anthony Wallace, *The Death and Rebirth of the Seneca*. Toronto: Random House of Canada, 1972.

27 See Anthony Wallace, "New Religions Among the Delaware Indians, 1600-1900," *Southwestern Journal of Anthropology* 12(1956): 1-21; Howard Peckham: *Pontiac and the Indian Uprising*. Princeton: Princeton University Press, 1947.

28 See William Fenton, ed., *Parker on the Iroquois*. Syracuse: Syracuse University Press, 1968; Elisabeth Tooker: "On the New Religion of Handsome Lake," *Anthropological Quarterly* 41(1968): 187-200; Anthony Wallace: "Cultural Composition of the Handsome Lake Religion," William Fenton and John Gulick, ed., *Symposium on Cherokee and Iroquois Culture*. Washington D.C., 1961; Wallace, *The Death and Rebirth of the Seneca*. One can find a version of the *Gaiwiio* of Handsome Lake in Sam Gill, *Native American Traditions. Sources and Interpretations*. Belmont: Wadsworth Publishing Company, 1983, pp. 146-151.

29 See Ake Hultkrantz, *Belief and Worship in Native North America*. Edited by Christopher Vesey. Syracuse: Syracuse University Press, 1981, pp. 264-281.

30 See James Mooney, *The Ghost Dance Religion and the Sioux Outbreak of 1890*. Chicago: The University of Chicago Press, 1965. Original edition: 1896.

31 See Michael Hitman, "The 1870 Ghost Dance at the Walker River Reservation: A Reconstruction," *Ethnohistory* 20(1973): 247-278.

32 See Hultkrantz, *Belief and Worship in Native North America*, pp. 212-234 (Tribal and Christian Elements in the Religious Syncretism Among the Shoshoni Indians of Wyoming). On the evolution of Amerindian eschatology, Hultkrantz, *Belief and Worship*, pp. 187-211 (The Problem of Christian Influence on Northern Algonkian Eschatology).

33 See Mooney, *The Ghost Dance Religion*; Paul Bailey: *Wovoka: The Indian Messiah*. Los Angeles: 1957; Gerald Kreyche: "The Ghost Dance Shirts," *Listening* 19(1984): 204-219. A description of Wovoka's message and of the Ghost Dance ritual can be found in Sam Gill: *Native American Traditions*, pp. 157-162.

34 See Andrew Rettig, "A Nativist Movement at Metlakatla Mission," *B.C. Studies* 46(1980): 28-39.

35 See David Mulhall, *Will to Power. The Missionary Career of Father Morice*. Vancouver: University of Vancouver Press, 1986.

36 See Robin Ridington, "Changes of Mind: Dunne-za Resistance to Empire," *B.C. Studies* 43(1979): 77-78; Anthony Wallace, "Revitalization Movements," *American Anthropologist* 58(1956): 264-281. The *Prophet Dance* goes back to prophet Smohalla, a Wanapum Indian from the Columbia Plateau who experienced visions in 1855. He predicted the total disappearance of the white race, the resurrection of all the Indians, and the restoration of the old traditions. He opposed agriculture and industrial mining which he considered a desacralization of the earth. The Religion of Smohalla or the *Prophet Dance*, an ensemble of rituals and symbols partially inspired by Christianity, spread rapidly in Canada via the Nez Perce Indians.

37 See Champagne, *Les débuts de la mission dans le Nord-Ouest canadien*, pp. 164-171.

38 See Martha McCarthy, *The Missions of the Oblates of Mary Immaculate to the Athapaskans, 1846-1870: Theory, Structure and Method*. Manitoba: Library of the University of Manitoba, Department of History, 1982 (Ph.D. Dissertation).

39 See Kerry Abel, "Prophets, Priests and Preachers: Dene Shamans and Christian Missions in the Nineteenth Century," *Historical Papers. Communications historiques*. Ottawa: Tanamac International Inc. and Mutual Press, 1986, pp. 211-224; Kerry Abel, *The Drum and the Cross*. Ph.D. Dissertation, Queen's University, 1984.

40 See Jean-Guy Goulet, "Representation of Self and Reincarnation Among the Dene-Tha," *Culture* 8(1988): 3-18.

41 See Aylward Shorter, *Jesus and the Witchdoctor. An Approach to Healing and Wholeness.* Maryknoll: Orbis Books, 1985.

42 See the Introduction by Harold Turner to Carl Starkloff, "Religious Renewal in Native North America: The Contemporary Call to Mission," *Missiology. An International Review* 13(1985): 81-82.

43 See Edward Spicer: "Yaqui," Edward Spicer, ed., *Perspectives on American Indian Culture Change.* Chicago: The University of Chicago Press, 1961, pp. 7-93; Edward Spicer: *Cycles of Conquest. The Impact of Spain, Mexico and the United States on the Indians of the Southwest 1533-1960.* Tucson: University of Arizona Press, 1967, pp. 46-85.

44 A complete list of James Mooney's documents and publications can be found in Omer Stewart, *Peyote Religion. A History.* Norman: University of Oklahoma Press, 1987, pp. 413-414.

45 For a detailed description of the historical evolution of peyotism, see Hazel Hertzberg, *The Search for an American Indian Identity. Modern Pan-Indian Movements*: Syracuse: Syracuse University Press, 1971, pp. 239-284; Omer Stewart, *Peyote Religion.* With detailed bibliography.

46 See Vittorio Lanternari, *The Religion of the Oppressed. A Study of Modern Messianic Cults.* New York: The American Library, 1965. Original Edition: *Movimenti religiosi di liberta e di salvezza dei popoli oppressi.* Milano: Feltrinelli Editore, 1960.

47 See Weston LaBarre, "Materials for a History of Studies of Crisis Cults: A Bibliography Essay," *Current Anthropology* 12(1971): 3-44.

48 See Anthony Wallace, "Revitalization Movements," *American Anthropologist* 58(1956): 264-281.

49 See Ralph Linton, "Nativistic Movements," *American Anthropologist* 45(1943): 230-240.

50 See David Aberle, *The Peyote Religion Among the Navajo.* Chicago: Aldine, 1966.

51 See Christopher Vecsey, *Imagine Ourselves Richly. Mythic Narrative of North American Indians.* New York: Crossroad, 1988, pp. 150-205. With extensive bibliography.

52 See Sven Liljeblad, *The Idaho Indians in Transition, 1805-1960.* Pocatello: Idaho State University, 1972, pp. 103-105.

53 See Paul Steinmetz, *Pipe, Bible and Peyote Among the Oglala Lakota. A Study in Religious Identity.* Knoxville: The University of Tennessee Press, 1990, pp. 101-107.

54 See Hertzberg, *The Search for American Indian Identity,* p. 282; Carl Starkloff, "Religious Renewal in Native North America," pp. 90-91.

55 See Steinmetz, *Pipe, Bible and Peyote,* pp. 153-162; 174-175.

56 See Charles Lillard, *Mission to the Nootka 1874-1900.* Reminiscences of the West Coast of Vancouver. Sidney (B.C.): Gray's Publishing Ltd., 1977.

57 Pierre Duchaussois, *Mid Snow and Ice: The Apostles of the North-West.* London: Burns Oates and Washbourne, 1932, p. 28.

58 See Jacques Rousseau, *Persistances païennes chez les Indiens de la forêt boréale* Montréal: Les Editions du Dix, 1953. In the United States of America the Sun Dance and other native religious ceremonies were forbidden by law between 1818 and 1933. In Canada, the Potlatch was forbidden by law between 1851 and 1951. See Rémi Savard and Jean-René Proulx, *Canada. Derrière l'épopée, les autochtones.* Montréal: L'Hexagone, 1982; Jean-Guy Goulet, "Liberation Theology in Canada," *Église et Théologie* 15(1984): 239-319.

59 See Adrian Tanner, *Bringing Home Animals. Religious Ideology and Mode of Production of the Mistassini Cree Hunters.* New York: St. Martin's Press; London: C. Hurst, 1979.

60 Roger Vandersteene, *Wabasca. Dix ans de vie indienne*. Gemmenich: Editions OMI, 1960, pp. 182-191.

61 See R.M. Vanderburgh, *I am Nokomis Too. The Biography of Verna Patronella Johnson*. Don Mills: General Publishing Co., 1977.

62 See Christopher Vecsey, *Traditional Ojibwa Religion in Its Historical Changes*. Philadelphia: American Philosophical Society, 1983.

63 See D. Morrisette, "Rencontre au Centre Monchanin avec Rémi Savard," *Recherches amérindiennes au Québec* 8(1978): 96.

64 See Jean-Guy Goulet, "Representation of Self and Reincarnation Among the Dene-Tha," *Culture* 8(1988): 3-18; Jean-Guy Goulet, "Religious Dualism Among Athapaskan Catholics," *Canadian Journal of Anthropology/Revue Canadienne d'Anthropologie* 3(1982): 1-18.

65 See Jean-Guy Goulet, "Visions et conversions chez les Dènès Tha. Expériences religieuses chez un peuple autochtone converti," *Religiologiques,* Automne 1992, No. 6, pp. 147-182.

66 A description of Alexis Seniantha's vision, as told by the prophet, can be found in Paul Hernou, "Même les oiseaux apportent des messages. Compte rendu d'une rencontre d'anciens tenue à l'Assomption (Alberta) du 12 au 15 août 1979," *Kerygma* 16(1982): 111-122.

67 See Nathalie Boisseau, "Un choc des cultures," *Maîtres* 2(1990): 11-18; Michael Asch and Patrick Macklem, "Aboriginal Rights and Canadian Sovereignty: An Essay on R.V. Sparrow," *Alberta Law Review* 24(1991): 498-517; Dora Wilson-Kenni, "Time of Trial: The Gitksan and Wet'suwet'en in Court," *B.C. Studies* 95(1992): 7-11. For an overview of the Gitksan-Wet'suwet'en spirituality and court case, see Terry Glavin, *A Death Feast in Dimlahamid*. Vancouver: New Star Books, 1990.

68 See Carl Starkloff, "The Anishnabe Ministry Training Project: Scriptural-Theological Formation," *Kerygma* 19(1985): 71-81.

69 See Achiel Peelman, "Christianisme et cultures amérindiennes. Présentation et analyse d'une démarche théologique interculturelle," *Église et Théologie* 22(1991): 131-156.

70 See William Powers, *Beyond the Vision. Essays on American Indian Culture*. Norman: University of Oklahoma Press, 1987, pp. 94-125 (Dual Religious Participation: Stratagems of Conversion Among the Lakota).

71 See Vine Deloria, Jr, *God is Red. A Native View of Religion. Second Edition*. Golden: North American Press, 1992, pp. 218-235.

72 See Powers, *Beyond the Vision*, p. 122. Only recently did the Lakota start sharing their visions with the missionaries. See William Stolzman, *The Pipe and Christ. A Christian-Sioux Dialogue*. Chamberlain, S.D.: Tipi Press, 1986.

73 See Steinmetz, *Pipe, Bible and Peyote*, p. 179.

74 See Steinmetz, *Pipe, Bible and Peyote*, pp. 170-200.

75 See Kenneth Morrison, "Discourse and the Accommodation of Values: Toward a Revision of Mission History," *Journal of the American Academy of Religion* 53(1985): 378; Kenneth Morrison: *The Embattled Northeast: The Elusive Ideal of Alliance in Abenaki-Euramerican Relations*. Berkeley: University of California Press, 1984.

76 See Sergei Kan: "Introduction," *Arctic Anthropology* 24, No. 1 (1987): 1-7. This issue contains proceedings from the Conference on Native Cultures and Christianity in the Circumpolar area of the American Anthropological Association, 1983.

77 Paul Tillich, *Theology and Culture*. New York: Oxford University, 1959, p. 42.

78 See Achiel Peelman, *L'inculturation. L'Église et les cultures*. Paris: Desclée - Ottawa: Novalis, 1988, pp. 9-7.

79 See Karl Rahner, *Le courage du théologien*. Paris: Les Éditions du Cerf, 1985, pp. 223-224.

80 See Carl Starkloff, "New Tribal Religious Movements in North America," *Toronto Journal of Theology* 2(1986): 157-171.

81 See the entire issue of *Missiology. An International Review* 13, No. 1 (1985).

82 See Robert Schreiter, "Faith and Cultures: Challenges to a World Church," *Theological Studies* 50(1989): 744-760.

83 See Kan, "Introduction," pp. 1-7.

84 See W.E. Windey, *Machetakonia. Pater Jan De Smet van Dendermonde bij de Indianen en de Amerikanen*. Dendermonde: Pater Jan De Smet Aktie Gelegenheidsuitgave. Drukkerij De Hauwere-Huau, 1984.

85 See René Fumoleau, *As Long as This Land Shall last. A History of Treaty 8 and Treaty 11, 1870-1939*. Toronto: McLelland and Stewart, 1973.

86 See Alan Tippet, "Christopaganism or Indigenous Christianity?," Charles Kraft and Tom Wisley, ed., *Readings in Dynamic Indigeneity*. Passadena: William Carey Library, 1979, pp. 400-421.

87 See Carl Starkloff, "God as Oppressor? Changing God's Name Among Contemporary Arapaho," *Kerygma* 17(1983): 165-174.

88 See Vincent Cosmao, *Changing the World. An Agenda for the Churches*. Maryknoll: Orbis Books, 1984, pp. 46-49.

89 See Arnulf Camps, "Four Key-Notions for a more Empirical Missiology," *Neue Zeitschrift für Missionswissenschaften* 29(1973), pp. 133-142.

90 See Jean-Guy Goulet, "The Church and Aboriginal Self-Government. Tradition and Change in the North Today," *Kerygma* 21(1987): 207-244.

91 See Mary Davis (e.a.), "Ambe! Ambe! Kitakwita! A Story of Adult Religious Education Among Native People," *Insight. A Journal for Adult Religious Education*. Ottawa: Canadian Conference of Catholic Bishops. National Office of Religious Education: 1987 Edition, pp. 42-49.

92 See the different models of syncretism in Leonardo Boff, *Igreja: Carisma e Poder. Ensaios de Eclesiologia Militante*. Petropolis: Vozes, 1982, pp. 145-171 (*Church: Charisma and Power. Liberation Theology and the Institutional Church*. New York: Crossroad, 1985).

93 See Judith Shapiro, "From Tupa to the Land without Evil: The Christianization of Tupi-Guarani Cosmology," *American Ethnologist* 14(1987): 126-139.

94 See Sergie Kan, "Russian Orthodox Brotherhoods Among the Tlinglit: Missionary Goals and Native Responses," *Ethnohistory* 32(1985): 196-223.

95 See Champagne, *Les débuts de la mission dans le Nord-Ouest canadien*, pp. 164-171; Trigger, *Natives and Newcomers*, passim; Grant, *Moon of Wintertime*, passim; Mulhall, *Will to Power*, passim.

96 See McCarthy, *The Missions of the Oblates of Mary Immaculate to the Athapaskans, 1846-1870*, passim.

97 See Powers, *Beyond the Vision*, pp. 147-168 (Beyond the Vision: Trends Toward Ecumenism in American Indian Religions).

98 See, for example, Carl Starkloff, "Keepers of Tradition. The Symbol of Power in Indigenous Ministry," *Kerygma* 23(1989): 3-120.

99 As early as 1959, the entire Semaine de Missiologie de Louvain (Belgium) was dedicated to the topic of inculturation.

100 See Peelman, *L'inculturation*, pp. 112-122.

101 See Achiel Peelman, "L'inculturation. Une vision nouvelle de l'évangélisation," *L'Église canadienne* 23(1990): 231-235; René Jaouen, "Conditions for Authentic Inculturation. Some Observations of a Missionary in Cameroon," *Kerygma* 19(1985): 3-15; Aylward Shorter, *Toward a Theology of Inculturation.* Maryknoll: Orbis Books, 1988.

102 John Paul II, "Celebration of the Word. Martyr's Shrine, Huronia. September 15, 1984," *Canadian Catholic Review* 2, No. 9 (1984): 368.

103 A.-M. Carré, ed., *Pour vous qui est Jésus-Christ?* Paris: Les Éditions du Cerf, 1970, pp. 140 (my translation).

104 See Normand Provencher, "Singularité de Jésus et universalité du Christ," Jean-Claude Petit et Jean-Claude Breton, eds., *Jésus: Christ universel? Interprétations anciennes et appropriations contemporaines de la figure de Jésus.* Montréal: Fides, 1989, pp. 9-24.

105 See Jacques Dupuis, *Christ at the Encounter of World Religions.* Maryknoll: Orbis Books, 1991, p. 191.

106 See, for example, Paul Knitter, *No Other Name? A Critical Survey of Christian Attitudes Toward the World Religions.* Maryknoll: Orbis Books, 1985.

107 See, for example, Hans Urs Von Balthasar, *A Theology of History.* New York: Sheed and Ward, 1963, pp. 77-107; Achiel Peelman: *Hans Urs Von Balthasar et la Théologie de l'histoire.* Bern: Peter Lang, 1978, pp. 300-331.

108 Walter Kasper, *Jesus the Christ.* Mahwah: Paulist Press, 1976, pp. 267-268; Dupuis: *Jesus Christ at the Encounter of the World Religions,* pp. 152-177.

Notes to Chapter 4

1 See Achiel Peelman, "Christianisme et cultures amérindiennes. Présentation et analyse d'une démarche théologique interculturelle," *Église et Théologie* 22(1991): 131-156.

2 In other areas of Canada, for example, such as the Roman Catholic Diocese of Thunder Bay (Ontario), Catholic Anishnabe are reflecting on how to bring together their traditional name-giving ceremony and the Christian baptism.

3 This summary is based on a report prepared by Denis Paquin, O.M.I., one of the animators of the session.

4 In this synthesis of the meetings which took place in Dryden, Fort Frances and Thunder Bay, all the names are fictitious.

5 See Jean-Guy Goulet and Achiel Peelman, *The Amerindian Reality and the Catholic Church in Canada.* Brussels: Pro Mundi Vita Bulletin 93, 1983.

6 Data provided by Sister Theresa Smith.

7 See Pat Moore and A. Wheelock, eds., *Myths and Visions. Dene Traditions from Northern Alberta.* Compiled by the Dene Wodih Society. Illustrated by Dia Thurston. Edmonton: The University of Alberta Press, 1990, p. 3 and p. 62.

8 See Paul Hernou: "Même les oiseaux apportent des messages. Compte rendu d'une rencontre d'anciens tenue à l'Assomption (Alberta) du 12 au 15 août 1979," *Kerygma* 16(1982): 122.

9 Quoted in *Spirit.* Baptism of the Lord, 3, No. 11 (1991): 2.

Notes to Chapter 5

1   See, in particular, Raymond DeMaillie, *Sioux Indian Religion*. Norman: University of Oklahoma Press, 1975; William Powers: *Oglala Religion*. Lincoln: University of Nebraska Press, 1975; J.B. Walker (ed. J. DeMaillie and Elaine Jahner), *Lakota Belief and Ritual*. Lincoln: University of Nebraska Press, 1982; Vivian One Feather, ed., *Ehanin Ohunkakan: Myths of the Walker Collection*. Spearfish, S.D.: Black Hills State College, 1974.

2   See William Stoltzman, *The Pipe and Christ. A Christian-Sioux Dialogue*. Chamberlain, S.D.: Tipi Press, 1986, pp. 166-179.

3   See Paul Steinmetz, "The Sacred Pipe in American Indian Religions," *American Indian Culture and Research Journal* 8(1984): 27-80; Jordan Paper: *Offering Smoke. The Sacred Pipe and Native American Religion*. Edmonton: The University of Alberta Press, 1989.

4   See Maureen Korp, *The Sacred Geography of the American Mound Builders*. Queenston/Lampeter: The Edwin Mellen Press, 1990.

5   See Stolzman, *The Pipe and Christ*, p. 169.

6   See Joseph Epes Brown, *The Sacred Pipe. Black Elk's Account of the Seven Rites of the Oglala Sioux*. Norman: University of Oklahoma Press, 1953 (1988). Black Elk, who told the legend to Brown in 1948, had told a shorter version to Neihardt in 1932. See John Neihardt, *Black Elk Speaks. Being a Life Story of a Holy Man of the Oglala Sioux*. Lincoln: University of Nebraska Press, 1961.

7   See Michael Steltenkamp, *The Sacred Pipe. Native American Religion and its Practice Today*. New York/Ramsey: Paulist Press, 1982, p. 24.

8   See Stolzman, *The Pipe and Christ*, p. 178.

9   See Gayla Twiss, "The Role of the Pipe in Dakota Religion," *Pine Ridge Research Bulletin*, No. 10, August 1969, p. 8.

10 See Paul Hernou, "Missionary Among the Cree of Northern Alberta: The Challenge of Inculturation," *Kerygma* 21(1987): 242.

11 See William Powers, *Beyond the Vision. Essays on American Indian Culture*. Norman: University of Oklahoma Press, 1987. Chapter 3: Counting Your Blessings: Sacred Numbers and the Structure of Reality.

12 "Baseline Data Study - Some Notes on Denominational Preferences Among the Oglalas," *Pine Ridge Research Bulletin*, No. 10, August 1969, pp. 1-6; Gordon McGregor: *Warriors Without Weapons*. Chicago: University of Chicago Press, 1946, pp. 91-98.

13 See Paul Steinmetz, *Pipe, Bible and Peyote Among the Oglala Lakota. A Study in Religious Identity*. Knoxville: The University of Tennessee Press, 1990. All further references to this book are quoted in the text.

14 See Mircea Eliade, "Methodological Remarks on the Study of Religious Symbolism," in Mircea Eliade and Joseph Kitagara, eds., *Essays in Methodology*. Chicago: University of Chicago Press, 1959, pp. 106-107.

15 See Paul Steinmetz, "Christian Meets Lakota Sioux," *Listening* 19(1984): 222.

16 See footnote 6.

17 See Stolzman, *The Pipe and Christ*, p. 208. All further references to this book are quoted in the text.

18 See Powers, *Oglala Religion*, p. 116.

19   See Roger Vandersteene, *Wabasca. Dix ans de vie indienne*. Gemmenich: Editions O.M.I., 1960. Adapted from the Dutch by Jacques De Deken. All further references to this book are quoted in the text.

20   See Hernou, "Missionary Among the Cree." The Cree pipes are made out of a rather soft stone of red or slate-grey colour. Some of these pipes are very old. The most frequently encountered bowl shape is the reversed T-shape. The rounded bowl is drilled in the vertical bar, while a hole for the stem is drilled in the horizontal bar. According to Jordan (*Offering Smoke*, pp. 94-97) the T-shaped pipes have been widely used by the Plains Indians since the nineteenth century. The standard T-shaped pipe is thus relatively modern, but is based on a widely-distributed shape of considerable antiquity whose religious significance is well-established.

21   See Achiel Peelman, "Christianisme et cultures amérindiennes. Présentation et analyse d'une démarche théologique interculturelle," *Église et Théologie* 22(1991): 131-156.

22   Hernou, "Missionary Among the Cree," pp. 240-241.

23   Vandersteene, *Wabasca*, p. 192 (my translation).

24   Information provided by Guy Lavallée, O.M.I.

25   See Leslie Crossingham, "Crowshoe says now is time to reveal our culture," *Windspeaker* 6, No. 3 (1988): 12.

26   See Walter Vogels, *God's Universal Covenant: A Biblical Study*. Ottawa: Saint Paul University, 1979.

27   See René Jaouen, "L'histoire des peuples non-chrétiens peut-elle servir d'Ancien Testament," *Kerygma* 20(1986): 229-238.

28   See the testimony of Eva Solomon in the previous chapter. Also, René Jaouen, "Le puits était profond ... (Jean 4:1-42)," *Communauté chrétienne* 1, No. 4 (1990): 18-21.

29   See "Dialogue and Proclamation: Reflections and Orientations on Interreligious Dialogue and the Proclamation of the Gospel of Jesus Christ, by the Pontifical Council for Interreligious Dialogue and the Congregation for the Evangelization of Peoples," *Origins* 21, No. 8 (1991): 121-135.

30   See Marcello Zago, "Day of Prayer for Peace. Assisi, 27 October 1986," *Kerygma* 21(1987): 100.

31   John Paul II, "To the Native Peoples. Ste-Anne-de-Beaupré, 10 September 1984," *The Canadian Catholic Review* 2, No. 9 (1984): 329.

32   John Paul II, "Celebration of the Word. Martyr's Shrine. Huronia, 15 September 1984," *The Canadian Catholic Review* 2, No. 9 (1984): 368.

33   John Paul II, "To the Native Peoples," *The Canadian Catholic Review* 2, No. 9 (1984): 380.

34   See the Pastoral Letter by Most Rev. James Griffin, Bishop of Columbus, Ohio, published on May 9, 1991: "Reflections on Evangelization Yesterday, Today and Tomorrow," *Origins* 21(1991): 57-66.

35   See Vine Deloria, "Religion and the Modern American Indian," *Current History* 67(1974): 253.

36   See Harold Cardinal, "There is no Reason for us to Fear Each Other," *Kerygma* 18(1984): 53-56.

37   Paul Hernou, "Même les oiseaux apportent des messages. Compte rendu d'une rencontre d'anciens tenue à l'Assomption (Alberta) du 12 au 15 août 1979," *Kerygma* 16(1982): 120.

38   See Secretariat for Non-Christians, *The Attitude of the Church Toward the Followers of Other Religions: Reflections and Orientations on Dialogue and Mission*. Rome: 1984, Nos. 28-35.

39   See Jacques Johnston, "Native Spirituality and the Catholic Faith. The Beginning of Dialogue," *Kerygma* 16(1982): 123-132.

40   See Jon Magnuson, "Echoes of a Shaman's Song: Artifacts and Ethics in the Northwest," *The Christian Century*, April 1987, pp. 406-408; "Affirming Native Spirituality: A Call to Justice," *The Christian Century*, December 1987, pp. 1114-1117.

41   See "The Church and American Indians: Towards Dialogue and Respect," *Origins* 6(1977): 766-769.

42   See Silvio Fittipaldi, "Open Forum and Reader Response. The Catholic Church and the American Indian," *Horizons* 5(1978): 73-75.

43   See Stolzman, *The Pipe and Christ*; Steinmetz, *Pipe, Bible and Peyote*.

44   See Chief John Snow, *The Mountains are our Sacred Places. The Story of the Stoney People*. Toronto-Sarasota: Samuel Stevens, 1977, pp. 142-149.

45   See Deloria, "Religion and the Modern Indian," *Current History* 67(1974): 251-252.

46   See Peelman, "Christianisme et cultures amérindiennes."

47   See Steinmetz, *Pipe, Bible and Peyote*, pp. 163-200.

48   See Achiel Peelman, "L'actualité des religions amérindiennes au Canada," *Revue Internationale d'Action Communautaire. International review of Community Development* 66, No. 26 (1991): 11-118.

49   See "Litany of the Lord's Prayer," *Cross and Feather News. Tekakwitha Conference National Center* 10, No. 1 (1991): 11.

50   See Powers, *Beyond the Vision*. Chapter 7: Beyond the Vision: Trends Towards Ecumenism in American Native Religions.

51   Zago, "Day of Prayer For Peace," p. 105.

52   The official viewpoint adopted by "Dialogue and Proclamation," No. 13, which refers to another recent document in which the question of the new religious movements is treated. The complete text of this document can be found in *Origins* 16(1986). French original in *La Documentation Catholique* 69 No. 1991 (1986): 547-554.

53   See John Paul II, "Voici pour vous l'heure d'une naissance nouvelle," *La Documentation Catholique* 69 No. 1932 (1987): 133-139; "Defense of the Rights of Aboriginal Peoples in Alice Springs, Australia, November 29, 1986," *Origins* 16(1986): 473-475.

54   "A New Covenant. Towards the Constitutional Recognition and Protection of Aboriginal Self-Government in Canada. A Pastoral Statement by the Leaders of the Christian Churches on Aboriginal Rights and the Canadian Constitution. February 1987," *Kerygma* 21(1987): 141-146. See also Achiel Peelman, "Le Défi du dialogue Amérindien-Chrétien au Canada," *S.C.H.E.C. Etudes d'histoire religieuse* 60(1994): 35-46.

Notes to Chapter 6

1   See Jacques Ellul, *The New Demons*. New York: Seabury Press, 1975, pp. 133-136. Original: *Les nouveaux possédés*. Paris: Fayard, 1983, pp. 170-174.

2   See Aylward Shorter, *Jesus and the Witchdoctor. An Approach to Healing and Wholeness*. Maryknoll: Orbis Books, 1985.

3   See Aylward Shorter, "Christian Healing and Traditional Medicine in Africa," *Kerygma* 20(1986): 51-58.

4   Shorter, *Jesus and the Witchdoctor*, p. 167.

5 See Richard Friedli, *Le Christ dans les cultures*. Fribourg (Suisse): Editions Universitaires - Paris: Éditions du Cerf, 1989.

6 This title comes from the Caribbean poet Aimé Césaire.

7 See Arnold Camps, "Four Key-Notions for a More Empirical Missiology," *Zeitschrift für Missionswissenschaften* 29(1973): 137.

8 See Shorter, *Jesus and the Witchdoctor*, pp. 110-111.

9 See Wolfgang Gilek, *Indian Healing. Shamanic Ceremonialism in the Pacific Northwest Today*. Surrey-Washington: Hancock House, 1982.

10 See David Young, Gran Ingram, Lise Swartz, *Cry of the Eagle. Encounters with a Cree Healer*. Toronto: University of Toronto Press, 1989.

11 See, for example, the "Summary Chart. The Gifts of the Four Directions," *The Sacred Tree*. Lethbridge: Four Winds Development Project, 1984.

12 See Hartley Burr Alexander, *The World's Rim. Great Mysteries of the North American Indians*. Lincoln: University of Nebraska Press, 1953, p. 46.

13 See Maggie Hodgson, "The Eagle Has Landed," *Kerygma* 23(1989): 195-203.

14 See Achiel Peelman, "Traditional Native Spiritual Practice in Canada's Federal Prisons," *Kerygma* 20(1986): 101-119.

15 See Christopher Vecsey, *Imagine Ourselves Richly. Mythic Narratives of North American Indians*. New York: The Crossroad Publishing Company, 1988, pp. 206-232.

16 See Eva Solomon, "The Sweat Lodge. Spiritual Rebirth for Men and Women Through the Revival of a Sacred First Nations Tradition," *Home Mission* 8, No. 3 (1989): 10-12.

17 See Vecsey, *Imagine Ourselves Richly*, p. 207.

18 See Etienne Trocme, *Jésus de Nazareth vu par les témoins de sa vie*. Neuchâtel: Delachaux et Niestlé, 1971, pp. 120-123; *La Formation de l'Évangile selon Marc*. Paris: Presses Universitaires de France, 1963, pp. 90-94.

19 See Michael Harper, *The Healings of Jesus*. London: Hodder and Stronghton, 1986; Helge Kjaer Nielsen, *Heilung und Verkündigung bei Jezus und in der ältesten Kirche*. Leiden: R.J. Brill, 1987; Morton Kefsey, *Psychology, Medicine and Christian Healing*. San Francisco: Harper and Row, 1988 (with extensive bibliography).

20 See Jean-François Six, *Jésus*. Paris: Editions Aimery-Simogy, 1972, pp. 81-88.

21 See Fritz Arnold, *Der Glaube der dich Heilt: Zur therapeutischen Dimension des christlichen Glaubens*. Regensburg: F. Pustet, 1983; Bernhard Häring, *Healing and Revelation: Wounded Healers Sharing Christ's Mission*. Slough: St. Paul Publications, 1984; *Vom Glauben der gesund macht: Ermutigung der heilenden Berufe*. Freiburg: Herder, 1987; Helmut Jaschke, *Psychotherapie aus dem Neuen Testament: Heilende Gegegnungen mit Jesus*. Frieburg: Herder, 1987.

22 See Hans Urs Von Balthasar, *Theology: The New Covenant (The Glory of the Lord: A Theological Aesthetics*, Vol. 7). Edinburgh: T.& T. Clark, 1989, pp. 115-161.

23 Hans Urs Von Balthasar, *La foi du Christ*. Paris: Aubier, 1968, p. 181 (my translation).

24 See François Varonne, *Ce Dieu censé aimer la souffrance*. Paris: Cerf, 1984.

25 See Balthasar, *Theology: The New Covenant*, pp. 69-79.

26 Richard Bergeron, "Libérateur ou Thérapeute?," *Communauté chrétienne* 28, No. 164 (1989): 112 (my translation).

27 Testimony by an Oblate missionary working among the Montagnais. *Pastoral Session*, Mingan (Québec), 1982. Personal fieldnotes.

28 Based on testimonies presented during the Session of the *Native Pastoral Council*, Diocese of Thunder Bay (Ontario), November 21-24, 1991. Personal fieldnotes.

29 Research on Amerindian Church, Beauval (Saskatchewan), April 6, 1983. Personal fieldnotes.

30 Albert Nolan, *Jesus Before Christianity*. Maryknoll: Orbis Books, 1978, pp. 35-36.

31 Grant Maxwell, "Culture, Religion Rooted in Respect for Nature," *Prairie Messenger*, January 11, 1988, p. 11.

32 George Leach and Greg Humbert, *Beedahbun. First Light of Dawn. Featuring the Paintings of Leland Bell*. North Bay: Tomiko Publications; Espanola: Anishnabe Centre, 1989, p. 80.

33 See Elaine O'Farrell, "Church Art Shows Indian Jesus," *Windspeaker*, February 17, 1989.

34 See James Axtell, *The European and the Indian. Essais in the Ethnography of Colonial North America*. Oxford: Oxford University Press, 1981, pp. 39-86; James Axtell, *The Invasion Within. The Contest of Cultures in Colonial North America*. Oxford: Oxford University Press, 1985, pp. 91-127; Lucien Campeau, *La mission des Jésuites chez les Hurons 1634-1650*. Montréal: Bellarmin - Rome: Institutum Historicum S.J., 1987, pp. 97-112; Bruce Trigger, *Natives and Newcomers. Canada's "Heroic Age" Reconsidered*. Kingston - Montreal: McGill - Queen's University Press, 1985, pp. 226-297; David Mulhall, *Will to Power. The Missionary Career Of Father Morice*. Vancouver: University of British Columbia Press, 1986, pp. 41, 53-55, 66, 71, 141-143, 150; Kerry Abel, "Prophets, Priests and Preachers: Dene Shamans and Christian Missions in the Nineteenth Century," *Historical Papers. Communications Historiques*. Ottawa: Tamarac International Inc. and Mutual Press, 1986, pp. 211-224.

35 While competing with the shamans for spiritual power, the same missionaries did not hesitate to appeal to images of the devil and hell to conquer the soul of the Indians. The devil was sometimes described as the most efficient missionary! See Jean-Guy Goulet, "Liberation Theology and Missions in Canada," *Église et Théologie* 15(1984): 293-319.

36 See Vittorio Lanternari, *The Religion of the Oppressed. A Study of Modern Messianic Cults*. New York: The American Library, 1965. Original Edition: *Movimenti religiosi di liberta e di salvezza dei popoli oppressi*. Milano: Feltrinelli Editore, 1960.

37 Shorter, *Jesus and the Witchdoctor*, p. 16.

38 See, for example, Shirley Shih-Hsin Chin, *Practices of Folk Religion and Christianity in Taiwan*. Ann Arbor: University Microfilms International, 1985; Gerardus C. Oosthuizen, ed., *Afro-Christian Religion and Healing in Southern Africa*. Lewiston: E. Mellen Press, 1989.

39 See Cécé Kolie, "Jésus guérisseur?," François Kabasele, ed., *Chemins de la christologie africaine*. Paris: Desclée, 1986, pp. 167-199.

40 Ake Hultkrantz, *Les religions des Indiens primitifs d'Amérique. Essai d'une synthèse typologique et historique*. Acta Universitatis Stockholmiensis. Stockholm: Studies in Comparative Religion, 1963. Volume 4; Young, *Cry of the Eagle*, p. ix.

41 All these elements can be found in Mircea Eliade, *Le chamanisme et les techniques archaïques de l'extase*. Paris: Payot, 1978. See also Danielle Vazeilles, *Les chamanes*. Paris: Cerf-Fides, 1991.

42 See, for example, Amanda Porterfield, "Shamanism: A Psychological Definition," *Journal of the American Academy of Religion* 55(1987): 721-739.

43 See Enrique Dussel, "Popular Religion as Oppression and Liberation: Hypotheses on its Past and Present in Latin America," *Concilium* 186(4/1986): 82-94.

44 See Hans Urs Von Balthasar, *Mysterium Paschale: The Mystery of Easter*. Edinburgh: T.& T. Clark, 1990, pp. 89-147.

45   See Frank Cassidy, "Aboriginal Government in Canada: An Emerging Field of Studies,"
      Canadian Journal of Political Science/Revue canadienne de science politique 23, No. 1 (1990):
      73-99.

46   See George Manuel and Michael Posluns, eds., *The Fourth World. An Indian Reality.* Don
      Mills: Collier - Macmillan Canada Ltd., 1975; Mel Watkins, ed., *Dene Nation - The Colony
      Within.* Toronto: University of Toronto Press, 1977.

47   See René Fumoleau, "The Challenge of Justice in the Canadian North," *Grail: An Ecumenical
      Journal* 1988, pp. 7-20.

48   These laws are the *British North America Act* (1867), the *Statute of Westminster* (1931) and the
      Constitution Act (1982).

49   See Brian Slattery, "Understanding Aboriginal Rights," *The Canadian Bar Review* 66(1987):
      727-783; William Pentney, "The Rights of the Aboriginal Peoples of Canada and the
      Constitution Act, 1982," *U.B.C. Law Review* 22 Vol. I (1988): 21-59; Vol. II: 207-279.

50   See Anthony Pagden, *The Fall of Natural Man. The American Indian and the Origins of
      Comparative Ethnology.* Cambridge: Cambridge University Press, 1982.

51   See Leslie Green and Oliva Dickason, *The Law of Nations and the New World.* Edmonton:
      University of Alberta Press, 1989.

52   James Muldoon, *Popes, Lawyers and Infidels. The Church and the Non-Christian World 1250-
      1550.* Philadelphia: University of Pennsylvania Press, 1979.

53   Pedro Casaldaliga, "The 'Crucified' Indians - A Case of Anonymous Collective Martyrdom,"
      Concilium 163 (3/1983): 51.

54   Quoted by Casaldaliga, "The 'Crucified' Indians," pp. 49-50; See also "Geneva 1977: A Report
      on the Hemispheric Movement of Indigenous Peoples," *A Basic Call to Consciousness* (edited
      by *Akwesasne Notes*, Mohawk Nation, Rooseveltown, N.Y., 1982), pp. 38-64.

55   "Les chemins de l'Évangile. 500ᵉ anniversaire de l'évangélisation des Amériques 1492-1992,"
      Univers, February 1991, p. 16 (my translation).

56   See Vine Deloria, "A Native Perspective on Liberation," Gerald Anderson and Thomas
      Stransky, eds., *Mission Trends No. 4. Liberation Theologies in North America and Europe.* New
      York: Paulist Press, 1989, pp. 261-270.

57   See "Les deux tendances actuelles de la théologie de la libération. Exposé et interview du P.
      Juan Segundo, S.J.," *La Documentation catholique* 88, No. 1881 (1984): 912-917.

58   See Gustavo Gutierrez, *The Power of the Poor in History: Selected Writings.* Maryknoll: Orbis
      Books, 1983.

59   See Walter Vogels, "Biblical Theology for the 'Haves' and the 'Have-Nots'," *Science et Esprit*
      39(1987): 193-210.

60   See Jean L'Hour, "The People of the Covenant Encounters the Nations. Israel and Canaan,"
      Mariasusai Dhavamony, ed., *Evangelization, Dialogue and Development. Selected Papers of
      the International Theological Conference. Nagpur (India) 1971.* Roma: Università Gregoriana
      Editrice, 1972, pp. 77-85.

61   See Robert Allan Warrior, "Cannanites, Cowboys and Indians. Deliverance, Conquest and
      Liberation Theology Today," *Christianity and Crisis,* September 11, 1989, pp. 261-265.

62   See Claus Gussmann, *Who do you say? Jesus Christ in Latin American Theology.* Maryknoll:
      Orbis Books, 1985, pp. 32-36.

63   William Baldridge, "Native American Theology: A Biblical Basis," *Christianity and Culture,*
      May 28, 1990, pp. 17-18. With a reply by Warrior.

64   "Les deux tendances actuelles ...", pp. 912-913.

65   Gutierrez, *The Power of the Poor in History*, p. 99.

66   See Marie-Dominique Chenu, *Une école de théologie: le Saulchoir*. Paris: Cerf, 1985.

67   See *Recovering the Feather. The First Anglican Native Convention. March 1989*. Reproduction
      of a text published in *Anglican Magazine*, December 1988.

68   See Harold Cardinal, *The Unjust Society. The Tragedy of Canada's Indians*. Edmonton: M.G.
      Hurtig Ltd., 1969; *The Rebirth of Canada's Indians. An Indian Declaration of Independence*.
      Edmonton: Hurtig Publishers, 1977.

69   See Anton Wessels *Images of Jesus. How Jesus is Perceived and Portrayed in Non-Western
      Cultures*. Grand Rapids: Eerdmans, 1990. Original: *Jezus zien. Hoe Jezus is overgeleverd in
      andere culturen*. Baarn: Ten Have, 1986; William Dyrness, *Learning About Theology from the
      Third World*. Grand Rapids: Academic Books, 1990, pp. 71-120.

70   Deloria, "A Native Perspective on Liberation," p. 263.

71   See Jon Magnuson, "Echoes of a Shaman's Song: Artifacts and Ethics in the Northwest," *The
      Christian Century* April 1987, pp. 406-408.

72   See Thomas Berry, "The Indian Future," *Cross Currents* 26(1967): 133-142.

73   See "A New Covenant. Towards the Constitutional Recognition and Protection of Aboriginal
      Self-Government in Canada. A Pastoral Statement by the Leaders of the Christian Churches on
      Aboriginal Rights and the Canadian Constitution. February 1987," *Kerygma* 21(1987): 141-
      146.

74   See Walter Principe, "Catholicity, Inculturation and Liberation Theology. Do They Mix?,"
      Franciscan Studies 47(1987): 24-43.

75   "Les chemins de l'Évangile," *Univers*, February 1991, p. 19.

76   See Achiel Peelman, "Christianisme et cultures amérindiennes. Présentation et analyse d'une
      démarche théologique interculturelle," *Église et Théologie* 22(1991): 131-156.

77   Mary Davies (e.a.), "Ambe. Ambe. Kitakwita. A Story of Adult Religious Education Among
      Native People," *Insight. A Journal for Adult Religious Education*. 1987 Edition. Ottawa:
      Canadian Conference of Catholic Bishops, p. 42.

78   See Jean-Guy Goulet, "The Church and Aboriginal Self-Government. Tradition and Change in
      the North Today," *Kerygma* 21(1987): 207-224.

79   See Gregory Baum, "Le pluralisme ethnique au Québec," *Relations* No. 570, May 1991, pp.
      117-119.

80   See Goulet, "Liberation Theology and Missions in Canada," pp. 293-319.

81   See, for example, the information published in 1991 by the Canadian Conference of Catholic
      Bishops, by the Aboriginal Rights Coalition and the Project North group of Vancouver.

82   See "Entrevue avec Dom Fragoso," *Univers*, February 1991, pp. 22-23 (my translation).

83   See Remi De Roo, "The Fourth World and the Christian Churches. Developing New Forms of
      Mission in Solidarity with Aboriginal People," *Kerygma* 17(1983): 115.

84   See "An Apology to the First Nations of Canada on Behalf of the 1200 Missionary Oblates of
      Mary Immaculate Living and Ministering in Canada," *Kerygma* 25(1991): 129-133; "A Public
      Declaration to the Tribal Councils and Traditional Spiritual Leaders of the Indian and Eskimo
      Peoples of the Pacific Northwest" by representatives of ten churches in the United States. See
      Jon Magnuson, "Affirming Native Spirituality: A Call to Justice," *The Christian Century*,
      December 1987, pp. 1114-1117.

85   See Mary Jo Leddy, "Where is here? Towards a Canadian Theology," *Home Mission* 8, No. 3
      (1989): 19-28.

Notes to Chapter 7

1   Karl Rahner: "Towards a Fundamental Interpretation of Vatican II," *Theological Studies* 40(1979), p. 721; see also *Le courage du théologien*. Paris: Les Editions du Cerf, 1985, pp. 223-224.

2   See Tissa Balasuriya, *Planetary Theology*. Maryknoll: Orbis Books, 1984.

3   See Gérard Siegwalt, "Cosmologie et Théologie. Pour une nouvelle coordination entre Science, Philosophie et Théologie," *Etudes théologiques et religieuses* 51(1976): 313-337.

4   Siegwalt, "Cosmologie et Théologie," p. 320.

5   See Claus Westermann, *Blessings in the Bible and in the Life of the Church*. Philadelphia: Fortress Press, 1978, pp. 1-14.

6   See Paul Tillich, *Systematic Theology*. Welwyn: J. Nisbet, 1960. Part II, II (The Reality of God); Karl Rahner, *Foundations of Christian Faith. An Introduction to the Idea of Christianity*. New York: Seabury press, 1978, pp. 44-89 (Man in the Presence of the Absolute Mystery). Original: *Grundkurs des Glaubens. Einführung in den Begriff des Christentums*. Freiburg: Herder, 1977.

7   See Balasuriya, *Planetary Theology*, pp. 2-10.

8   See Evode Beaucamp, *The Bible and the Universe. Israel and the Theology of History*. Montreal: Palm Publishers, 1963. Original: *La Bible et le sens religieux de l'univers*. Paris: Editions du Cerf, 1959; Piet Schoonenberg, *Covenant and Creation*. London: Sheed and Ward, 1968. Original: *Het geloof van ons doopsel*. Chapters 1-4: *Verbond en Schepping*. 's-Hertogenbosch: L.G.C. Malmberg, 1955-56; Claus Westermann, *Creation*. London: S.P.C.K., 1974. Original: *Schöpfung*. Stuttgart: Kreuz-Verlag, 1971.

9   See Walter Vogels, *God's Universal Covenant. A Biblical Study*. Ottawa: University of Ottawa Press, 1986.

10 See Jean-François Bonnefoy, *Christ and the Cosmos*. Paterson, N.J.: St. Anthony Gould Press, 1965. Original: *La primauté du Christ selon l'Écriture et la Tradition*. Rome: Herder, 1959; André Feuillet, *Le Christ Sagesse de Dieu d'après les Épîtres Pauliniennes*. Paris: J. Gabalda, 1966; Franz Mussner, *Christus, das All und die Kirche. Studien zur Theologie des Epheserbriefes*. Trier: Paulinus-Verlag, 1955; Anton Vogtle, *Das Neue Testament und die Zukunft des Kosmos*. Düsseldorf: Patmos-Verlag, 1971.

11 See Marie-Emile Boismard, *St. John's Prologue*. London: Blackfriars Publications, 1957. Original: *Le Prologue de saint Jean*. Paris: Editions du Cerf, 1953; François-Marie Braun, *Jean le Théologien*. II. Sa Théologie. III. Le Christ, Notre Seigneur, hier, aujourd'hui, toujours. Paris: Librairie Lecoffre, J. Gabalda, 1972; Henri Van Den Bussche, *Jean. Commentaire de l'Évangile spirituel*. Bruges: Desclée De Brouwer, 1967. pp. 65-106.

12 See Hans Urs Von Balthasar, *Eludications*. London: S.P.C.K., 1975. pp. 50-56. Original: *Klarstellungen. Zur Prüfund der Geister*. Freibuer: Herderbücherei, 1971; *A Theology of History*. New York: Sheed and Ward, 1963, pp. 79-90. Original: *Theologie der Geschichte*. Einsiedeln: Johannes Verlage, 1950 (New edition 1959).

13 See George Sioui, *Pour une Autohistoire amérindienne. Essai sur les fondements d'une morale sociale*. Québec: Les Presses de l'Université Laval, 1989.

14 John Paul II, "Celebration of the Word. Martyrs' Shrine, Huronia," *Canadian Catholic Review* 2, No. 9 (1984): 368.

15 See Joseph Epes Brown, *The Spiritual Legacy of the American Indian*. New York: Crossroad, 1982.

16 See Claude Levy-Strauss, *Anthropologie structurale*. Paris: Plon, 1958, pp. 205-206.

17   See the title of the book by Serge Bramly, *Terre Wakan. Univers sacré des Indiens d'Amérique du Nord*. Paris: Robert Laffont, 1974.

18   See William Stolzman, *The Pipe and Christ. A Christian-Sioux Dialogue*. Chamberlain, S. D.: Tipi Press, 1986, pp. 116-130.

19   See the different testimonies in Chapter IV.

20   See Tom Roach, "An Anishnabe Artist's Unified View of Reality. Leland Bell's Way of the Cross Speaks Pointedly of the Universality of Christ," *Social Compass* 8, No. 4 (1990): 45-46.

21   See his testimony in Chapter IV.

22   Helmut Riedlinger, "How Universal is Christ's Kingship?," *Concilium* I, No. 2 (1966): 56.

23   Rahner, *Le courage du théologien*, p. 97.

24   See Allan D. Galloway, *The Cosmic Christ*. London: Nisbet & Co., 1951; George A. Maloney, *The Cosmic Christ. From Paul to Teilhard*. New York: Sheed and Ward, 1968(1951); James A. Lyons, *The Cosmic Christ in Origen and Teilhard de Chardin. A Comparative Study*. Oxford: Oxford University Press, 1982, pp. 7-73; Jaroslav Pelikan, *Jesus Through the Centuries. His Place in the History of Culture*. New Haven: Yale University Press, 1985, pp. 56-70; Matthew Fox, *The Coming of the Cosmic Christ. The Healing of Mother Earth and the Birth of Global Renaissance*. San Francisco: Harper and Row, 1988.

25   See Joseph A. Sittler, "Called to Unity," *The Ecumenical Review* 14(1962): 177-187.

26   Sittler, "Called to Unity," p. 178.

27   See Wilhelm Anderen, "Jesus und der Kosmos. Missiologische Uberlegungen zu New-Dehli," *Evangelische Theologie* 23(1963): 471-493; Carl F. Hallencreutz, *New Approaches to Men of Other Faiths 1938-1968. A Theological Discussion*. Geneva: World Council of Churches, 1970, pp. 56-62; Jürgen W. Winterhager, "New-Dehli und die Anfänge einer Ökumenischen Theologie," *Theologia Viatorum*. Berlin: Walter De Gruyter, 1962, pp. 299-311.

28   See Horst Bürkle, "Die Frage nach dem kosmischen Christus als Beispiel einer ökumenischen orientierten Theologie," *Kerygma und Dogma* 11(1965): 103-115.

29   See Paul D. Devanandan, "Called to Witness," *The Ecumenical Review* 14(1962): 154-163; Thomas Madathilparampil, *Risking Christ for Christ's Sake: Towards an Ecumenical Theology of Pluralism*. Geneva: World Council of Churches, 1987, pp. 85-106 (Paul Devanandan - The Historical Universality of the New Creation in Christ).

30   See Theo Witvliet, *A Place in the Sun. An Introduction to Liberation Theology in the Third World*. Maryknoll: Orbis Books, 1985, pp. 156-159. Original: *Een plaats onder de zon. Bevrijdingstheologie in de derde wereld*. Baarn: Ten Have, 1984.

31   See Choan-Seng Song, "From Israel to Asia: A Theological Leap," Gerald Anderson and Thomas Stranzky, eds., *Mission Trends No. 3. Third World Theologies*. New York: Paulist Press, 1976, pp. 211-212.

32   See Kosuke Koyama, "Adam in Deep Sleep," Emerito P. Nacpil and Douglas J. Elwood, eds., *The Human and the Holy. Asian Perspectives in Christian Theology*. Maryknoll: Orbis Books, 1978, pp. 36-61; Kosuke Koyama, *Waterbuffalo Theology*. Maryknoll: Orbis Books, 1974; Choan-Seng-Song, "Theology of Incarnation," Gerald Anderson, ed., *Asian Voices in Christian Theology*. Maryknoll: Orbis Books, 1976, pp. 147-160; Choan-Seng-Song, "The Divine Mission of Creation," in Douglas J. Elwood, (ed.), *Asian Christian Theology: Emerging Themes*. Philadelphia: Westminster, 1980, pp. 187-188; John S. Mbiti: "Some African Concepts of Christology," Stanley J. Samartha, ed., *Living Faiths and Ultimate Goals: A Continuing Dialogue*. Maryknoll: Orbis Books, 1975, pp. 108-119; François Kabasele, Joseph Doré, René Luneau, eds., *Chemins de la Christologie africaine*. Paris: Desclée, 1986; François Kabasele, Joseph Doré, René Luneau, eds., *Pâques africaines d'aujourd'hui*. Paris: Desclée, 1989.

33   See Mircea Eliade, *Traité d'histoire des religions*. Paris: Payot, 1974.

34   See Edwin O. James *The Tree of Life. An Archeological Study.* Leyden: E.J. Brill, 1966; Roger Cook, *The Tree of Life, Image of the Cosmos.* London: Thames and Hudson, 1974.

35   See Carl Jung, *Alchemical Studies* (Collected Works, Vol. 13). London: Routledge and Kenan Paul, 1967, pp. 251-349; Carl J. Jung, *Mandala Symbolism.* Princeton: Princeton University Press, 1973; Carl J. Jung (e.a.), *Man and his Symbols.* Garden City, N.Y.: Doubleday & Co., 1971(1964).

36   See Carl Starkloff, *The People of the Center. American Indian Religion and Christianity.* New York: Crossroad, 1974.

37   See Joan M. Vastokas, "The Shamanic Tree of Life," *Arts Canada. The Thirtieth Anniversary Issue. Stones, Bones and Skin. Ritual and Shamanic Art* 184-195-196-187(1973-74): 125-149.

38   John G. Neihardt, *Black Elk Speaks: Being the Life Story of a Holy Man of the Oglala Sioux.* New York: Pocket Book, 1972, p. 230.

39   For a detailed description of the vision, see Neihardt, *Black Elk Speaks,* p. 36. For the interpretation of the vision, see Kenneth Lincoln: *Native American Renaissance.* Berkeley: University of California Press, 1983, pp. 86-95; Paul Steinmetz, *Pipe, Bible and Peyote Among the Oglala Sioux. A Study in Religious Identity.* Knoxville: The University of Tennessee Press, 1990, pp. 181-189.

40   See, in particular, Hartley Burr Alexander, *The World's Rim. Great Mysteries of the North American Indians.* Lincoln: University of Nebraska Press, 1953, pp. 25-41; Hyemeyohsts Storm, *Seven Arrows.* New York: Ballantine Books, 1972, pp. 14-27.

41   It seems that the sacred meaning of the totem poles as *axis mundi* or tree of life was gradually given a more secularized meaning even before the Europeans arrived. It came to symbolize the social stratification and hierarchical structure of the native communities. See Vastokas, "The Shamanic Tree of Life," pp. 142-148.

42   See Ruth Landes, *Ojibwa Religion and the Midewiwin.* Madison: University of Wisconsin Press, 1968.

43   Adam Cutland, "A Native Anglican Priest Speaks," *Interculture* 15, No. 1, Cahier 74 (1982): 38.

44   For an overview of this tradition and a selection of representative texts, see Henri De Lubac, *Aspects du bouddhisme.* Paris: Éditions du Seuil, 1950, pp. 55-79; Sebastien Steckx, *Introduction au monde des Symboles.* Sainte-Marie de la Pierre-qui-vire: Zodiaque, 1966, pp. 25-49; 365-373; Pierre Nautin, "Une homélie inspirée du traité sur la Pâque d'Hippolyte," *Homélies pascales* I. Paris: Editions du Cerf, 1950, pp. 177-179; Hugo Rahner, *Greek Myths and Mystery.* London: Burns & Oates, 1963, pp. 46-68. Original: *Griechische Mythen in christlicher Deutung.* Darnstadt: Wissenschaftliches Buchgesellschaft, 1966, pp. 55-73.

45   See Marjoris Reeves, *Joachim de Flore and the Prophetic Future.* London: S.P.C.K., 1976; Marjoris Reeves and Warnick Gould, *Joachim de Flore and the Myth of the Eternal Evangel in the Nineteenth Century.* Oxford: Clarendon Press, 1978; Henri De Lubac, *La postérité spirituelle de Joachim de Flore.* Paris: Editions Lethielleux, 1979-80 (2 volumes).

46   See Stolzman, *The Pipe and Christ,* pp. 189-205; Steinmetz, *Pipe, Bible and Peyote,* p. 177.

47   See Joseph Ratzinger, *The Theology of History in St. Bonaventura.* Franciscan Herald Press, 1971. Original: *Die Geschichtstheologie des Heiligen Bonaventura.* München: Schnell & Steiner, 1959; Hans Urs Von Balthasar, *Studies in Theological Style: Clerical Styles (The Glory of the Lord: A Theological Aesthetics,* Vol. 2). San Francisco: Ignatius Press, 1984, pp. 260-362 (Bonaventure). Original: *Herrlichkeit. Eine theologische Aesthetik.* Bd. II: *Fächer der Stile.*

48   For a reproduction of this painting, see Cook, *L'Arbre de la vie, image du cosmos,* p. 81.

49   For a colour reproduction of this painting, see Mary B. Southcott, *The Sound of the Drum. The Sacred Art of the Anishnabe*. Erin: The Boston Mills Press, 1984. Plate 15.

50   See Alexander, *The World's Rim*, p. 151.

51   See Douglas Schwarz, *Plains Indian Theology. As Expressed in Myth and Ritual and in the Ethics of the Culture*. Ann Arbor: University Microfilms International, 1984, pp. 154-156.

52   See, for example, Joseph Jorgensen, *The Sun Dance Religion. Power of the Powerless*. Chicago: University of Chicago Press, 1972. This book offers a political and economic analysis of the sun dance of the Shoshoni and Ute Indians, and a comparative study of the modern versions of the ritual.

53   See Ake Hultkrantz, "Tribal and Christian Elements in the Religious Syncretism Among the Shoshoni Indians of Wyoming" and "The Traditional Symbolism of the Sun Dance Lodge Among the Wind River Shoshoni," Christopher Vecsey, ed., *Belief and Worship in Native North America*. Syracuse: University of Syracuse Press, 1981, pp. 212-234; 235-236.

54   Brown, *The Spiritual Legacy of the North American Indian*, p. 101.

55   See William Powers, *Oglala Religion*. Lincoln: University of Nebraska Press, 1975, p. 95; Stolzman, *The Pipe and Christ*. p. 158.

56   See Starkloff, *The People of the Center*. p. 58; Alexander, *The Word's Rim*. p. 140.

57   Alexander, *The World's Rim*. p. 85 and p. 92.

58   See Joseph Epes Brown, *The Sacred Pipe. Black Elk's Account of the Seven Rites of the Oglala Sioux*. Norman: University of Oklahoma Press, 1988(1953). pp. 67-100.

59   Alexander, *The World's Rim*. p. 139.

60   See Robert Bunge, *An American Urphilosophie. An American Philosophy BP (Before Pragmatism)*. Lanham: University of America Press, 1984. This study deals directly with the Sioux (Lakota, Dakota, Nakota), not with the sun dance as such.

61   Brown, *The Spiritual Legacy of the American Indian*, p. 105.

62   See J.R. Walker, "The Sun Dance and other Ceremonies of the Oglala Division of the Teton Dakota," *American Museum of Natural History. Anthropological Papers*, Volume XVI, Part II, 1917, pp. 78-92; 152-158; William Powers, *Beyond the Vision. Essays on American Indian Culture*. Norman: University of Oklahoma Press, 1987. Chapter 3: Counting Your Blessings. Sacred Numbers and the Structure of Reality.

63   See Hultkrantz, "Tribal and Christian Elements," p. 222.

64   See Jorgensen, *The Sun Dance Religion*, pp. 210-211.

65   See Hultkrantz, "Traditional Symbolism," p. 259.

66   See Hultkrantz, "Traditional Symbolism," p. 261.

67   See Steinmetz, *Pipe, Bible and Peyote*, pp. 30-39; Sylvain Lavoie: "Worship Without Walls," *Kerygma* 23(1989): 147-251.

68   See Hultkrantz, "Traditional Symbolism," p. 251.

69   See Stolzman, *The Pipe and Christ*, pp. 151-165.

70   See Frank Speck, *Naskapi. The Savage Hunters of the Labrador Peninsula*. Norman: University of Oklahoma Press, 1935.

71   Robert Lowie, *An Introduction to Cultural Anthropology*. New York: Rinehart, 1947, p. 312.

72   See Ake Hultkrantz, "The American Indian Vision Quest: A Transition Rite or a Device for Spiritual Aid?," Ligo Bianchi, ed., *Transition Rites. Cosmic, Social and Individual Order. Proceedings of the Finnish-Swedish-Italian Seminar held at the University of Rome La Sapienza, 24-28 March 1984*. Rome: L'Erma di Bretschneider, 1986, pp. 29-43.

73 See Achiel Peelman, "Christianisme et cultures amérindiennes. Présentation et analyse d'une démarche théologique interculturelle," *Église et Théologie* 22(1991), pp. 131-156. Between 1983 and 1987 we undertook the vision quest four times with approximately fifteen other persons, mostly Catholic priests, who were involved in a process of interreligious dialogue with native elders and medicine men.

74 See the classical works of Irvin Hallowel, *Culture and Experience.* New York: Schocken Books, 1955; Ruth Landes, *The Ojibwa Women.* New York: Columbia University Press, 1938; *Ojibwa Religion and the Midewiwin.* Madison: University of Wisconsin Press, 1968. For an overview of the historical evolution of the ritual, see Christopher Vecsey, *Traditional Ojibwa Religion and Its historical Changes.* Philadelphia: The American Philosophical Society, 1983.

75 Basil Johnson, *Ojibway Heritage. The Ceremonies, Rituals, Songs, Dances, Prayers and Legends of the Ojibway.* Toronto: McLelland and Stewart, 1976(1982): 119.

76 Because of the very private or individualized character of the vision quest, there are few systematic studies on the ritual, especially on the nature of the vision itself. For a presentation of the ritual, see Brown, *The Sacred Pipe,* pp. 44-66; Richard Erdoes, *Crying for a Dream.* Santa Fe: Bear & Company, 1990, pp. 24-28. A Teton Sioux Indian of South Dakota offers an exceptional description of his own vision quest experience. See Arthur Amiotte, "Eagles Fly Over," Sam Gill, *Native American Traditions. Sources and Interpretations.* Delmont: Wadsworth Publications, 1983, pp. 90-114. Also published in *Parabola* 1, No. 3 (1976): 28-41.

77 See Achiel Peelman, "Christianisme et cultures amérindiennes," Stolzman, *The Pipe and Christ,* pp. 1-12; Michael Steltenkamp, *The Sacred Vision. Native American Religion and its Practice Today.* New York: Paulist Press, 1982, pp. 35-49.

78 See Stolzman, *The Pipe and Christ,* pp. 74-84.

79 See Pierre Teilhard de Chardin, *Hymne de l'Univers.* Paris: Editions du Seuil, 1961, pp. 39-58 (Le Christ et la matière); Pieter Smulders, *The Design of Teilhard de Chardin.* Westminster, Md.: Newman Press, 1967. Original: *Het Visioen van Teilhard de Chardin. Poging tot theologische waardering.* Brugge: Desclée de Brouwer, 1962; Norbertus Wildiers, *An Introduction to Teilhard de Chardin.* London: Collins, 1968. Original: *Teilhard de Chardin: Een inleiding in zijn denken.*

80 See Francisco Bravo, *Christ in the Thought of Teilhard de Chardin.* Notre Dame: Notre-Dame University Press, 1967; George Maloney, *The Cosmic Christ. From Paul to Teilhard.* New York: Sheed and Ward, 1968; Christopher Mooney, *Teilhard de Chardin et le mystère du Christ.* Paris: Aubier, 1968. Attila Szekeres, ed., *Le Christ cosmique de Teilhard de Chardin.* Paris: Seuil, 1969.

81 See Hultkrantz, "The American Indian Vision Quest," p. 42.

PRINTED BY
IMPRIMERIE D'ÉDITION MARQUIS
IN AUGUST 1995
MONTMAGNY (QUÉBEC)